Women's Work in Rural China

Cambridge Modern China Series

edited by William Kirby, Harvard University

Women's Work in Rural China

Change and Continuity in an Era of Reform

TAMARA JACKA

School of Humanities
Murdoch University

PUBLISHED BY THE PRESS SYNDICATE OF THE UNIVERSITY OF CAMBRIDGE
The Pitt Building, Trumpington Street, Cambridge CB2 1RP, United Kingdom

CAMBRIDGE UNIVERSITY PRESS
The Edinburgh Building, Cambridge CB2 2RU, United Kingdom
40 West 20th Street, New York, NY 10011–4211, USA
10 Stamford Road, Oakleigh, Melbourne 3166, Australia

© Tamara Jacka 1997

First published 1997

Typeset in Times 10/13 pt

National Library of Australia Cataloguing in Publication data

Jacka, Tamara.
Women's work in rural China: change and continuity in an
era of reform.
Bibliography.
Includes index.
ISBN 0 521 59928 8 (pbk.).
ISBN 0 521 56225 2.
1. Rural women – China. 2. Sexual division of labor –
China. 3. Women in rural development – China. 4. China –
Politics and government – 1976– . I. Title. (Series:
Cambridge modern China series).
306.36150951249

Library of Congress Cataloguing in Publication data

Jacka, Tamara, 1965–
Women's work in rural China: change and continuity in an
era of reform/Tamara Jacka.
    p.   cm. – (Cambridge modern China series)
Includes bibliographical references and index.
ISBN 0 521 56225 2 (alk. paper) – ISBN 0 521 59928 8 (pbk.:
alk. paper)
1. Rural women – China – Social conditions. 2. Women – Employment –
China. 3. China – social conditions – 1976– . I. Title. II. Series.
HQ1767.J33   1997
306.3'615'0951–DC20   96–41501

A catalogue record for this book is available from the British Library

ISBN 0 521 56225 2 hardback
ISBN 0 521 59928 8 paperback

Transferred to digital printing 2004

Contents

Tables

Acknowledgements

This study began its life as a doctoral dissertation at the University of Adelaide. Over the several years in which it has slowly taken shape, numerous people have helped to make it possible. I owe thanks first of all to my supervisors, Professor Andrew Watson and Dr Susan Magarey. Andrew Watson, in particular, was a most valuable source of advice and support and provided a much appreciated critique of my arguments.

For their generous help with my fieldwork in China, and for discussing their research with me, I wish to thank Li Ling from the Rural Development Institute, the Chinese Academy of Social Sciences; Ran Moying, Ning Dong and Duan Chende from the Research Office of the Sichuan Provincial Women's Federation; Xu Min and Xu Tianqi from Hangzhou University; and Wang Jingling from the Zhejiang Academy of Social Sciences.

I wish to thank Associate Professor Beverley Hooper, Associate Professor Tim Wright, Dr Susan Young and Sally Sargeson for support and advice; Katryn Obenhaus for invaluable help with the preparation of tables and Jocelyn Grace for proof reading. Dr Delia Davin gave me much encouragement and made helpful comments on the manuscript, for which I am very grateful. I would also like to thank my anonymous readers for their valuable comments.

I am particularly grateful to my mother, Eleanor Jacka, for her advice and help with editing, and to her and Josko Petkovic for being so supportive.

Funding for fieldwork carried out in 1989 was provided by two travel grants for which I thank the University of Adelaide. I am also grateful to Murdoch University and to the Australian Research Council for two grants provided in 1995.

Finally, and above all, I would like to thank the numerous rural women that I talked to in Beijing, Hangzhou, Shandong and Sichuan, who gave me their time and support, and who taught me so much. Without them, this study would not have been possible. I alone, though, am responsible for any weaknesses in the final product.

Earlier and briefer versions of parts of Chapters 2, 3, 6, 7 and 8 appeared in 'The public/private dichotomy and the gender division of rural labour', in Andrew Watson, ed., *Economic Reform and Social Change in China*, Routledge, London and New York, 1992, pp. 117–143.

Abbreviations

ACWF   All-China Women's Federation

CCP   Chinese Communist Party

FNGZ   *Funü Gongzuo [Woman-work]* (An internal periodical, produced monthly for members of the ACWF)

NMRB   *Nongmin Ribao [Peasants' Daily]*

PRC   People's Republic of China

RMRB   *Renmin Ribao [People's Daily]*

SWB   *Summary of World Broadcasts* (BBC)

ZGFN   *Zhongguo Funü [Chinese Women]* (A periodical published monthly by the ACWF for mass consumption)

ZGFNB   *Zhongguo Funü Bao [Chinese Women's Daily]*

ZGNMB   *Zhongguo Nongmin Bao [Chinese Peasants' Daily]*

Introduction

IN 1978 the Chinese Communist Party (CCP) embarked upon a new path toward modernisation and development, rejecting much that was central to the previous Maoist political philosophy, and implementing a range of reform policies. Through the course of the 1980s and 1990s these policies have engendered major social, political and economic changes. Not the least of these has been a greater degree of openness, which has allowed for new opportunities for social scientists in China and elsewhere to observe change in Chinese society, and to theorise about how such change occurs. Scholars have, for example, analysed the interactions between different interest groups and how these shape politics and economic change; the relationship between political or ideological reforms and changes in the economy; and the effect of economic reforms on different sectors of society and how these in turn feed back into reforms.[1]

A number of valuable studies of gender relations in the post-reform period have been published, drawing our attention to the fact that in a general sense Chinese women have not benefited from the process of reform to the same extent as men, and that in numerous ways the subordination of women has been reinforced and increased since the reforms were introduced.[2] An issue that remains problematic, however, is that of the *mechanics of change* in gender relations. We have yet to understand, in other words, the exact causal links between economic reform and change in gender relations, the mechanisms and processes through which such change occurs, and, in particular, how changes in gender relations are legitimated and come to be seen as 'natural'.

This book aims to further our understanding of these issues by examining the changes that have occurred in gender relations in rural areas since reforms were introduced. It will concentrate, in particular, on women's work and gender divisions of labour and the complex interrelations between these and other aspects of gender relations.

By 'gender relations' I mean both the social organisation of people into the categories 'man' and 'woman', and the interactions between members of these two different categories. In discussing divisions of labour between 'men' and 'women' I use the term '*gender divisions* of labour' rather than the more

1

common '*sexual division* of labour' as a way of emphasising that there is not one division but many, and that these divisions are not a natural or inevitable consequence or reflection of sexual differences.

Much of this work will necessarily be concerned simply with charting the ways in which particular gender divisions of labour have changed since 1978, while others have not. However, my main aim will be to try to understand *how* the perpetuation of some divisions and the changes in others have taken place, and what implications these patterns have had for gender relations.

In particular, I wish to show how the effects of structural reforms on gender divisions of labour have been shaped, firstly by existing social structures and, secondly, by already current values and assumptions about work and about what it means to be male or female in rural China. In addition, I am concerned with changes to social values that have been promoted by the state alongside structural reforms, because these too have contributed to newly emerging divisions of labour and to the acceptance, by and large, of these divisions as legitimate and natural. Finally, I will address the question of the extent to which women have benefited from the reforms by examining the impact of new gender divisions of labour on the nature of work undertaken by women, women's participation in family decision making, political affairs and education, and on values and assumptions about women's identity and their position in society.

Women's work and gender divisions of labour have, in different ways, been issues of major concern in both Chinese Marxist and western feminist, especially socialist feminist, approaches to gender inequalities. Thus, it is hoped that this study, apart from contributing to a western understanding of Chinese society, will contribute to both the discussions of gender relations and the development of strategies to overcome gender inequalities within China, and will generate new reflections on, and insights into, gender relations in other societies.

What I believe will be of particular value in the approach taken here is the integration of an analysis of material causes and effects of gender divisions of labour with an examination of the values and meanings surrounding those divisions. In the course of the book I will develop a model of gender divisions of labour in rural China which sees them as being constructed and operating through a number of conceptual dichotomies which are connected with what is perceived as a dichotomy between 'male' and 'female'. The two dichotomies which I focus on as being of particular importance are between 'outside' ('*wai*') and 'inside' ('*nei*') domains of work and between 'heavy' ('*zhong*') and 'light' ('*qing*') work. I will show that in some instances a dichotomy between 'skilled' or 'technical' ('*jishu*') and 'unskilled' or 'manual' ('*shougong*') work also operates. In each of these the first element is seen as associated with men, and the second with women.

2

My contention is *not* that the actual work of women and men in rural China falls strictly into separate categories according to these dichotomies. Rather that the latter can be thought of as sets of values and assumptions, or as stereotypes, shaping the work opportunities and choices of women and men, the ways in which work is recognised, and the ways in which notions of gender identity are maintained. These stereotypes are reproduced at all levels of society, from children's education through to the recruitment policies of rural industry employers and the work patterns of individual women and men.

However, values and stereotypes are not static. Thus, outside/inside, heavy/light and skilled/unskilled dichotomies have a range of meanings and associations in rural China, and, in addition, the relations between them and the actual work women and men do have been changing over time.

Heavy/light is a relatively straightforward dichotomy between 'heavy' work, or work demanding a high degree of physical strength, and 'light' work that is often also tedious, time-consuming and intricate. Concomitant with this is a categorisation of men as physiologically more able to undertake heavy work and of women as being more capable of lighter work and work which involves dexterity and patience. It is important to note, however, that despite the common recourse to differences between male and female physiology as an explanation of this dichotomy, there are major inconsistencies and variations in local definitions of what types of work are 'heavy' and what types of work are 'light'. As I will show in Chapter 7, in relation to agriculture, negotiations and contestation over these definitions have played an important part in the determination of remuneration rates for male and female labour.

In addition, the introduction of new technology has commonly been accompanied by a submergence of the idea that 'heavy' work should be undertaken by men, and 'light' work undertaken by women, and a greater emphasis placed on a dichotomy between 'skilled' and 'unskilled' work. This latter dichotomy, apparent in both agriculture and industry, has served to legitimate and maintain a gender division of labour in which the use of certain types of labour-saving machinery is dominated by men, whilst women are concentrated in more menial, labour-intensive tasks.

The outside/inside dichotomy has a range of meanings which it is important to identify, but which nevertheless overlap and reinforce each other. Taking, for the moment, a relatively ahistorical approach, the following levels of meaning have been attached to the inside/outside dichotomy at different times, with varying degrees of emphasis and in different combinations in rural China during this century.[3] Firstly, the dichotomy separates work according to physical location. Thus, in pre-1949 China, according to Confucian ideals, women were responsible for work *inside* the walls of the family house or compound, and their

3

movement beyond those walls was restricted, while men's domain was *outside* the house. I will show, however, that since 1978 the 'inside' domain has been extended to include work in the fields, while 'outside' work refers to work involving travel out of the village for extended periods.

Secondly, the outside/inside dichotomy refers to a division between family and non-family. Before the revolution it was assumed that women would interact and work mostly with other family members and that their interactions with outsiders, especially men, would be limited. Women could be involved in family businesses, but activities, such as arranging business deals, involving substantial interaction with non-family people would be undertaken by men. Indeed, any formal representation of the family to the outside world, for example in village politics, was considered the responsibility of the male head of the family. This set of ideas, I argue, is still of major influence in shaping gender divisions of labour today.

A third set of meanings attached to the outside/inside dichotomy is a distinction between 'work' and 'care for the family', or between 'production' and 'reproduction'. These meanings have, I argue, been transposed onto the outside/inside dichotomy as a result of Communist intervention into rural structures and values.

A final set of meanings attached to the outside/inside dichotomy, also as a result of Communist intervention, is a distinction between work undertaken for the collective, and work undertaken for family consumption and cash profit. As a result of reforms introduced since 1978, however, this particular set of meanings has lost its earlier significance.

It is widely recognised that in the first half of the twentieth century women were culturally defined as inferior to men, and in practice also, were subordinated in a number of ways. Gender divisions of labour, shaped by conceptual dichotomies between 'outside' and 'inside', and 'heavy' and 'light' work, played an important part in reproducing this devaluation and subordination. For example, restrictions on women's movement and on their interactions with non-family members made them more vulnerable within the family and in this sense contributed to their lack of power. In addition, the perception that females could not undertake 'heavy' field work contributed to the view that girl babies were less desirable than boys.

Communist intervention in gender relations and the rural economy after 1949 involved challenges to gender divisions of labour and the conceptual dichotomies which framed them. In particular, large numbers of women were drawn into 'outside' production. As will be discussed in Chapter 2, this played an important role in reducing women's vulnerability and powerlessness in the family. At the same time, though, a failure to completely overcome or change

4

gender divisions of labour, combined with a reinforcement, and in some cases an alteration, of the conceptual dichotomies informing those divisions, meant that some other aspects of women's subordination were left untouched and some new ones were created. For example, a failure to reduce women's domestic workload to any significant extent resulted in a serious 'double burden' for women. Furthermore, the introduction of a Marxist ideology, combined with the reorganisation of the rural economy into a primary collective sector and a secondary private sector had the effect of both reinforcing a distinction between 'inside' and 'outside' spheres, and of adding new negative connotations to the former, resulting in a further devaluation of women's work in that sector. In the 'outside' sphere of collective production the implementation of the work-point system was often accompanied by local struggles over remuneration in which gender divisions of labour between relatively low paid 'light' or 'unskilled' 'women's work' and more highly paid 'heavy' or 'skilled' 'men's work' were strengthened, or in some cases newly created.

Through the course of this book I argue that, as a result of reforms initiated by the state in 1978, marked changes have occurred in the conceptual dichotomies between outside/inside, heavy/light and skilled/unskilled. Nevertheless, these dichotomies, and the lower value assigned to the 'female' side of the dichotomies, still operate, and indeed in some ways have been strengthened in the process of reform. This has, in turn, contributed to the creation and maintenance of gender divisions of labour through which women's subordination continues to be reproduced.

SCOPE AND METHOD OF RESEARCH

This work is concerned mainly with an analysis of the situation of *rural* women of Han nationality. However, I will also discuss the rural/urban division and the changes that have occurred there, because these have been important factors in shaping divisions of labour and other aspects of social relations in rural China in recent years.

By 'rural' women I mean here those women with rural household registration (*hukou*). This category is primarily comprised of women who live and work in villages and small townships. However, it also includes women whose permanent residence is rural, but who live and work on a temporary basis in a town or city. The household registration system and the impact it has on divisions of labour is discussed in Chapter 7.

Readers looking for an in-depth, localised ethnographic study will be disappointed in this book. Rather than take such an approach, this study aims to delineate and to understand patterns and shifts in gender divisions of labour across the whole of China, paying attention, of course, to broad regional variations. To this end, it draws both on interviews with rural Chinese women, officials and social scientists, and on Chinese newspapers, journals and academic reports.

Each of these sources has its limitations. Taken together, however, they provide a wealth of information. In most instances in this study I have been able to base my discussion on information gained not just from one source, but from many. Thus, when discussing phenomena reported in the media I have generally been able to draw on a number of articles, or have confirmed the validity of media reports by reference to my own fieldwork (see below). Similarly, in discussing my fieldwork findings, I have made comparisons with the findings of other scholars, or with reports published in the Chinese media.

The journals *Zhongguo Funü [Chinese Women]*, *Hunyin yu Jiating [Marriage and the Family]*, and (since its inception in 1993) *Nongjianü Baishitong [Rural Women Knowing All]*, the newspapers *Nongmin Ribao [Peasants' Daily]* and *Zhongguo Funü Bao [Chinese Women's Daily]*, and the compilation of media clippings published every two months by the People's University entitled *Funü Zuzhi yu Huodong [Women's Organisations and Activities]* have proved to be the most useful documentary sources of short reports and human interest stories relating to women in rural China. Many of the articles report 'success' stories, for example of female entrepreneurs. These cannot be taken as representative of the situation of rural women, but they do give an indication of the parameters shaping the fortunes of women and the degree to which they are able to benefit from reform. Not all reports present a rosy picture. Common also are articles discussing particular problems faced by women. In recent years, reports on crimes against women and the rarity of women involved in formal politics have been particularly numerous. Such reports are often useful in their discussion of the factors contributing to these problems, and how the state or local authorities are addressing them. However, they most commonly provide only very localised statistics, and give little indication of how widespread the problems are.

The internal journal of the Women's Federation, *Funü Gongzuo [Woman-Work]*, has been a valuable source of discussions on the approach of the Women's Federation to gender relations in rural areas, and of reports on surveys of the situation of rural women, conducted by the Federation. These surveys are mostly small in scale, however, and issues such as sample size and survey methodology are poorly documented in the reports.

Academic monographs and articles published in journals such as *Nongye Jingji Wenti [Issues in Agricultural Economics]*, *Renkou yu Jingji [Population and the Economy]*, and *Shehui Kexue* (a condensed version of which is also

6

published in English as *Social Sciences in China*), contain more detailed reports and analyses of surveys of various aspects of rural society and, in particular, of the rural economy. Over the last fifteen years numerous very thorough surveys of the rural economy have been conducted, but usually they do not break down statistics according to gender. Few surveys, outside those undertaken by the Women's Federation, focus on gender relations, or on women's position in society. A major exception, one I refer to in this book, is the *Sample Survey on the Status of Women in Contemporary China*, conducted by the Institute of Population Studies, the Chinese Academy of Social Sciences, in conjunction with the Population Research Institute of the East–West Center, USA, with support from the United Nations Population Fund. The survey was based on data collected in 1991 from questionnaires distributed to married couples in urban and rural areas in five provinces and one municipality.[4]

Except when specifically indicated, all quotations from Chinese have been translated by myself. Transcriptions of Chinese are in pinyin.

Apart from documentary sources, this book draws on fieldwork undertaken between August and December 1989 in Beijing, Shandong and Sichuan, and to a lesser extent on interviews and discussions held in Hangzhou between August and November 1995. In 1989 I conducted a total of 60 interviews with rural women in Huairou County in Beijing Municipality, Ling County in Shandong Province, and Xindu, Jinniu, Wenjiang, Guan and Mianyang Counties, all of which are in the vicinity of Chengdu, in Sichuan Province. In each county, I visited a few different villages. My interviewees were selected beforehand by local officials. My request that I be allowed to talk to women of varying ages and occupations was granted in each county. However, my sample included only married or widowed women, and the number of women running specialised households or private enterprises was disproportionately large.

Interviews were generally conducted in the woman's home. The questions I asked related mainly to family membership, to the family's economic activities, income and expenditure, to divisions of labour in the family and family decision-making processes, and to women's perception of their work and of gender relations. Usually I was accompanied by one or more officials and in some cases the woman's husband or other family members were also present. The presence of these various people provided some useful insights into official–peasant and intrafamily relations, but probably also inhibited the women from speaking freely in some instances, as no doubt my identity as a foreigner also did.

In addition to interviewing individual rural women, in most counties I visited two township enterprises where I interviewed managers, and in some cases women's representatives and small numbers of female workers. These visits gave me an insight into the experiences of women working in township

7

enterprises, as well as providing information on the recruitment of workers, occupational segmentation, wages and labour protection policies.

Background information on the situation of rural women, and on state policies affecting women, was obtained in interviews with officials and scholars in Beijing and Chengdu, and with officials at provincial, county and village level.

In 1995 I was based in Hangzhou. There I interviewed some thirty young rural women from various parts of China who had come to the city to work as nannies, factory labourers, shop assistants and waitresses. Their accounts have informed the discussion of rural women's experience of employment in urban areas in Chapter 9.

In all cases, interviews were conducted primarily in Mandarin, with interviewees also sometimes using their local dialect.

In Chapter 1 I discuss the intellectual origins of my approach to unravelling the complexities of gender divisions of labour in post-reform rural China. These origins can be divided primarily between the analyses of western feminists, which are concerned mainly with ideology and culture as the determinants of gender relations on the one hand, and on the other, of the views of Chinese Marxists and western socialist feminists, which focus on the position of men and women within production as a determinant of gender relations. Although I consider none of the theoretical approaches in these works to be fully satisfactory, an examination of the advantages and the limitations of each, combined with a reflection on recent poststructuralist insights has, I believe, enabled me to synthesise a more sophisticated and politically useful theoretical framework for analysing change and continuity in gender relations in contemporary rural China.

The chapter serves two purposes. First of all, it provides an introductory description and critique of the theory underlying the CCP's approach to gender relations, which has, of course, had major consequences for gender divisions of labour in rural China, and the meanings and values associated with them. Second, by making explicit the theoretical traditions out of which my ideas have developed, and the concerns and assumptions which frame the study presented here, this chapter paves the way for others to use, critique, develop or adapt my theoretical approach in their own attempts at advancing our understanding of gender relations.

I provide a historical perspective in Chapter 2 by examining gender relations and state policies on gender relations before 1978. Chapter 3 then sketches out the key features of the reform process initiated by the state in 1978 and signals questions and themes relating to the impact of reform on gender relations to be taken up in subsequent chapters.

Chapters 4 and 5 discuss women's position in the family and their participation in education and politics. The aim of these two chapters is to examine the ways in which gender divisions of labour and the conceptual dichotomies informing them are shaped by, and reproduced through, other aspects of gender relations, and how, in turn, these are affected by gender divisions of labour and changes in those divisions.

Chapters 6 to 9 focus on the issue of change and continuity in women's work, gender divisions of labour and conceptual dichotomies relating to work and gender in the post-Mao era. Through an examination of the impact of reform in each of the areas of domestic work, agriculture, the courtyard economy and industry, these chapters seek to understand the relationship between general social and economic change and change in gender divisions of labour, and the implications of such change for rural women and for gender relations in rural China. I conclude by demonstrating in Chapter 10 how the findings of my study support and elucidate the position which I take on the theoretical issues outlined above and in the next chapter.

1

Theorising Gender

IN this chapter I begin by exposing some of the flaws in the Marxist analysis of gender relations as expounded by Friedrich Engels in his work *The Origin of the Family, Private Property and the State*, first published in 1884. Whilst it may at first seem far removed from our concerns here, a consideration of Engels' work is in fact of central importance to this study because it has been the starting point for both Chinese Marxist and western socialist feminist analyses of gender relations. Understanding the weaknesses in Engels' arguments will thus help us to understand why it is that despite professing a commitment to gender equality, the CCP has far from achieved this goal. In addition, a critique of the arguments of Engels and of those who followed in his footsteps, as it were, will provide a basis from which to develop a more satisfactory theoretical approach to the questions raised in this book.

In *The Origin* . . . Engels undertook a historical materialist analysis in which he linked the emergence of women's subordination with changes in the social relations of production.[1] His work provided both Chinese revolutionaries and feminists in the West with a valuable framework for challenging assumptions that women's subordination to men stems directly from biological differences between the sexes, and hence is natural and, by extension, inevitable and right.

In China, the Marxist approach, based on Engels' arguments, has undeniably been very useful for tackling key areas of women's oppression. Yet the approach has also had severe limitations, in part because of one-sided interpretations or the incomplete implementation of Engels' suggestions, and in part because of limitations inherent in Engels' original formulation, and the unsuitability of the formulation for the Chinese context.

Here I wish to draw attention to just three related aspects of the Marxist approach that I see as particularly limiting theoretically.[2] These are, first of all, a narrow conception of 'production'; second, a failure to problematise gender divisions of labour; and, third, a failure to theorise adequately the relations between economic processes on the one hand, and social organisation and culture on the other.

In the preface to *The Origin* ... Engels argued that 'the determining factor in history is, in the final instance, the production and reproduction of immediate life. This again is of a twofold character: on the one side, the production of the means of existence, of food, clothing, and shelter and the tools necessary for that production; on the other side, the production of human beings themselves, the propagation of the species'.[3]

However, in most of the writing of Marx and Engels 'production' is more narrowly conceived than it appears here, referring only to the production of material goods, or, in some cases, to the production of material goods for 'surplus value', that is, for profit, rather than for consumption.[4] The 'economy' is defined as the organisation of the production of material goods, and is regarded as the material 'base' of a society, determining ultimately what happens in the non-economic realm, or 'superstructure'.[5] Marx and Engels, however, see women primarily as child bearers and child rearers, working in a family sphere that is separate from the 'economy'. From a feminist perspective, this set of ideas is problematic, firstly because it obscures the reality that women (and men) are in fact engaged in both of the areas of production that Engels outlines. Secondly, by relegating them to 'the family' in the way that they do, they effectively cast women and their work as the objects, but not the subjects, of historical change.[6] A corollary of this is that the organisation of women's work and the relations between women and men within the family are not regarded as important issues, nor are the interconnections between the organisation of work within the family and in the 'economy' recognised as playing a part in determining social relations.

The second limitation in orthodox Marxist approaches to gender issues is a failure to regard gender divisions of labour as part of, or related to, the problematic of women's subordination. In *The Origin* ..., Engels claimed that in 'primitive communal' society the division of labour by sex was a 'natural' one that did not lead to inequality.[7] This notion of an original, 'natural' division of labour between the sexes is also suggested in other passages in the works of both Engels and Marx.[8]

Engels did, however, give a detailed description of the social processes through which, over time, the 'original', 'natural' division of labour between the sexes became oppressive, and it was in the context of this description that he made his now-famous claim that 'the emancipation of women becomes possible only when women are enabled to take part in production on a large social scale, and domestic duties require their attention only to a minor degree'.[9]

The implication here is that the division of labour by gender, in which women are excluded from 'production', can and should be abolished. Yet the force of this argument is weakened by the earlier references to the natural basis of these divisions. Moreover, elsewhere, Marx and Engels appear to argue explicitly *against* the complete removal of divisions of labour between women and men, with the suggestion that such divisions have both biological and moral foundations.[10] Thus, while Marx and Engels argue for the possibility and the desirability of an emancipation of women which relies heavily on women's participation in 'production', at the same time they see limitations to that participation as 'natural', and also desirable.

This inconsistency in their argument is further compounded by a lack of recognition that within 'production' there are major gender divisions of labour through which women continue to be subordinated to men in a number of ways, such as lower occupational status, lower wages, and poorer working conditions, and a failure to make connections between these divisions and what is perceived to be 'natural' divisions in the family.

In the appropriation by the CCP, and other Communist parties around the world, of Marx's and Engels' approach to gender inequalities, the analysis of gender divisions of labour has not been improved. Rather, Communist parties have exploited the ambivalence toward such divisions so as to maximise the use of women's labour within particular economic strategies, and in such a way that the force of the historical materialist approach to understanding women's subordination is blunted.

Thus, in China under the CCP, while women have been drawn into 'productive' labour on a large scale and some efforts have been made to persuade men to share domestic work, there has been no serious challenge to the notion that child care and other aspects of domestic work are the 'natural' responsibility of women. Furthermore, although equal pay legislation has been enacted, and although periodic efforts have been made (with limited success) to draw women into areas of production, such as heavy industry, which were previously regarded as men's work, under the slogan 'what men can do, women can do too', these moves have not been accompanied by any serious analysis of, or attempts to overcome, the inequalities faced by women in production as a result of gender divisions of labour.

As will be discussed in Chapter 3, since 1978 the rhetoric of 'what men can do, women can do too' has been abandoned, and 'natural' or 'biological' differences between the sexes have been given primacy in discussions of women's work and their position in society, in a way that affirms the inevitability and desirability of particular gender divisions of labour within 'production', as well as women's roles as mothers and domestic workers. This appears to sit awkwardly in what otherwise is professed to be a Marxist historical materialist approach to social relations. However, as the preceding discussion suggests, there is less incongruity in this stance than one might suppose, given the ambivalence that Marx and Engels themselves displayed over the question of gender divisions of labour.

A third problem with Marxist approaches to women's subordination, and indeed to social relations more generally, has been a failure to account fully for culture and individual consciousness, and the links between economic processes and culture, or in Marxist terms, between 'base' and 'superstructure'. This is, of course, a very complex and multifaceted issue and this is not the place to address it in detail. However, there are two specific aspects of this question that I wish to mention briefly here. The first is that orthodox Marxist approaches cannot fully account for either change in, or reproduction of, women's subordination because they do not consider the ideological processes through which such subordination is made to appear legitimate or 'natural'.[11]

Second, orthodox Marxist approaches do not adequately address the complexity of relations between women's position in the economy, their cultural (de)valuation, and social structures and practices, including such things as arranged marriage, footbinding and rape, through which women are subordinated, emphasising, instead, the determining role of economic factors. Consequently, in China, as Kay Ann Johnson has pointed out, Engels' emphasis on changing relations of production and women's exclusion from 'productive' work as the causes of women's oppression has provided the basis for a very conservative and politically inactive approach toward aspects of political, social and family relations through which women are subordinated.[12]

Much of the driving force behind the initial development of socialist feminism came from a concurrent recognition of the values of an historical materialist approach to the analysis of gender relations and attempts to overcome the three key limitations in orthodox Marxist approaches to women's subordination outlined above. Michelle Barrett, for example, claimed that in the most general terms, it was the task of socialist feminism (or, as she terms it, Marxist feminism) to 'explore the relations between the organisation of sexuality, domestic production, the household and so on, and historical changes in the mode of production and systems of appropriation and exploitation'.[13]

During the 1970s and early 1980s socialist feminism inspired numerous analyses of women's subordination in which explorations of gender divisions of labour across the spectrum of work undertaken by men and women were central. These analyses made important advances in understanding the nature of women's subordination in different societies and the mechanisms through which that subordination is reproduced.

Included amongst them were three germinal works on women in China: Delia Davin's *Woman-Work. Women and the Party in Revolutionary China* (1976), Elisabeth Croll's *Feminism and Socialism* (1978) and *The Unfinished Liberation of Chinese Women 1949–1980*, by Phyllis Andors (1983). Following a number of somewhat simplistic and overly optimistic accounts of women's liberation under Chinese socialism,[14] these monographs succeeded in showing, through detailed description and analysis, that – although it improved their situation enormously – the Chinese Communist revolution did not completely liberate Chinese women.

However, as in socialist feminist studies of women's subordination in other societies written in this period, an understanding of the mechanisms through which women's subordination is reproduced was limited in these analyses by a failure to examine the social meanings of gender divisions of labour, and the connections between gender divisions of labour and the 'superstructural' aspects of women's subordination. Davin, Croll and Andors highlight the inconsistencies and the limitations of the CCP's practical approach to gender issues, but they make little attempt either to justify or to critique the theoretical principles guiding that approach. Thus, while they demonstrate that the CCP did not consistently meet its commitment to reduce women's domestic work and to draw them into 'production' on a large scale, they do not explain, to my satisfaction, the importance of women's domestic work in their subordination, the exact reasons why women's entry into 'production' should be liberating, and the relationships between this change in the gender division of labour and changes in women's participation in politics, their education, their decision-making power in the family and values and beliefs concerning the 'proper' place of women in the family and society.[15]

However, this problem is not confined to analyses of women's position in China, nor indeed, to the largely empirical works on women in other countries, written in the 1970s and early 1980s. In more theoretical socialist feminist texts of this period also, it is apparent that the problem of the relationship between 'base' and 'superstructure' has by no means been solved.[16] Iris Young, for example, argues for the need for a theoretical approach to social and economic relations in which a consideration of the gender division of labour is central.[17] However, she presents conflicting views on the significance of the gender division of labour and the relations between this division and ideology, culture and individual consciousness. On the one hand she cites the economistic Marxist argument that individuals' consciousness, behaviour and relations with others can be explained by their place in the division of labour.[18] In another section, however, she seems to be arguing that ideology and culture precede and condition the gender division of labour when she says that 'any account of the gender division of labour ... presupposes that there are genders – that is, sociocultural division and classification of people according to their biological sex'.[19] We therefore need, she claims, an account of 'the origins, symbolic and ideological significance and implications of gender differentiation'.[20]

In attempting to move away from the awkwardness of the 'base'/ 'superstructure' problematic, or what one might term a Marxist and socialist feminist version of the 'chicken and egg' dilemma, so apparent in Iris Young's conflicting statements, I have found it useful to consider the work of Michelle Rosaldo and Sherry Ortner. These two American feminist anthropologists have been concerned primarily with understanding cultural perceptions of women and men, rather than material aspects of their relations. I would argue, however, that they also suggest a way in which the two concerns might be addressed in a more integrated fashion than has yet been achieved by Marxist or socialist feminist analysts such as those discussed above. I must stress, however, that there are also serious problems with Rosaldo's and Ortner's theories.

In an influential paper published in 1974 Michelle Rosaldo set out to explain what she regarded as 'a universal asymmetry in cultural evaluations of the sexes'[21] by means of a structural model which relates key aspects of human psychology, culture and society to an opposition between the 'domestic' orientation of women and the 'public' orientation of men.[22]

For Rosaldo, a dichotomy between 'domestic' and 'public' spheres is a broad description of a universal fact of social organisation. This fact has both material and symbolic consequences for all aspects of gender relations. She argues, for example, that men are universally judged primarily in terms of their achievement in the 'public', or 'social' sphere, and hence are associated with 'culture'. Women's lives, on the other hand, appear to be irrelevant to the articulation of social order, and their status is derived primarily from their biological role as mothers. Consequently, one finds a recurrent link in cultural systems between woman and 'nature' and, often, disorder.[23]

This point is further elaborated by Sherry Ortner in her paper 'Is female to male as nature is to culture?' Like Rosaldo, Ortner argues that the universal devaluation of women can be explained in terms of the fact that women are regarded as closer to nature than men, whilst men are seen as being associated with culture.[24] Ortner stresses, however, that 'nature' and 'culture' are conceptual categories – 'one can find no boundary out in the actual world between the two states or realms of being'.[25]

Rosaldo and Ortner made an important contribution to feminist anthropology by suggesting a framework for analysing gender relations with which the complexity of the links between gender ideologies and stereotypes, broader cultural systems, social institutions, social behaviour and personal experience could be explored.[26] As I will discuss in the following paragraphs, their arguments have also come in for an enormous amount of criticism. To my mind, however, this criticism does not entirely negate the value of their work. Rather, by taking their theoretical approach as a starting point, and by examining the criticisms of that approach, it is possible to develop a more sophisticated framework for understanding gender relations.

First of all, they have been criticised primarily for a narrow conception of nature/culture and domestic/public dichotomies in western culture, and secondly, for an ethnocentrism which leads them to attribute a false universalism both to women's subordination, and to the dichotomies they outline.

In a critique of attempts, such as those of Ortner, to impute to other people's thought systems a dichotomy between 'nature' and 'culture' and a view of women as being closer to nature, Marilyn Strathern begins by examining western perceptions of male and female, nature and culture. She points out that in western thought there is in fact no single, consistent dichotomy between nature or culture, but rather a matrix of contrasts,[27] and argues that in discussing another society in terms of a single dichotomy drawn from our own mix of overlapping concepts, 'we are at best making prior assumptions about the logic of the system under study, and at worst using symbols of our own as though they were signs; as though through them we could read other people's messages, and not just feedback from our own input'.[28]

In similar fashion, other writers have suggested that in attributing a domestic/public dichotomy either to the actual organisation, or to the culture of the society they are observing, western anthropologists are merely reproducing an ideological construct belonging to their own culture. Following criticism of her paper on the domestic/public dichotomy, Rosaldo herself acknowledged that most modern western social thinking is based on the work of turn-of-the-century social theorists who absorbed, quite uncritically, the Victorian doctrine of separate male and female spheres.[29] Amongst these social theorists is Engels, whose depiction of the origins of women's subordination and prescriptions for their liberation, as Rosaldo suggests, are based on assumptions that women's reproductive role has everywhere confined them to a 'domestic' sphere, distinct from a 'public' sphere of production. These assumptions, in turn, reflect Victorian ideals of femininity and masculinity which are bound up with industrialisation and a contrast between a natural, nurturing, moral, domestic sphere and a competitive, progressive, heartless public sphere.[30]

Turning to the second order of criticism of Rosaldo's and Ortner's theses, numerous writers have undermined their claims to the existence of the universal subordination of women based on domestic/public and nature/culture dichotomies with ethnographic evidence from other societies.

Strathern and MacCormack, for example, claim that the Hagen people of the Papua New Guinea Highlands draw a contrast between wild (*romi*) and domestic or planted (*mbo*) things, but deny other writers' suggestions that this can be equated with the nature/culture contrast. Nor, they argue, do Hageners make the same associations between these contrasting categories as are made between the male/female, nature/culture contrasts found in western thought. Men are associated with that which is prestigious (*nyim*), and women with that which is rubbish (*korpa*), but these categories are not linked with those of the planted and the wild.[31]

Studies such as this repudiate Rosaldo's and Ortner's claims for the universal existence of gender-linked dichotomies of domestic and public domains, and nature and culture, primarily with empirical evidence. However, equally important, and not dissimilar, criticisms of their work can also be made from a more theoretical standpoint. A particularly serious weakness in both Rosaldo's and Ortner's arguments lies in their conception of the nature of the dichotomies, and of their significance.

In Rosaldo's case, the domestic/public contrast is, as noted, taken to be a description of a universal aspect of social organisation which has a particular, singular set of cultural consequences and, although Rosaldo points out that 'biological research may illuminate the range in human inclinations and possibilities, but it cannot account for the interpretation of these facts in a cultural order', she nevertheless argues that 'biology dictates that women will be mothers' and claims that everywhere 'women become absorbed primarily in domestic activities because of their role as mothers'.[32] Apparent in Rosaldo's approach are three conceptual leaps that must be questioned. The first is the assumption that biology or physiology is everywhere perceived or categorised in the same way (for example, that women's reproductive capacities are everywhere taken as the basis for their categorisation in a single social group); the second is the assumption that biology or physiology leads to particular forms of social organisation; and the third is the assumption that similar forms of social organisation are everywhere linked with the same sets of values or meanings.

In contrast to Rosaldo, Ortner speaks of the nature/culture dichotomy as a conceptual one. However, as Olivia Harris points out, she too 'slides into unargued assumptions about the universal implications of certain physiological and physiology-related characteristics'.[33] Thus, while claiming that biological facts 'only take on significance of superior/inferior within the framework of culturally defined value systems', she also argues that women everywhere are devalued because of their closer association with nature, which stems directly from women's 'greater bodily involvement with the natural functions sur-rounding reproduction'.[34]

In Ortner's argument, universal associations between women and nature, men and culture, are made at the level of the unconscious. Such associations may not be explicitly drawn within any given culture, but are implicit in all cultural thought. It is apparent from her paper that Ortner draws heavily on Lévi-Strauss' discussion of the distinction between 'nature' and 'culture' as a fundamental element in all cultures and, more generally, on structuralist linguistic theories according to which all human beings construct meaning through the perception of oppositions and contrasts, and in which it is held that underlying all human thought and behaviour is a single basic structure of binary thinking.[35] While this is not the place for a detailed critique of structuralism, there are two limitations of this approach that I wish to highlight here. Firstly, because it refers to the unconscious, it is difficult to validate; and secondly, by attempting to reduce all cultures to a universal set of binary oppositions, this approach does more to obscure than to explain changes in perceptions and values within a given society, and the differences between societies: for example, in their interpretation of physiology and their valuation of 'male' and 'female'.

Drawing on poststructuralist theories of language and power, one could summarise the underlying problems in Rosaldo's and Ortner's conceptions of domestic/public and nature/culture dichotomies in terms of an assumption of a direct correspondence between the world around us (whether 'natural' or 'social') and the construction of a single set of meanings. Rather than assuming such a correspondence, one of the frequent consequences of which is, as we have seen, the perpetuation of ethnocentric understandings, we need to ask *how*, that is through what social processes and relations of power, meanings and values are acquired in specific societies at specific times, and how those meanings and values change.[36]

Adopting such an approach does not necessarily mean discarding in their entirety Rosaldo's and Ortner's theses on domestic/public and nature/culture dichotomies. Rather, it implies exploring more deeply the implications of Ortner's claim that these dichotomies must be seen, not as descriptions of a universal reality, but as 'conceptual' categorisations, that is, as elements of thought systems through which people seek to organise and understand their world, that vary from one society to another and change over time. It suggests that in societies other than our own where male/female, domestic/public or nature/culture dichotomies seem to operate, we need to be open to the possibility that they may have very different meanings and values attached to them.

We need also to consider that in the meaning systems of some other societies these particular dichotomies may not operate, while in others they may be central. This insight is, of course, the basis for my exploration of outside/inside and heavy/light dichotomies in contemporary rural China. Initial research suggested that a conceptual dichotomy between domestic and public domains was an important factor in ordering and legitimating gender divisions of labour and changes to those divisions. Further study revealed, however, that the complex of meanings surrounding the dichotomy in rural China was somewhat different from that of the domestic/public dichotomy in contemporary western society, and could be better represented by the indigenous terms 'inside' and 'outside', although these must also be viewed only as shorthand for a more complex and changing set of concepts. At the same time, it appeared that in some situations two other very important organising principles for the work of rural Chinese women and men and the relations between them were conceptual dichotomies between 'light' and 'heavy', and 'unskilled' and 'skilled' work.

Pushing these ideas yet further, it is, I would suggest, possible that societies exist, or have existed, in which distinctions between the sexes are not regarded as being of any particular social significance (just as in our society the distinction between brown eyes and blue eyes is not regarded as significant), and are not connected, symbolically or otherwise, with any other distinctions. Thus, I make no attempt to argue in this thesis that gendered dichotomies of any kind are universal.

Ethnographic studies strongly suggest, however, that in societies in which people *are* regarded as being divided into the two separate and contrasting categories of 'male' and 'female', that division is most commonly entangled with, and reproduced through, other conceptual dichotomies or contrasts which play central roles in organising social life.[37] And in this book I will draw on a large body of evidence to show that *in rural China* notions of gender identity and cultural understandings of what people do are shaped by, and intertwined with, conceptual dichotomies, in particular, between inside/outside, light/heavy and unskilled/skilled work. These conceptual dichotomies must, I argue, be taken into account if we are to understand the changes that have occurred in gender divisions of labour and the links between these changes and other aspects of gender relations. It is necessary, first of all, to take account of the ways in which the conceptual dichotomies have contributed to the existing cultural perception of women as subordinate or inferior to men and how they both shape, and are reproduced in, the structures and processes through which women are subordinated in practice. Second, we must pay attention to the ways in which modifications of the conceptual dichotomies have shaped and legitimated changes in gender divisions of labour.

This, then, is the approach adopted in the following study, beginning, in the next chapter, with a brief discussion of gender divisions of labour in rural China before 1978.

2

Patterns from the Past

GENDER relations in rural China in the post-Mao era are the result of a complex blend of continuities and discontinuities with the more recent past, that is the Maoist era, and with pre-revolutionary society. Therefore, before examining the reforms introduced by the state in the late 1970s, and the impact these reforms had on gender relations, it is necessary to step back for a longer perspective, which puts the contemporary period in the context of the history of gender relations in twentieth-century China.

This chapter aims for such a perspective. Rather than attempting a comprehensive history, however, it focuses on certain issues of lasting significance for the discussion developed in this book.[1] The first section of the chapter provides a brief outline of gender divisions of labour in rural China in the early twentieth century, and of the key values and structures that shaped those divisions. The second section outlines the origins of the CCP's theoretical approach to gender issues, and the ways in which that approach was moulded by practical experience and expediency in the early years of CCP power. The final section of the chapter sketches the fluctuations in state policy toward women between 1949 and 1978, and indicates in broad terms the changes in gender relations, especially in gender divisions of labour, that occurred in rural areas during this period.

GENDER DIVISIONS OF LABOUR IN EARLY TWENTIETH-CENTURY RURAL CHINA

The bulk of the time and labour of most families in rural China in the early twentieth century was spent in subsistence agriculture and domestic work. In addition, activities such as the production of handicrafts, small-scale animal husbandry and farm labour for other families were undertaken to supplement the family's diet or cash income, or both. John Buck, undertaking a survey of Chinese farms in the 1930s, found that, not including domestic work which he neglected to investigate, agriculture involved the full-time labour of just over two-thirds of the farm population, subsidiary work one-eighth and agriculture and subsidiary work combined one-fifth.[2]

Gender divisions of labour in the rural economy were, and indeed continue to be, partly shaped by certain Confucian ideals and family structures. In particular, the notion that women are to serve and be subordinate to men and to the demands of the patrilineal family was both expressed and partially enforced through the belief that ideally women should be confined to an 'inside' sphere of family and home. Thus, one of the words for wife – *'neiren'* – literally meant 'inside person', and it was commonly claimed that *'nan zhu wai, nü zhu nei'* ('men rule outside, women rule inside'). According to Confucian ideals, 'good' women limited their interactions with people outside the family, especially men. Representation of the family to the 'outside' world, for example in community politics or in business transactions, was considered the responsibility of the male head of the family. In more literal terms, also, women's movement was ideally restricted to within the bounds of the home. The most visible expression of this ideal was the practice of footbinding, in which a young girl's feet were wrapped tightly to prevent them from growing beyond three-inch stumps. This meant that for the rest of the girl's life walking would be slow and painful.

Whilst families maintained control over women, in part by confining them to an 'inside' sphere, another key element in women's subordination and in the maintenance of particular gender divisions of labour was, ironically, their status as 'outsiders' to the patrilineal family. Marriages in rural China were most commonly arranged by the older generation or by a matchmaker, and were usually patrilocal, that is to say, the woman joined the man's family upon marriage.[3] In most places same-surname and same-village marriages were also prohibited. These practices meant that women were treated as temporary members of their family before marriage, and as outsiders to the family after marriage. Since a family lost its daughters' labour power when the girls married (generally in their early teens), daughters were treated as less valuable than sons and, even in well-to-do families, were very rarely educated. In times of hardship they were sometimes drowned at birth or later sold as slaves, prostitutes or wives. Patrilocal marriage and surname and village exogamy also meant that as a new wife a woman was somewhat isolated and vulnerable.

The Confucian ideal of women being confined to the 'inside' sphere of family and home contributed to a division of labour such that domestic work was largely done by the women of the family, or in households of the gentry, by female servants. However, in peasant families, although some domestic work was performed within the home, it also included activities outside the home, involving travel and contact with outsiders. Thus, peasant women not only cleaned the house, washed clothes, repaired and made clothes, prepared food and looked after young children and the sick and elderly, they also had to fetch water, often a few times a day and from considerable distances, collect firewood or crop residues for fuel, tend domestic animals, grow vegetables, and buy goods from pedlars or in the market. As Marion Levy has written, peasant women, by necessity, led far less secluded lives than their sisters of the gentry: 'Light inside their houses was poor, and peasant women frequently sat on their doorsteps or along the street to do sewing and similar jobs ... Since they had no servants to shop and market for them, the peasant women and their daughters who accompanied them came into more contact with local shopkeepers and peddlers than did their gentry counterparts.'[4]

In agriculture, women worked far less than men, on average. Buck estimated that 24 per cent of rural women worked in the fields and they performed only thirteen per cent of all field labour, most of which was done in the busy seasons of harvesting and planting.[5] Women's low participation rate in agriculture was once again related to Confucian ideology, in the sense that it was considered improper for women to work in the fields. This ideal, combined with the patrilocal marriage system meant, in addition, that parents were unwilling to train their daughters in farming techniques. Women, therefore, did not know how to do some agricultural tasks.

These restrictions on women's participation in agriculture were further bolstered by popular religion, in which women were associated with pollution and destruction. It was widely believed, for example, that if a woman went near a well that was being dug, no water, or only bad water, would be found, and if a menstruating woman walked through a paddy field she would cause the rice shoots to shrivel.[6]

It must be recognised, however, that while women's participation rate in agriculture was, everywhere, lower than men's, it varied considerably according to economic necessity and between different classes and different parts of China. In general, the total absence of women from agriculture could only be afforded by the gentry and the wealthiest peasant families, and the poorer the family the more often its women would work in the fields, especially during the busy seasons.

John Buck analysed Chinese rural land and labour utilisation in terms of two major regions – the wheat region of north China and the rice region of south China. He found that in the rice region as a whole women performed 16 per cent of field labour, as compared to only nine per cent in the wheat region.[7] He suggested that the amount of work done by women was partly associated with the extent to which women's feet were bound, so that in the rice region, where the practice of footbinding was less strictly adhered to, women performed more field work than in the wheat region of the north. It may be, however, that, as Delia Davin has suggested, the variations in footbinding practices were more an effect than a cause of the differentials in women's field work.[8] But in any case, the correlation between footbinding practices and the extent of women's field work does not hold in all cases. As Buck himself pointed out, 'in the Spring Wheat Area where foot binding is very prevalent and where it is so tight as to compel women to do the field work on their knees, fourteen per cent of the labour is done by women'.[9] Nor can this relationship explain the existence of variations in women's field work between areas with similar footbinding practices.[10]

Another factor in determining variations in women's field work was that of variations in labour requirements. For example, since the cultivation of rice was particularly labour intensive, women's participation rates in field work were highest in the double-cropping rice area. In addition, despite a general discouragement of women's involvement in agriculture, there were certain agricultural tasks, such as tea cultivation and sericulture, that were considered women's work, and where such work was common, women's agricultural participation rates were higher. Variations between local customs also had an impact. Hakka women, for example, worked a great deal in the fields.[11]

Within agriculture there was a good deal of variation in gender divisions of labour. In general, it was considered that men should do more of the heavier work, while women performed the lighter tasks. However, there were considerable differences in the meanings attached to the terms 'heavy' and 'light' work, and in the strictness with which work was differentiated. This is illustrated by the following three examples, all from Yunnan in the 1940s. Francis Hsu claimed that in 'West Town', 'men do the comparatively heavier jobs, such as carrying the crops from the fields or spreading fertiliser. Women do the planting, gathering, weeding, and threshing. But either men or women may do any work that is most convenient at the moment'.[12]

In contrast, Fei Hsiao-Tung and Chang Chih-I claimed that in 'Yuts'un' there was a very clear division between the sexes:

> During the transplantation of rice the men pull the shoots from the nursery beds and transport them to the main fields, where the women plant them. In the rice harvest the women cut the grain, tie it, and transport it to the threshing box. The men do the threshing and carry the threshed grain to the storehouse.[13]

In this village the work that men did was considered to require more strength and energy than that undertaken by women, and male hired labourers were remunerated at twice the rate received by women.

In another village in Yunnan, however, Fei Hsiao-Tung and Chang Chih-I reported that 'the sex differentiation in work is not very strict here. We ourselves have seen women digging the soil'.[14]

Despite intensive farming, peasant families frequently found that their small plot of land was not enough to support them, and so the labour power not being

24

used in the fields was turned to developing subsidiary activities, such as spinning and weaving, basket-making, animal husbandry, and vegetable growing, the products of which were sold in nearby markets.[15] These activities were small-scale and undertaken at home or in village workshops. As the saying '*nan geng nü zhi*' ('men plough, women weave') suggests, subsidiary activities, especially spinning and weaving, were an important area of employment for women. Sidney Gamble found, for example, that in Ding County, Hebei, 95 per cent of spinners were women and 82 per cent of weavers were women. Eighty-eight per cent of home industry workers were engaged in spinning or weaving or both.[16] Fei Hsiao-Tung and Chang Chih-I reported that in 'Yuts'un' in Yunnan, weaving was done only by women. Of 201 adult women in the village, 151 undertook weaving. Almost all young girls learnt how to weave from their mothers or other older women, and were given a loom as part of their dowry. Most of the women engaged in weaving were middle-aged and from middle-income families (the rich generally did not bother with it and the poor often could not afford the necessary materials). Weaving in this village was of low profit: working full-time a woman could not earn her subsistence. Generally women only undertook it as a subsidiary occupation in addition to farming and domestic work. This nevertheless brought in an important income for the family, serving as a buffer against starvation when, for example, the main crops failed, or the male worker became ill.[17]

According to John Buck, women performed 16 per cent of all subsidiary activities in the early 1930s. However, under 'subsidiary occupations' Buck included those of merchant, hired farm-hand, unskilled labour, skilled labour, professional occupations, scholar, official and soldier, as well as those in home industry.[18] His figures obscure the fact that in a number of these occupations, particularly those of soldier, and those such as official and scholar, requiring a high level of education, the numbers of women were negligible, whereas in home industry their participation rate was high.

The notion that women belong in the 'inside' sphere did not prevent rural women in the early twentieth century from being involved in commerce or trading. Generally, however, women involved in such activities travelled shorter distances than men and their transactions were on a smaller scale. Francis Hsu reported that in 'West Town' there were more women than men in the markets, selling all sorts of products. However, women traded within a radius of no more than 15 miles, while a large number of men made trips to places as far away as Burma, Indo-China, Hong Kong and Shanghai. Hsu claimed also that women worked in small family shops that occupied a part of their home, but were rarely found in the larger shops located on separated premises and employing people outside the family.[19]

In this brief examination of women's and men's work in early twentieth-century rural China I have shown that gender divisions of labour were constructed and maintained in part through conceptual dichotomies, in particular between 'inside' and 'outside' spheres, and also between 'light' and 'heavy' work. These dichotomies and the ways in which they shaped gender divisions of labour varied, however, from one region to another. They also intersected with, or were modified by, popular beliefs, for example relating to the so-called polluting effects of women, class divisions, and the requirements of the family economy.

The picture I have so far drawn of gender relations and gender divisions of labour is a somewhat static one. Even within the period covered by the above account, however, gender relations underwent a good deal of disruption and change. Scholars generally agree that from the eighteenth to the mid-twentieth century, living conditions for Chinese peasants were gradually worsening.[20] In part this was due simply to increasing population pressure on the land. In the two hundred years from 1651 to 1851 China's population tripled, from 120–140 million to 350–430 million, and by the early 1950s it had reached approximately 580 million people.[21] Despite increases in cultivated acreage due to improved farming methods and the planting of new crops, and the migration of millions of southerners overseas and of northerners to Manchuria, this population explosion put severe strains on the land and the rural economy, and consequently on social relations. In the first half of the twentieth century, shortage of land, increasing exploitation of tenant farmers by landowners, and natural disasters resulted in starvation, mass migration, banditry and rebellions, and these were further compounded by foreign imperialism.[22]

These socio-economic disruptions made it extremely difficult for poor peasants to attain the Confucian ideals of the family and of gender relations: children died, sons left home to look for work elsewhere and daughters and wives were sold to pay for the survival of the rest of the family. Many poor young men could not afford to marry, and women whose husbands had died or, for one reason or another, could not support them, were forced out to earn food for themselves and their children, often through begging or prostitution. Opium, sold by the British from the eighteenth century onwards, made numerous families destitute. Men became addicts, were unable to support their families and sold all their possessions and even wives and children in order to obtain the drug.[23] Some other imported goods competed with local products and dealt a severe blow to certain rural home industries. Cotton spinning, the largest handicraft industry in the nineteenth century, and one involving numerous peasant women working at home, suffered most. Other handicraft industries, however, such as weaving, were relatively unaffected.[24]

26

As the most vulnerable and insecure members of society, women suffered most from poverty and dislocation, yet they also gained some independence through it. In addition to the women who were forced to earn a living for themselves, some young women were sent to work in the textile and light industry factories newly established in the big cities. For most, this was a miserable experience, characterised by exploitation and appalling living and working conditions.[25] However, these young women did gain some independence from their families and were exposed to new ideas about individual freedom. In the 1920s some rural women industrial workers participated in strikes, and in the Guangzhou silk factories young women banded together and refused the marriages that their families arranged for them.[26] On the whole, however, new ideas and behaviour in the cities scarcely affected the vast rural population.

EARLY CCP POLICIES ON GENDER RELATIONS, 1921–1949

This, then, was the setting in which the CCP, founded in 1921, first formulated policies concerning gender relations in rural China.

As in other areas, the CCP initially followed closely the approach taken by the Soviet Union. Thus, it held firstly, that, as Engels had argued, women's liberation is dependent on their involvement in non-domestic production and the reduction of their domestic workload. Secondly, the CCP regarded the particular oppression of women as far less important than the oppression of the worker and poor peasant classes, and, like the Russian Bolshevik Party, was wary of any separate organisation that represented women's interests *as women*, fearing that this would disrupt the unity between women and men in the revolutionary movement.[27]

In the years to come, the CCP did not always adhere to the first point mentioned above. For one thing, with the exception of the Great Leap Forward period (1958–1960), the CCP's adoption of Engels' maxim has always been lop-sided, with the reduction in women's domestic work receiving far less attention than their participation in non-domestic production. CCP policies have not been limited to the latter concern, however. They have also included, at times, measures aimed at the establishment of equal rights and the direct reform of values and social structures that oppress women, that have been more in line with the concerns of earlier Chinese feminists influenced by western liberalism. At other times, both the participation of women in non-domestic production and the reform of oppressive social attitudes and structures have been actively discouraged. What has remained constant throughout CCP history is that, while the Party has always claimed to be committed to gender equality, a concern for

27

gender equality for its own sake has always been subordinated to other concerns, in particular, peasant support for the revolution, economic growth, and class struggle, and has been modified, downplayed or compromised in strategies designed to achieve these latter goals.

Between the 1920s and the 1940s the CCP emphasised that the most important task for the activists in its Women's Department was to draw as many women as possible into production, political activities, and support work for the Red Army.

In the Jiangxi Soviet area in the early 1930s, women's rights issues received some attention with the introduction of the Land Law and the Marriage Law. Under the former, land was to be taken from landlords and distributed among the peasants. Peasant women were to have equal rights with men to land allotments, a move which, it was expected, would give women the economic independence necessary for their liberation. According to the Marriage Law introduced in 1934, marriage was defined as a legal tie between a man and a woman, to be forged without the interference of other parties, and to be ended by mutual agreement or upon the insistence of either spouse. After divorce, a woman was to retain her full property rights and, in a radical break with patrilineal custom, women were to be favoured over men in the custody of children.[28]

These laws were important because they symbolised the CCP's commitment to new values and goals for social change. Implementation of the laws was, however, uneven and imperfect. Indeed, in Yan'an between 1937 and 1945, such implementation was actively discouraged, and all work with women that did not directly contribute to an increase in their productivity was downplayed.

This initially may have been a temporary measure adopted by a party struggling for survival in the difficult period of civil war and war against the Japanese. However, it was also the beginning of a longer-term pattern in which efforts to change gender relations were limited by the CCP's reluctance to jeopardise the support of the poor peasantry, who resisted strongly any attempts to dismantle the Confucian family model.

To the urban intellectuals who had been active in the formation of the CCP, revolution was a chance for individuals to fight free of what they saw as the stifling restrictions of the Confucian ideal. Poor peasants saw it in a very different light, though. During the early twentieth century, the disintegration of many peasant families in the face of poverty and socio-economic disruptions had resulted in severe hardship and indignity. Consequently, when the CCP and the Red Army became active in rural areas, peasants supported them, not in the hope of destroying family and other social structures, but of restoring some semblance of Confucian family order. They were, therefore, opposed to any moves on the part of the CCP that might lessen their power to achieve this Confucian ideal, in particular, moves, such as the implementation of the Marriage Law, which would give more autonomy to young women.[29]

Kay Ann Johnson has pointed to conflicts and compromises between the individualist theoretical approaches of Chinese Marxist intellectuals and the family oriented concerns of the Chinese peasantry as major forces shaping CCP social policies after the 1949 revolution, as well as before.[30] Johnson suggests that the CCP is not 'a Marxist leadership deterministically trapped by its inheritance of a disrupted but largely untransformed "feudal social base" in the countryside',[31] but neither has it completely destroyed or changed that base. Rather, it has sought to reform certain aspects of society, but to accommodate or make use of other aspects which are useful for, or at least not in conflict with, the achievement of its major priorities.

For women, the result of this process has been, as Johnson shows, that some very major improvements in their lives have been made, but these improvements have nevertheless been limited because certain fundamental aspects of peasant society have been left unchallenged. This was clearly illustrated by the land reform campaigns begun in Yan'an in 1945. Under these campaigns peasant women, as well as men, were to be granted property rights. Many peasant women believed that ownership of land would make them economically independent from their fathers and husbands, thus improving their bargaining power within their families, and, under the most oppressive circumstances, enabling them to leave.[32] This potential effect of land reform was blocked, however, because, due to the family-oriented nature of rural society, women's land was considered family land, and land reform authorities, unless strongly challenged by a local women's group, automatically gave women's land deeds to the male family head. During the 1940s the value of separate land rights for women was particularly limited because of the difficulty women had in obtaining divorce. This issue would be tackled by marriage reform workers in the 1950s, but until the end of the 1940s marriage reform issues were considered too divisive to be pursued with any vigour.

STATE POLICIES AND GENDER RELATIONS IN RURAL CHINA, 1949–1978

In March 1949, seven months before the CCP assumed leadership of the whole of China, the All-China Democratic Women's Federation was established and held its first national congress. The congress passed draft regulations for the Federation and described, in a general way, its formal structure. It was not until the third congress held in September 1957 that the Federation's organisational structure was spelt out fully, however, at which time its name was also changed to the All-China Women's Federation. At the latter congress it was announced that the Federation would have representative groups at each level of government from the level of township (*xiang*) or street committee, to that of county, province and national congress. Each group would elect the members of the group above it.[33]

As a mass organisation, the dual task of the Women's Federation was to mobilise mass support for CCP policies, and to defend and further the interests of women. In subsequent years the actions and policy statements of the Federation were to reveal a shifting and uneasy tension between these aims. The rhetoric of both the Women's Federation and the CCP leadership has been that there is no conflict between the two, but from an outsider's point of view this can be seen to have sometimes resulted in an acceptance by the Women's Federation of Party policies that are in fact detrimental to women's interests, and a failure, on its part, to tackle problems for women that the Party itself does not acknowledge, or regards as unimportant.

The first law promulgated by the CCP after Liberation was the Marriage Law of May 1950. This was followed in June by the Agrarian Reform Law, which was to guide land reform in those areas, amounting to approximately 75 per cent of the country, in which it had not already been accomplished.[34]

The content of the 1950 Marriage Law was similar to that of the 1934 law, but this time more effort was put, by the Women's Federation especially, into the implementation of the law, and to propaganda and education on gender equality and freedom of marriage and divorce. For all this, the law achieved limited success in the countryside. In many areas cadres outside the Women's Federation were reluctant to implement it. Despite the fact that the Agrarian Reform Law and the Marriage Law were promulgated at the same time, and despite the limitations for women of having the former without the latter, many land reform cadres continued to find that marriage reform was far too difficult and divisive an issue to tackle until *after* land reform had been fully accomplished. Even then, those trying to implement the Marriage Law faced formidable resistance from peasants, resulting in some cases in severe physical violence against Women's Federation cadres and young peasant women. There was also a sharp increase in female suicides. By mid-1953, the persistence of resistance to the reforms led the CCP to the conclusion that direct political pressure was causing too much social unrest and disaffection among peasants, and that marriage reform would be a much slower process than they had previously expected it would be.[35]

During the First Five-Year Plan period of 1953–1957 there was a major change in policy on women in urban areas, and although their situation was very different, this also affected rural women. In the cities, the previously much publicised notion that a precondition for women's liberation was their participation in non-domestic production was quietly pushed aside, and instead, the housewife's role as a servicer of those who participated directly in production was glorified. In 1954 the Women's Federation's magazine *New Women of China [Xin Zhongguo Funü]*[36] published a series of articles entitled 'How housewives can serve socialism', and in 1956 the Women's Federation mounted a 'five good' family (*Wu hao jiating*) campaign to reward families in which women contributed to socialism by uniting with neighbourhood families for mutual aid; doing domestic work well; educating children well; encouraging the family in production, study and work; and working well themselves.[37] This shift in policy was the state's response to urban unemployment problems. Unemployment, endemic in urban areas at liberation, continued during the 1950s because the growth of industry could not match the enormous population growth, which was due both to natural increase and to migration from rural areas.

The First Five-Year Plan period was not the only time when the state revoked its emphasis on women's participation in paid labour in urban areas. In fact, since 1949 there has been a rough pattern in which state policies related to women's work have swung from an emphasis on women's participation in non-domestic labour in one period, to a de-emphasis on their non-domestic labour and a greater emphasis on their domestic labour in the next. Thus, the years 1949–1952, 1957–1960, and 1966–1978 were periods in which strong efforts were made to increase the number of women in non-domestic production, while the years between 1953 and 1957, and between 1961 and 1965, and the period following reforms in 1978, were periods in which women's participation in non-domestic production was de-emphasised. This pattern corresponds roughly to shifts between 'left' and 'right' economic and political strategies.[38]

With the exception of the Great Leap Forward period, national policies on women and the propaganda of the Women's Federation (for example, their magazine *ZGFN*) have been dominated by a concern for urban women. Consequently, the fluctuations in CCP attitudes to urban women that I have outlined above have also carried over into the work of Women's Federation cadres in rural areas, even though rural and urban situations have generally been very different. Thus, in the early 1950s attempts were made in rural areas as well as cities to improve the image of the housewife, and the 'five good' family campaign was also carried out in the countryside.

In the countryside, however, unemployment was not the problem that it was in urban areas, and much stronger attempts were made to draw rural women into non-domestic work. Indeed, the expansion of opportunities to employ labour profitably in non-domestic production, generated through collectivisation, was as important a motive for drawing women into the collective labour force as beliefs about women's liberation.

The collectivisation of agriculture and rural industry began once land reform had been completed. Families were organised into larger and larger production groups, and much of the ownership of the means of production was taken over by these groups. This process was undertaken gradually at first, but under the Great Leap Forward of 1958–1960 the pace of collectivisation was enormously increased.

The Great Leap Forward was a development strategy put forward by Mao Zedong that was characterised by the policy of 'walking on two legs'. Under this policy, modern, large-scale urban-centred heavy industry would receive the greatest proportion of investment, but the agricultural sector would also be developed and become self-sufficient by relying on the mass mobilisation of rural labour for work in the fields, on large-scale construction and water control projects, and in local, small-scale industries. It was found that the existing collectives lacked sufficient labour power and resources to meet these requirements and consequently they were regrouped into communes. By the end of 1958, 99 per cent of all peasant families were members of rural people's communes, comprising an average of about 4,600 families.[39]

Although few reliable statistics are available, it appears that during the collectivisation period, and especially during the Great Leap Forward, rural women's participation in 'outside' work increased significantly. According to Marina Thorborg's calculations, between 1929 and 1954, 30 to 50 per cent of rural women worked in collective agriculture. In 1955 the range was 40 to 55 per cent, and it rose to 60–70 per cent in 1956, 50–65 per cent in 1957, 80–95 per cent in 1958 and 1959 and 70 to 80 per cent in 1960.[40] The time each woman spent in the fields also increased. In 1957 a survey of 228 Agricultural Producers' Cooperatives across the country found that women worked, on average, 166 workdays per year, while men worked 220 workdays. In 1959 women worked 250 workdays, while men worked 300.[41]

An important result of collectivisation for women was a loosening of the authority of the (usually male) head of the family over other family members. Under the collective system, the production team leader, rather than individual male heads of families, made the important decisions concerning the use of women's labour power in 'outside' production. In many places this played an important role in improving the situation of women, since Party policy put pressure on production team leaders to treat women and men equally. In addition, women's participation in 'outside' production, and the contribution to the family income made by the work-points they earned in such work, helped to improve their bargaining power in the family. In most cases, however, women did not have

32

control over their earnings. Although their work-points were listed separately, payment was not made to individual women, but rather was added to that of other family members and handed to the head of the family.[42]

A further aspect of the collectivisation drive of the late 1950s particularly important to rural women was that for the first, and to date the last, time in the history of the CCP, encouragement of women's participation in the 'outside' sphere was accompanied by large-scale efforts to reduce women's work in the 'inside' sphere by socialising domestic work. Marina Thorborg estimated that, whereas in 1956, seven to ten per cent of children whose mothers took part in field work were taken care of in busy-farm-season child-care stations, in 1959, 53 to 73 per cent of such children were taken care of in child-care stations that functioned all year round.[43] Other services developed on a wide scale during this period included sewing workshops, grain mills, health services, maternity centres and communal dining halls.

Another move which had the effect of lessening women's work in the 'inside' sphere was the discouragement of what were called 'domestic sidelines' (*jiating fuye*). When communes were first established, they took over all ownership of the land and almost all the means of production, and employed peasants to work in production teams in return for work-points entitling them to a share of the total output of the team. At the same time, though, peasant families were assigned small private plots of land (*ziliudi*) and retained ownership of scattered fruit trees, domestic livestock and small farm tools. They were allowed to use time outside collective work hours and the labour of family members not engaged in collective work to gather wild plants, cultivate vegetables and fruit trees on their private plot or in their courtyard, rear small numbers of domestic livestock, and make handicrafts on a small scale. Much of the work involved in these domestic sidelines was done by women.[44]

State policies towards domestic sidelines fluctuated from the 1950s to the late 1970s between cautious encouragement and repression. On the one hand, they were regarded by the state as competition with, and a threat to, the collective economy, and as an area where class inequalities could re-emerge. On the other hand, they were a concession to the peasant population which, on the whole, was opposed to collectivisation, and, in addition, they could provide an important supplement to collective production. In most periods the latter considerations won out. Peasants generally obtained grain from collective distribution, but a large proportion of other food items and cash they obtained from domestic sidelines. This was reflected in the peasant saying 'We depend on the collective for grain, but on ourselves for cash'.[45] During the Great Leap Forward, however, domestic sidelines were officially discouraged or banned, and many communes confiscated private plots without compensation.[46]

The liberation of women was not a central focus of the Great Leap Forward. However, the demands of the Great Leap Forward strategy did mean that efforts made to fulfil what had been Engels' two main requirements for women's liberation – involvement in 'social production' and release from domestic work – were greater during this period than at any other time. As a consequence, the Great Leap Forward offers a particularly clear picture of the problems and limitations of the Chinese adoption of Engels' approach.

One problem was that the programme for the socialisation of domestic work ran into difficulties because of the financial costs. Tasks formerly performed by women as unpaid domestic work continued to be done mainly by women, but became collective services that had to be paid for out of collective funds. In many areas the costs of such services were considered too high and they functioned for only a short time. After the end of the Great Leap Forward, a large proportion of collective services in rural areas ceased.

Other limitations of women's liberation during the Great Leap Forward were due to the fact that, as in the land reform campaign, certain attitudes and social structures remained unchallenged. No attempt was made, for example, to challenge the continued practice of patrilocal marriage in rural areas. This practice had a whole host of negative consequences: the mistreatment of young daughters and a reluctance to teach them skills that would be lost to another family and, resulting from this and from the fact that upon marriage they moved to an alien environment, an inability on the part of many young women to participate in production outside the home and in the political affairs of the commune.

Another phenomenon that remained largely unchallenged was the gender division of labour between 'inside' and 'outside' work. The establishment of collective child care and other services lessened individual women's burden of domestic work, but it left untouched the notion that domestic work was women's responsibility, not men's. The staff of collective services were almost all women, and where such services were minimal, individual women bore the entire responsibility for domestic work. Consequently, many women shouldered a heavy double burden during the Great Leap Forward.

Not only did the Great Leap Forward not eliminate the gender division of labour between 'inside' and 'outside', it also created a low opinion of 'inside' work and hence reinforced the devaluation and subordination of women. This, I would argue, was due largely to the fact that some of the assumptions on which the original Marxist approach to women's liberation was based were at odds with the Chinese situation.

Engels' claim that women's liberation was dependent upon their participation in social production and the reduction of their domestic duties was based, first of all, on his belief that men's domination over women stemmed from the fact that in what he termed the middle stage of barbarism men began domesticating animals and were able to produce more than was needed for consumption. Consequently, 'all the surplus now resulting from production fell to the man; the woman shared in consuming it, but she had no share in owning it ... The woman's housework lost its significance compared with the man's work in obtaining a livelihood. The latter was everything, the former an insignificant contribution'.[47] Underlying Engels' claim was also what I discussed in Chapter 1 as a Victorian ideological dichotomy between a 'private', 'feminine' family sphere and a 'public', 'masculine' sphere of production.

Recent research has thrown doubt on Engels' version of world history. For example, there is much anthropological data which suggests that it was women, rather than men, who first developed horticulture and thereby generated productive surplus.[48] This problem aside, Engels' conception of gender divisions of labour clashes with what we know about women's work in rural China in the nineteenth and twentieth centuries. As discussed in the first section of this chapter, in rural China before collectivisation a conceptual dichotomy between 'inside' and 'outside' spheres resulted in gender divisions of labour such that women's work was relatively concentrated in the home and family, and field work was undertaken largely by men. The dichotomy did not, however, also involve a distinction between 'family care' and 'production' and, in practice, some aspects of women's 'inside' work, such as weaving and raising domestic livestock, did involve the production of material goods, both for consumption and for surplus value. Furthermore, there is no evidence to indicate that in pre-revolutionary China work such as cooking and child care was devalued as 'non-productive', or that it was recognised as any less necessary to the family economy than other work.

Thus, in adopting Marxist theoretical approaches, Chinese leaders in the 1950s added new, negative connotations to the 'inside' work undertaken largely by women. These connotations were then inscribed in the organisation of rural families into collectives and the subsequent distinction drawn between collective production and work undertaken for the individual family. Domestic work was devalued because it was seen as non-productive and as not contributing to the collective economy. Women's work in domestic sidelines was devalued both because of its association with 'unproductive' domestic work and, ironically, because it was, in fact, productive, and was part of a private market economy regarded as a threat to the collective economy.

During the Great Leap Forward there were also a number of problems surrounding women's work in the 'outside' sphere. There were numerous complaints from the Women's Federation, for example, of women being overworked and of practices, such as assigning heavy work to pregnant women, which resulted in serious damage to women's health. It was claimed that some production team leaders regarded the protection of women's health as an impediment to fulfilling production quotas, rather than as a sound investment in these workers.[49]

In addition, a division was generally maintained in the 'outside' sphere between the work of men and that of women, and women's work was under-valued and remunerated less well than men's, despite the often repeated slogan of 'equal pay for equal work'. The evaluation process for the work-point remuneration system adopted in Chinese communes varied considerably from place to place. Apart from taking into account the number of hours a worker spent in collective labour, work-points were sometimes assigned according to the 'heaviness' or difficulty of the tasks performed and sometimes according to the skill or physical abilities of the worker. Almost invariably, however, the definition of terms such as 'skill', 'heaviness' and 'physical ability' was such as to discriminate against women. As in parts of rural China before 1949, work which was seen as involving heavy labour, usually done by men, was rewarded more than work done by women that required dexterity or stamina. For example, ploughing with a cow was defined as 'heavy' work and was done by men. As such, it was rewarded more than harvesting grain with a sickle, which was women's work and was considered 'light', even though it was considerably more tiring.[50]

Rural men often strongly resisted equal remuneration for women's and men's work and put pressure on local officials to divide work tasks in such a way that women would receive less pay. In some instances, where there was not already such a classification in place, they called for certain tasks to be classified as 'heavy' work, to be done by men only, and to be remunerated at rates higher than those for tasks undertaken by women.[51] Consequently, as will be discussed in Chapter 7, the gender divisions of labour between 'light' and 'heavy' work apparent in agriculture in the post-Mao era are a result, in part, of struggles over remuneration that occurred under the collective system.

Where rural industry was developed, or capital construction works under-taken, women generally took over agricultural work, so that men could be freed for the new tasks. Through the 1960s and 1970s this pattern was repeated, and after 1978, with a marked increase in rural industrialisation, it became even more evident. The implications of this are discussed in Chapter 7.

The Great Leap Forward ended in economic disaster in 1960, and in the subsequent economic recession between 1960 and 1963 numerous collective services were closed down, rural employment opportunities contracted, and rural women's labour force participation rate declined to 50–60 per cent. As the economy strengthened in the mid-1960s, more rural industries developed, employing mainly men, and more women were absorbed into agricultural work. Women's labour force participation rate rose to 60–70 per cent during these years, and remained at about 70 per cent through to the mid-1970s.[52]

After the Great Leap Forward the All-China Women's Federation shifted its attention from a concern primarily with women's participation in production as the key to their liberation, to a greater concern with ideology. In the early 1960s it initiated a movement aimed at raising the ideological consciousness of women, believing that women's social inferiority was grounded in traditional ideology, and that in order to solve this problem women had first to increase their own self-awareness.[53] Many articles in *ZGFN* at this time addressed women's problems of combining participation in paid work with domestic duties and, while recognising that these problems were indeed considerable, claimed that with a strong will and 'correct thinking' they could nevertheless be overcome. The assumption was, of course, that domestic work would neither be thoroughly socialised, nor shared with men, but would remain the responsibility of individual women.

Although the attempts by the Women's Federation to improve the ideological consciousness of women corresponded in a general way with the growing emphasis of the state leadership during this period on ideology and politics, during the second half of the 1960s they received harsh criticism because they were seen to conflict with attempts to raise women and men's class consciousness. Subsequently, the Women's Federation, along with other mass organisations, was branded revisionist and was disbanded. During the three years of the Cultural Revolution there was no separate work carried out among women.

Despite this, young women did play a major role in Red Guard activities and there was strong encouragement of women's participation in political affairs and in all areas of 'outside' production during this period. Notions that women were not fit for 'outside' roles were countered with the slogans, 'Times have changed, men and women are equal', 'What men can do, women can do too' and 'Women hold up half the sky', and with stories of model women working alongside men or in 'Iron Girls' teams' in areas of production from which women had been previously excluded, such as heavy industry.

The negative side to this propaganda was that women's lives as mothers and wives and the problems of combining 'inside' work demands with those of 'outside' work were ignored. In media accounts, model women's families were either not mentioned, or else 'selfish' concerns for the individual family were sacrificed for the revolutionary cause. Women were still expected to undertake all domestic work, but this contribution to the economy was not recognised. The proposition that 'What women can do, men can do too', or that both women and men should do domestic work, was not raised.[54]

Rural inhabitants were on the whole less affected by the turmoil of the Cultural Revolution than those of the cities. However, one policy that had a major impact on rural areas was the *xia-xiang* policy, in which, altogether, some twelve million urban school-leavers were sent to the countryside to learn from the peasants.[55] The policy, which ran from 1968 until Mao Zedong's death in 1976, was unpopular, both with the urbanites who regarded it as akin to a sentence of hard labour, and with the peasants who considered the young urban people a burden and a nuisance. Young women, both urban and rural, did sometimes benefit from the policy, however. Educated young urban women, for example, sometimes had greater opportunity to exercise their skills and gain positions of respect in rural industry and rural politics than they would have had in competing with their male counterparts in the cities. At the same time, they provided a new model for young peasant women to emulate, and helped to break down rural prejudices about women.[56]

Following the end of the Cultural Revolution in 1969, separate work among women was given attention once more, and by 1973 the Women's Federation was re-established up to the provincial level throughout most of the country.[57]

The revival of separate political work with women[58] was partly due to a major new attempt to reduce population growth (this being seen as largely women's responsibility). Such attempts had been made in the mid-1950s and early 1960s, but were given relatively little emphasis and had been discontinued during the Great Leap Forward and the Cultural Revolution. In the early 1970s a national population policy aimed at reducing the birth rate to two per cent was implemented. Late marriage was promoted (24 to 26 for women, 26 to 29 for men), two or three children were recommended as the maximum, and a spacing of at least four years between births was urged. Health workers and those involved at all levels of the political system, but especially members of the Women's Federation, were mobilised to educate the population on the need for family planning.[59]

The greatest increase in woman-work during the 1970s was due, however, to the 'criticise Lin Biao and Confucius' campaign which ran from 1973 to 1976. This campaign resulted in a uniquely concentrated attempt to challenge the obstacles that Confucianism continued to create for the realisation of gender equality. In study groups across the country women read and criticised Confucian classic texts, in particular the *Classic for Girls [Nüer jing]*, and identified and analysed the effects of Confucianism on their own lives.

During these years some more direct and practical steps were also taken towards reducing gender inequalities in rural areas. For example, for the first time, a fairly strong propaganda effort was made to persuade men to share the burden of domestic work, local leaders were urged to improve women's representation in collective decision-making bodies, matrilocal marriages were encouraged, and unequal work remuneration was challenged. In some areas these efforts were moderately successful. Kay Ann Johnson reports that in Hebei, for example, Women's Federation statistics recorded an increase in the work-point ratings of women, an increase in the proportion of production brigades funding public child care, and an increase in the number of women working in full-time agriculture. They also noted an improved willingness on the part of men to do domestic work.[60]

William Parish and Martin Whyte claim, though, that although the official ideal of equal sharing of domestic work was known in the Guangdong villages they studied, no indication was given of any concrete attempts made to involve more men in domestic work.[61] This suggests that the 'criticise Lin Biao and Confucius' campaign, which was conducted at the time of the Parish and Whyte interviews, had little impact on gender relations in Guangdong.

Whatever the extent of the successes in realising gender equality engendered by the 'criticise Lin Biao and Confucius' campaign, they were, in any case, short-lived. After Mao Zedong's death and the fall of the 'Gang of Four' in 1976, there was a backlash against the campaign, as there was against everything that the new leadership chose to describe as a project of the Gang of Four. Emily Honig suggests, for example, that one reason for the surprising strength of belief in women's biological inferiority among Chinese people in the 1980s was that a suggestion to the contrary might evoke the accusation that one was espousing the principles of the Gang of Four.[62]

3

Post-Mao Reforms

A FTER Mao Zedong's death and the arrest of the Gang of Four in 1976, Deng Xiaoping, and other leaders whom the Gang of Four had opposed, rose to prominence. They promoted values and goals very different from those espoused under the previous regime, and introduced policies for radical economic and social reform. In rural areas, this turn around was to have an impact on the economy and on social relations as profound as that caused by the collectivisation drive of the 1950s, which it was now reversing.

SHIFTS IN STATE IDEOLOGY

In the first phase of post-Mao reform, between 1978 and 1980, the state leaders' attention was concentrated on the consolidation of their own power, and structural reforms were implemented only gradually.[1] During this early period, nevertheless, important shifts in state ideology and political and economic theory were expressed.[2] The Deng leadership distanced itself from the previous regime by criticising the latter's 'excessive' political radicalism and egalitarianism, promoting instead the depoliticisation of ordinary life, economic pragmatism, an improvement of living standards and balanced economic growth. The latter two goals were to be achieved through the 'four modernisations'[3] a greater opening to the outside world, more attention to the development of agriculture, consumer industries and services, greater division of labour and specialisation, and the promotion of material incentives and individual striving.

These broad shifts in ideology paved the way for radical structural change. Then, once structural change and social adjustment got under way, new concepts and slogans were developed, in some cases to legitimate changes that had already begun, and in others, to contain undesired consequences of those changes.[4]

This is not the place for a detailed account of these processes. Instead, in the following paragraphs, I wish to focus upon the 'gendered' nature of the shifts in ideology. As will become apparent, whether motivated by a desire to effect

40

change, to legitimate change already under way, or to guide it into new directions, the shifts in state ideology that have occurred have included, as a core element, a reconfiguration of notions of womanhood and of women's position in society. These, in turn, have had a powerful impact on actual gender relations, and the ways in which gender relations have been affected by structural change.

I will also argue, however, that the images of womanhood created in the post-Mao era are not solely an imposition by the central state leadership, but have received powerful support from a range of people in different social positions, including women as well as men.

One of the symbols of Cultural Revolution 'radicalism' against which the Deng leadership, and indeed the ordinary population, have reacted most vehemently is that of the woman who is active in the 'outside', 'male' sphere of politics – the 'Red Guard Lady', epitomised, in particular, by Mao Zedong's wife and a member of the Gang of Four, Jiang Qing. As will be discussed in Chapter 5, a key mechanism through which Jiang Qing's radicalism, and by extension, the Gang of Four and their policies, have been discredited by the current regime has been through a portrayal of Jiang Qing as a 'white-boned demon', a witch and a prostitute – a woman who acted outside the bounds of 'natural', 'proper' gender roles. The message to the Chinese people is two-fold: that the Gang of Four was bad; and that, as Marilyn Young has put it, 'there is something in the natural order of things that does not love a woman exercising public power'.[5]

A rejection of the Cultural Revolution and the Gang of Four also takes the form of denunciation and scorn at the 'Iron Girls' of the period, and a repudiation of the slogan 'What men can do, women can do too'.[6] Whereas during the late Maoist period women were exhorted to behave like men, it now insisted that women and men are different, and each have their special characteristics and abilities. As Emily Honig and Gail Hershatter point out, there is now a vast amount of media articles and other forms of popular literature providing advice on the physiological and psychological differences between women and men.[7]

As will become apparent through this book, this discourse has reinforced gender inequalities in a number of ways. It should also be noted, however, that it is supported by women themselves, and that this is not merely a case of 'false consciousness'. For many women as for men, living through the 'ten years of turmoil' (1966–1976) resulted in an equation between attempts at radical social and political change and chaos and suffering, and Deng Xiaoping's restoration of order and of the 'natural order' were met with relief. Women also welcomed the chance to move away from the masculine-style asceticism of the Maoist era and to enjoy the more traditional pleasures of femininity – changing out of their shapeless, worn Mao suits into colourful dresses, perming their hair and putting on make-up. And, finally, whilst some women, for example those who had been

Red Guards, looked back on the late 1960s and early 1970s as a time of excitement and freedom from the restrictions of traditional femininity,[8] many others reflected that 'equality' during this period merely meant their having to work twice as hard as men, whilst receiving fewer work-points in the fields and no recognition for their domestic work.

Yet there is more to the post-Mao discourse on gender difference than either a state or a popular rejection of political radicalism. On the one hand, as the billboards around China's cities testify, the rise of a commodity economy and consumerism has seen the image of woman as sex object being manipulated in the burgeoning advertising industry in much the same way as it has been in the West.

On the other hand, an emphasis on women's roles as mothers, and by extension, as the guardians of social order and morality, has been a central element in the state's attempts to combat post-Cultural Revolution cynicism and discontent amongst young people, to curb what are seen as the undesirable consequences of the 'open door policy' and the promotion of a market economy; that is, excessive materialism, selfishness, and 'spiritual pollution', and to promote values and standards of behaviour conducive to social stability and modernisation. As the then Party Chairperson, Hu Yaobang, put it in 1982: 'Women are not only an important force in national economic construction; they also have a particularly significant role to play in the building of socialist spiritual civilisation.'[9] As I have discussed elsewhere, the primacy of the image of woman as mother has also been bolstered through the argument, seen frequently in the media in the 1980s, and acted upon by numerous employers, that women working in state-run factories should take extended maternity leave or should 'return to the kitchen' permanently in order to relieve pressure on urban employment. [10]

Finally, as I suggest in my discussion of gender segregation in vocational education in Chapter 5, an emphasis on gender difference contributes to a greater division of labour in the economy. For this reason it has been encouraged by the state in its attempts to improve efficiency and to meet contrasting demands, in particular, for modernisation on the one hand, and employment generation on the other. The notion of gender difference has also been reinforced through the policies of the state and of employers in particular sectors of the economy. For example, as I suggest in Chapter 8, domestic sidelines and the 'courtyard economy' have been promoted by the state in the post-Mao era as an area of work 'particularly suited to women's special characteristics', in part as a way of relieving female underemployment, and in part as a way of taking full advantage of the cheap and flexible labour of women working at home. And in township enterprises manufacturing textiles, employers hire a majority of female workers because, they claim, they are more nimble-fingered and patient than men, whilst in heavy industries, employers hire more men because, they claim, the work is too heavy for women.

I will now turn to examine the reform policies in rural areas, the structural changes that they have initiated, and, briefly, the effects on rural society that these structural changes have had.

The introduction of the production responsibility system

According to the post-Mao leadership, a major drawback of the collective system was that it did not provide incentives for workers to improve their productivity. Consequently, at the Third Plenum of the Eleventh Central Committee, held in December 1978,[11] a form of what later became known as the 'production responsibility system' (*shengchan zerenzhi*) was introduced, with the aim of improving production incentives by linking production and remuneration more closely. It allowed a system of 'contracting output to the group' (*bao chan dao zu*), in which the production team signed a contract with a smaller work group stipulating the inputs, production quotas and work-point remuneration for a particular piece of work. Accounting, planning, control of tools and draught animals, irrigation and capital construction projects continued to be the production team's responsibility, but the internal distribution of work-points among its members was undertaken by the group.[12] This was the first in a number of different types of production responsibility system which became universal in rural areas by the early 1980s.

In September 1980 the CCP Central Committee issued Document 75, 'Announcement regarding several issues concerned with the further strengthening and perfection of the production responsibility system in agriculture'. The document allowed two other forms of household contracting to be implemented in poor and backward areas and in places where contracting to the household had already occurred. Under the first of these systems, known as 'contracting output to the household' (*bao chan dao hu*), the household signed a contract with the production team which stipulated an allocation of land to the household and a proportion of produce that the household was to give the team in return for a specified number of work-points. Machinery and draught animals were either managed by the team or divided between households.[13] Land was usually allocated according to the number of people or the number of labour powers in the household, or according to both.[14] In theory, any changes to the population of the household, such as a birth or death, the exit of a daughter or the entry of a wife, were to be followed by an adjustment of the household's land holdings. However, this system resulted in enormous management problems, and in subsequent years was therefore replaced by other schemes, a common one involving the reassessment and readjustment of the land holdings of all villagers every few years. As will be discussed in Chapter 4, however, there continue to be serious problems relating to the allocation of land to women, especially divorcees and widows, under the new systems.

Under the second type of production responsibility system, known as 'contracting everything to the household' (*bao gan dao hu* or *da bao gan*), the household took over all responsibility for production management, simply handing over land tax and a sales quota of a particular crop (usually grain) and paying a levy to the production team to help maintain basic collective services. Land was contracted in the same way as under the *bao chan dao hu* system, and tools and draught animals were distributed among households.[15]

Like other aspects of the reforms, the production responsibility system was not introduced uniformly across the country as part of a national policy. Even before the Third Plenum, forms of organisation other than that approved at the plenum were being tried out in some places,[16] and it was in view of these experiments that Document 75 was introduced. Thereafter, there was a good deal of regional variation in the timing of the introduction of the production responsibility system and the type of system adopted. In some places local cadres and peasants strongly resisted the decentralisation of production management that the new system implied.[17] More commonly, though, pressures from peasants desiring a return to family farming pushed the implementation of the system faster and further than the central authorities had originally planned.[18]

By October 1981 approximately 98 per cent of all collective accounting units had adopted some form of production responsibility system. At that time seven per cent had adopted the *bao chan dao hu* system and 38 per cent had adopted the *bao gan dao hu* system.[19] By late 1984 the *bao gan dao hu* system had been adopted by approximately 95 per cent of collective units, with the remainder using other forms of the production responsibility system.[20]

As will be noted below, collectives have not entirely given up their role in economic management since the introduction of the production responsibility system. Nevertheless, an important consequence of this reform has been that most decisions over work and the allocation of tasks have once more become internal to the family. An examination of family relations is, therefore, of particular importance for an understanding of the gender divisions of labour that have emerged in the post-Mao era. This topic will be pursued in Chapter 4.

Changes to political and administrative institutions

As household contracting spread, it became clear that a re-examination of the role and structure of commune and sub-commune institutions of administration and governance was needed. Between 1982 and 1985, attempts were made by the central leadership to effect a separation between governmental and economic administration, and to reduce the role of the Party in day-to-day administration and management. Governmental responsibilities of communes were taken over by township (*xiang*) and town (*zhen*) governments, and were formally separated from the township Party committee. Economic functions were transferred to economic management committees (*jingji guanli weiyuanhui*), subordinate to township governments. Similarly, production brigades were converted into administrative villages (*xingzhen cun*) led by villagers' committees (*cunmin weiyuanhui*) with governmental responsibilities and in some places 'joint cooperatives' or 'corporations' (*nong-gong-shang lianhe gongsi*) with economic functions. Production teams were renamed village groups (*cunmin xiaozu*), but became largely redundant, except where they coincided with a natural village.[21]

Despite these formal changes, however, there continues to be a good deal of overlapping between Party, government and economic institutions, both in terms of personnel and activities, and in general, people who held positions as local-level Party cadres before decollectivisation have tended to retain most control over local government and economic administration under the new arrangements. As one peasant put it, 'they are holding up a sheep's head, but they are selling the same old dog meat'.[22]

Across China there have been wide variations in the roles of township and village-level institutions and leaders, and their relations with peasant families. These variations result, at least in part, from differences in farmers' and local leaders' relative access to, and control over, resources. In more wealthy areas, leaders are able to offer assets, such as cheaper farm inputs and jobs in local factories, in return for peasants' compliance with demands, such as the delivery of crop quotas, and contributions to welfare funds. However, in these wealthier areas, limitations on leaders' ability to shape peasant behaviour arise from the existence of alternative channels, for example for the purchase of farm inputs, and the sale of produce. In poorer areas, local leaders have access to fewer assets to use as 'bargaining chips' in their relations with peasants. On the other hand, poorer households may be more reliant for their livelihood on these minimal assets, and may therefore be compelled to follow leaders' directives.[23]

In recent years, in some more wealthy townships and villages in particular, local leaders have played a major role in controlling or guiding the economy, for example by making village-wide decisions on crop planting,[24] by obtaining loans and investing in township- or village-run enterprises, by ensuring the provision of credit and other inputs and arranging sales outlets for peasant entrepreneurs, and by advising peasant families on profitable ventures. These

45

townships and villages have, in addition, made use of their revenue, obtained in particular from township enterprises and levies on agriculture, to provide production, welfare and education services, and to maintain public works such as roads and irrigation.[25]

Reports suggest, however, that in many places the role of the collective has greatly declined. Victor Nee and Su Sijin claim, for example, that in 15 of the 30 villages in Fujian that they studied in 1985, there was no sign of any collective activity. Public works were not being maintained and welfare services, such as aid to the poor and health insurance, were not being provided. Eleven villages reported some collective activity, but at a level much lower than before decollectivisation.[26]

For rural women, the lack of collective services has particular significance. As will be discussed in Chapter 5, for example, many rural families have responded to the rising costs of education, resulting from declining collective subsidies, by withdrawing their daughters from school. In addition, scarcity of child care facilities increases the workload on individual mothers and grandmothers (see Chapter 6).

Pricing adjustments, and the encouragement of diversification and specialisation in the rural economy

Concurrent with reforms in rural organisation and management have been changes in the pricing of agricultural products, and attempts to encourage diversification and specialisation in the rural economy. The Third Plenum of the Eleventh Central Committee in 1978 decided that, in order to stimulate agricultural production, the state purchase price for grain would be raised by 20 per cent, and the price for the amount purchased above the quota would be raised by an additional 50 per cent. The purchase price for various economic crops and agricultural subsidiary products would also be increased, and the cost of farm machinery, chemical fertiliser, insecticides and other agricultural inputs would be reduced.[27] In subsequent years other price changes followed, so that between 1979 and 1984 the average annual increase in the purchase price of agricultural and subsidiary products was 7.62 per cent and between 1985 and 1989 it was 13 per cent, although in the latter period there were also sharp increases in the cost of agricultural inputs.[28] At the same time, the state progressively decreased its direct control over, and intervention into, the marketing and pricing of agricultural products, to the extent that by the end of 1992 agricultural production, with the exception of cotton, oil crops and grain, was regulated almost solely by the market.[29]

The Third Plenum also reaffirmed peasants' rights to engage in domestic sidelines,[30] and encouraged local governments to invest, and expand, employment in rural industries, or township enterprises (*xiangzhen qiye*), as they came to be known.[31] These moves were part of a broad shift in which the state abandoned its earlier policy of aiming for self-sufficiency in grain in each region in favour of an encouragement of peasant involvement in cash-cropping, forestry, animal husbandry, fishing, processing, manufacturing and services. This trend toward diversification has both led to, and has itself been further increased by, improvements in agricultural productivity and the consequent release of 'surplus' labour from crop production (see Chapter 7), the opening of free markets, an improvement of transport and service facilities, and an increase in the movement of labour both within rural areas and between rural and urban areas.

In addition to promoting diversification of the rural economy, the state has encouraged peasant families to set up their own businesses, specialising in single areas of agricultural production, or in non-agricultural production, for the market. In order to make it easier for peasants to develop 'specialised house-holds' (*zhuanyehu*) and 'private enterprises' (*getihu* and *siying qiye*) as they are termed, local governments often provide them with subsidised fertiliser and other inputs, and help them to market their produce. In addition, the state has made major changes to laws concerning the hiring of labour and the sub-contracting of land. Document No.1 of 1983 allowed peasant families to hire labour, and Document No.1 of 1984 allowed peasant families engaged in non-agricultural production to subcontract their land to other families to farm for them, in return for a cash payment or a share of produce.[32]

Changes in rural employment patterns

The introduction of the production responsibility system, combined with the encouragement of diversification and specialisation in the rural economy, has given peasant families more freedom to make their own decisions about what areas of production to engage in, according to their particular abilities and the interplay of local prices, supply and demand. The net income to be earned from growing grain crops has generally been much lower than that in other areas of agriculture, so there has been a strong incentive for peasants to move out of grain production. Similarly, non-agricultural activities, such as processing, commerce and transport, are more profitable than agriculture.[33] These factors have led some peasant families to specialise in one area of agricultural production, or to abandon agriculture altogether. For most, though, the potential profitability of such a move has been offset by a lack of specialised technical skills, market information and capital, the risks involved in moving from largely subsistence agriculture to a new line of commodity production, and the uncertainties surrounding government policy, as well as by pressures to meet targets for crop production set by local leaders. In addition, land is generally regarded by peasants as their most important form of economic security and they have been reluctant to abandon it entirely in favour of more lucrative, but less secure, non-agricultural production. Most commonly, peasant families manage these conflicting factors by keeping a finger in each pie, as it were, with men and women in the family undertaking different economic activities. A woman might, for example, grow grain and vegetables, whilst her husband runs a private enterprise mending bicycles and their son and daughter work in nearby factories. This kind of division of labour was common amongst the rural families that I visited in 1989, and is clearly illustrated in the summaries contained in Appendix 1.

Significant changes in rural employment patterns have occurred, nevertheless. In particular, the 1980s and 1990s have seen large numbers of rural inhabitants shift from agricultural to non-agricultural occupations. Thus, whereas between 1952 and 1977 China's rural non-agricultural employment grew by only 2.4 per cent per annum, between 1978 and 1990 it grew at a rate of 13.3 per cent per annum. In 1977 total rural non-agricultural employment stood at 17.32 million people, or 5.6 per cent of total rural employment, but by 1990 it had increased to 87.56 million people, or 20.5 per cent of total rural employment.[34] As will be discussed in Chapter 9, however, significantly fewer rural women than men are employed outside agriculture.

It is also important to note that although, in terms of their basic thrust, the economic reforms have been implemented right across rural China, the details of their implementation and the changes they have effected have differed from place to place. The most obvious difference has been between areas on the eastern coast and around large cities, and areas inland and far removed from large cities. In the former areas industries are now well developed, as are trade networks with other parts of China and with overseas markets. A relatively large proportion of peasants work at non-agricultural occupations and families are fairly well-off. In the latter areas the market economy and industries are as yet relatively underdeveloped, and most peasants rely on agriculture for their livelihood, and are relatively poor.[35]

Income distribution

In the first half of the 1980s the economic reform policies introduced in rural China resulted in rapid improvements in peasant incomes and living standards. After 1985, however, real incomes stagnated. According to the State Statistical Bureau, net per capita rural income in 1978 was 133.57 *yuan*, of which 116.06 *yuan* or 86.9 per cent went on living expenditure. By 1984 net per capita rural income had increased to 355.33 *yuan*, of which 273.80 *yuan* or 77.1 per cent went on living expenditure. Thereafter, net incomes continued to rise, but the effects of inflation and rising living costs meant that the proportion of peasant income spent on living expenditure increased. Thus, by 1988 net per capita rural income had risen to 544.94 *yuan*, of which, however, 476.66 *yuan*, or 87.5 per cent, went on living expenditure. At the end of 1993 net per capita rural income was 921.62 *yuan*, of which 769.65 *yuan* (83.5 per cent) went on living expenditure.[36]

Roughly in tandem with these trends, the gap between rural and urban incomes and consumption narrowed in the early 1980s but then widened again in late 1980s and 1990s. Thus, according to the State Statistical Bureau, the ratio of peasant (*nongmin*) consumption to non-agricultural urban (*feinongye jumin*) consumption increased from 1:2.9 in 1978 to 1:2.2 in 1985, but then declined to 1:3.0 in 1991.[37]

Income inequalities within rural areas have been increasing since the early 1980s. According to studies undertaken by the World Bank, rural Gini ratios decreased from 0.32 in 1978 to 0.22 in 1982, but then increased to 0.27 in 1984 and 0.31 in 1986. Another large-scale study undertaken by a team of western economists found that in 1988 the rural Gini ratio was 0.34.[38]

Much of the inequality in rural income distribution has been due to increasing regional variations in the reform period. According to one report, for example, in 1979 per capita incomes in China's central and western regions were respectively 69 per cent and 56 per cent of the per capita income in the eastern region. By 1988 these figures had declined to 52 per cent and 43 per cent.[39]

In addition, inequalities in the distribution of income between families and between individuals have increased as a result of increased occupational differentiation. Amongst the wealthiest families are those who run specialised households and private enterprises. As will be discussed in Chapter 8, such families are commonly larger than the average, have above average levels of education, and have connections with local government. In more general terms, as noted by the 1988 study mentioned above, wages are the most significant factor in income inequalities between families and individuals. Some 62 per cent of income from wages is received by the richest 10 per cent of the population, and the poorest 20 per cent of the population receive only one per cent of their income from wages.[40]

As will be discussed in Chapter 9, rural women are much less likely than men to have jobs in industry or other areas of wage employment. This goes a long way towards explaining the fact that in general terms, rural women earn lower incomes than rural men, and the majority of the poorest rural people are women. This feminisation of poverty is well illustrated by the *Sampling Survey Data of*

Women's Status in Contemporary China, conducted in 1991. The survey found that 32.7 per cent of rural wives earned a monthly income of 50 *yuan* or less, and 65.2 per cent earned 100 *yuan* or less. In contrast, only 8.6 per cent of rural husbands earned 50 *yuan* or less, and 33.5 per cent earned 100 *yuan* or less. At the other end of the scale, those earning more than 300 *yuan* per month included 16.4 per cent of rural husbands, but only 4.5 per cent of rural wives.[41]

Focusing only on rural wage earners, it appears that the inequalities between male and female incomes, while significant, are not as stark. The 1988 survey found, for example, that amongst rural wage earners, the mean monthly wage of women (103.8 *yuan*) was 81 per cent of that of men (127.9 *yuan*). In urban areas, in comparison, the survey found that on average, women's wages were 80 per cent of men's.[42] These figures help to confirm findings, discussed in Chapter 9, that income distribution within rural industries is relatively equitable.

THE ONE-CHILD FAMILY POLICY

One final reform which needs to be considered in an examination of women's work and gender divisions of labour in the countryside since 1978 is the CCP's one-child family policy. Under this policy, which was introduced in 1979, various forms of economic incentives have been given to couples who, after the birth of their first child, pledge to have no more, and penalties, often in the form of fines, have been imposed on couples who have a second or third child.[43] In urban areas, a relatively long history of family planning education, combined with socio-economic pressures for having fewer children, such as housing shortages, has made the implementation of the one-child family policy relatively easy. In rural areas, however, the policy has met with enormous resistance.

One reason for this discrepancy between urban and rural areas has been that there are few welfare services in the countryside. Most elderly peasants do not receive a pension, and children (or more particularly sons, because under the patrilocal marriage system daughters leave their native village upon marriage) are considered vital for the care they will provide their aging parents. For elderly peasants without relatives to support them, the collective does provide what is known as 'the five guarantees' (*wubao*): that is guarantees of subsistence requirements of food, health care, shelter, clothing and funeral costs. However, at the beginning of the 1980s only three per cent of people in rural areas aged 65 or over received the five guarantees, and since then the proportion has declined even further, both as a result of declines in collective welfare funding and because of an increase in the proportion of the elderly in the population.[44]

To some extent, the lack of social support for elderly peasants will in the future be mitigated by a voluntary rural pension plan established in 1991, into which farmers and those working in township enterprises pay a portion of their income. At least in the near future, however, this will only provide for a minority of better-off rural inhabitants. Up until 1995, fifty million peasants had joined the plan.[45]

A second reason for the resistance to the one-child family policy in rural areas has been that, to a great extent, the economic prosperity of a rural family depends on the amount of labour power it can muster. This has become more critical following the introduction of the recent economic reforms, since the closer link between remuneration and work performance, and the diversification of the rural economy, mean that labour power can now be used more effectively to generate income. In addition, the increased autonomy of the family relative to the collective and the state has meant that CCP cadres have lost much of their authority over peasants' lives and their exhortations for family planning have often been ignored, although draconian enforcement through abortion and sterilisation has been reported.

Implementation of the one-child policy has had some serious negative effects on gender relations and on women's lives. For example, despite the state's attempts at education, women are still sometimes blamed for the sex of the children they bear and there have been numerous reports of husbands and in-laws abusing, beating or abandoning women following the birth of a girl.[46] It is women, also, who bear the brunt of conflicting pressures from relatives and officials over whether to carry through an 'out of plan' pregnancy, and of course it is they who suffer from forced or late abortions.

Perhaps most seriously, peasant desires for boys, combined with pressures from the state to have only one child, have led to sex testing of foetuses and sex-specific abortions, failure to report the birth of girl babies and, in the most extreme cases, the abandonment and killing of girl babies.[47]

In recent years, in reaction to problems such as these, the Chinese state has, in a sense, given up on the one-child family policy. Since 1989, all provinces except Sichuan and Anhui and the municipalities of Beijing and Shanghai, have allowed peasant families to have a second child if their first was a girl.[48] This change of policy is perhaps preferable to female infanticide. Unfortunately, however, it reinforces the attitude that females are inferior to, or less valuable than, males, and does not address the reasons for peasant desires for sons rather than daughters.

Family planning and the one-child family policy have brought some benefits to women. For example, the difficulties in implementing the policy, combined with a recognition of a link between women's status and fertility levels, have at least drawn attention to, and raised concern over, the persistence of gender inequalities. To some extent, as Elisabeth Croll and Delia Davin suggest, this has

51

lent support to the efforts of the Women's Federation to combat discrimination and violence against women, and to improve women's education and employment opportunities.[49] As will be discussed in Chapter 5, however, the Women's Federation's work continues to be hindered by a lack of resources and power. Furthermore, the involvement of Women's Federation cadres in family planning work makes them unpopular amongst peasants, and hence actually compounds their difficulties in protecting and furthering women's interests.[50]

A more direct benefit to rural women of family planning is that reducing the number of children they bear reduces strains on their health. Fewer children may also mean a reduction in women's domestic workload, although it is doubtful that this is so in all cases, since the lesser workload resulting from fewer children is often offset by the lack of older children's contribution to domestic work tasks and the care of their younger siblings. In addition, in the long run, if the one-child policy succeeds, this will be offset by an increase in women's work in looking after four elderly parents.

Regardless of their actual effect on women's child care and domestic workload, family planning and declines in fertility appear to have had little impact on the widespread perception that motherhood and domestic work are women's chief roles in life. Indeed, I would argue that any such impact has been completely overshadowed by the reinforcement in the media and in state pronouncements of the image of woman as mother and guardian of social morality, stability and order. As will become apparent in later chapters, this perception of women as mothers, first and foremost, plays a central role in creating, maintaining and legitimating gender divisions of labour in which women are concentrated in the 'inside' sphere of domestic work, agriculture and home-based industry, and their involvement in the 'outside' sphere of large-scale industry, business, and political and economic leadership is limited.

In this chapter I have given a brief introduction, firstly, to the ideology framing the post-Mao leadership's reform policies and the centrality of gender difference in that ideology; and secondly, to the reform policies introduced by the state in rural China and their broad consequences for economic, political and social relations.

While space allows me to do little more than outline key shifts in state ideology and policy and some of the main consequences of these, it should be apparent that the reform process is a complex one, in which outcomes stem not just from policies imposed on society by the state, but from interactions in which actors from different sections of state and society put pressure on each other, and respond to each other's moves, either by accepting them, by making compromises, or by resisting.[51]

The establishment of the production responsibility system is a clear example of this process. In some areas, in response to peasant demands for family farming, local leaders introduced the production responsibility system before it had been given central state approval. In others, however, local cadres and peasants delayed the implementation of the system. In this case, the central state overcame local-level resistance. In the case of family planning, however, the policy limiting peasant families to only one child was met with so much resistance that it was eventually relaxed.

The emergence of a powerful discourse on sexual difference in the post-Mao era is another example of state–society interaction. As discussed in this chapter, this discourse has, in part, been propagated by the state in attempts to bolster its legitimacy and its reform programme. However, it has also been supported and furthered by other elements in society, including both men and women.

In subsequent chapters I will examine in greater detail the ways in which state–society interactions in the process of reform have shaped gender divisions of labour in rural China, paying attention, in particular, to the changes in meaning and significance of gendered dichotomies between different spheres of work.

Before undertaking a direct examination of work patterns and gender divisions of labour, however, it is necessary to look at other aspects of gender relations and the ways in which they have been affected by reform, both in order to understand how these influence gender divisions of labour, and how, in turn, changes to gender divisions of labour affect other aspects of gender relations. This, then, is the aim of the following two chapters, in which I will discuss women's position in the family, and their involvement in politics and education.

4

Families

IN rural China today, as in times past, 'the family' (*jia*) is central to women's and men's perceptions of themselves, their work patterns and their relations with others. As in other cultures, however, the Chinese concept of family is fluid. Associated with it are a range of meanings and spheres of significance.

On the one hand, women and the family have commonly been linked in discussions of one particular set of issues – woman as wife, mother and daughter-in-law, as domestic worker, and as belonging to, and being most strongly identified with, the 'inside' sphere. In this sense the family has been 'both central and delimiting for women's lives',[1] and has been defined in opposition to the 'outside' domain of men. At other times, women have been cast as outsiders to the family, here defined in terms of patrilocality, patrilineality, networks of male kinship ties and the importance of male descendants.

In this chapter I will examine the significance of the family in these two senses for an understanding of women's work patterns and gender divisions of labour, and the links between these and other aspects of gender relations. These, I argue, are both affected by gender divisions of labour, and, at the same time, play a part in determining and maintaining particular gender divisions of labour, and the meanings which these divisions have for women.[2]

FAMILY SIZE AND STRUCTURE

When asked about the members of their family ('*jia li you shenme ren?*'), peasant women commonly discuss close relatives who share a common budget and live in the same house or compound of dwellings. They may also mention other close relatives who are living elsewhere but share the same budget: for example, a husband working away from home as a temporary labourer.[3]

As can be seen in Table 4.1, the average Chinese family is now smaller than it was before the 1949 revolution. In 1947 average family size was about 5.4 persons. This declined to about 4.3 persons by 1953. Between the 1950s and the 1980s average family size remained at between 4.1 and 4.4 persons. Thus, the most abrupt shift in family size occurred in the early 1950s. As the following

Table 4.1   *Average family size*

Year	Average Family Size	
	National	Rural
1911	5.17	
1912	5.31	
1928	5.27	
1933	5.29	
1936	5.38	
1947	5.35	
1953	4.3	4.26
1964	4.29	4.35
1982	4.43	4.57
1987		4.4
1990	4.06	

Sources: 1911–1982: Guojia Tongjiju Shehui Tongjisi [Social Statistics Department, Bureau of Statistics], *Zhongguo Shehui Tongji Ziliao [Chinese Social Statistics]*, Zhongguo Tongji Chubanshe, Beijing, 1987, p. 30. 1987: Guojia Tongjiju [State Statistical Bureau], *Zhongguo Tongji Nianjian, 1989 [Statistical Yearbook of China, 1989]*, Zhongguo Tongji Chubanshe, Beijing, 1989, p. 93. 1990: Guojia Tongjiju Renkou Tongjisi [Population Statistics Department, State Bureau of Statistics], *Zhongguo Renkou Tongji Nianjian, 1991 [Chinese Population Statistical Yearbook, 1991]*, Zhongguo Tongji Chubanshe, Beijing, 1992, p. 25.

discussion indicates, this was primarily due to an increase in the proportion of nuclear families, rather than a decline in birth rates.

Table 4.2 shows that in the second half of the twentieth century families in rural China were most commonly nuclear or stem families. Since 1949, the number of nuclear families has been greater than before and the number of stem and grand families smaller.[4] Improved health care and living standards after 1949 led to declines in infant mortality and an increase in life expectancy. However, a tendency for brothers to establish separate families after marriage or the birth of children, combined with the fact that more brothers were surviving, led to an increase in the number of nuclear families.[5] The number of grand families has greatly declined as a result of the fact that married brothers are now less likely than before 1949 to live in the same family for a long period of time. The stem family, however, continues to be an important family type because the prevalence of co-residence between parents and one married child has remained constant.

The changes in the total number of different types of family that have occurred do not necessarily imply that individuals' living arrangements have changed dramatically, but may be due, at least in part, to changes in the size and

Table 4.2 *Percentages of rural households consisting of single persons, nuclear families, stem families and grand families*

Year		Single Person	Nuclear	Stem	Grand
1930	(a)	3.0	34.0	63.0	
1973	(b)	12.0	50.0	37.0	2.0
1978	(c)	2.7	65.4	26.8	2.9
1982	(d)	7.6	69.3	16.4	5.8
1986	(c)	2.2	73.3	19.7	1.6
1987	(e)	0.6	71.4	22.5	2.6

Sources: (a) Lewis and Smythe 1935, cited in William Parish and Martin Whyte, *Village and Family in Contemporary China*, University of Chicago Press, Chicago and London, 1978, p. 134. Survey conducted in South China, N = 2,422.

(b) Parish and Whyte, *Village and Family in Contemporary China*, p. 134. Survey conducted in Guangdong, N = 131.

(c) Liu Ying, '*Xianshi yu lixiang de chaju – tan nongcun jiating jiegou bianhua*' ['The gap between reality and ideals – a discussion of changes in family structure'], *Hunyin yu Jiating [Marriage and the Family]*, no. 1, 1989, pp. 38–39. Survey conducted in 14 provinces and municipalities, N = 7,285.

(d) Zhang Qiti, '*Shixi wo guo de jiating leixing ji qi chengyuan goucheng*' ['An examination of China's family types and their membership'], *Renkou yu Jingji [Population and Economy]*, no. 6, 1988, p. 48. Results from 10 per cent sample survey of China, 1982. Non-family households not included in this table amounted to one per cent of the total surveyed.

(e) Zhao Xishun, ed., *Nongmin Hunyin – Sichuan Nongcun Hunyin Yanjiu [Peasant Marriage – Research into Rural Marriage in Sichuan]*, Sichuan Renmin Chubanshe, Sichuan, 1990, p. 238. Survey conducted in Sichuan, N = 1,911. 'Other families' not included in this table amounted to 2.9 per cent of the total surveyed.

structure of the population. For example, as one Chinese analyst has pointed out, an increase in the number of nuclear families in the 1980s may have been caused simply by the fact that the particularly large cohort of people born in the 1960s before rigorous family planning campaigns were begun were, in the 1980s, entering childbearing age, that is, the period in which they were most likely to establish nuclear families separate from their parents.[6]

This suggests that although the total number of women living in nuclear families may have been higher in the post-Mao era than previously, women as they grew older experienced the same sequence of family arrangements as experienced by women in previous decades. This was confirmed by a sample survey of 2,000 families undertaken in rural Sichuan in 1987.[7] The survey found that over the preceding fifty years women at the same stage in their life cycle were to be found in the same types of family.

Working from the results of this survey, and from other information, we can construct a model indicating the type of family a woman has been most likely to find herself in at different stages of her life over the last fifty years, and can make some comments on the consequences of these patterns for the nature and extent of her involvement in domestic work and the paid workforce.

Throughout this period, young, unmarried women have lived most commonly in nuclear or stem families. School-age girls, whilst being largely supported by their parents, are also usually expected to help their mothers with domestic work and care of their younger siblings. Once they have completed their education, which for most means attending no more than junior secondary school, young rural women usually make a substantial contribution to domestic work, and also work full time in some form of paid employment. For the majority this means working in the fields, at home undertaking some form of domestic sidelines, or in local industry. In the 1980s and 1990s, however, a small but growing proportion of young women have lived and worked away from home, for example as nannies or temporary workers in large cities (see Chapter 9).

Marriage is nearly universal in China, and about 98 per cent of rural women are married by the age of 29.[8] The legal marriage ages are now 22 for men and 20 for women, but a large number of marriages also occurs before these ages.[9] Earlier marriage allows for earlier and more frequent childbirth, and is in part a strategy adopted by rural families as a way of gaining more labour, thereby maximising the economic benefits of the return to family farming.

As in the past, most rural marriages are exogamous and patrilocal, which means that the bride and groom are from different villages and that, upon marriage, the woman moves from her natal family into her husband's family. The new couple may continue to live indefinitely in the man's family, especially if he is the youngest or the only son, in which case he and his wife will be expected to care for his parents as they grow old. Otherwise, the family will commonly divide its property and the young couple will establish a new family, often just after the birth of their first child.

In families where mothers- and daughters-in-law live together, it is most common for them to share domestic work. The particular division of labour varies from one family to another. In some families the young woman works during the day in a nearby township enterprise and her mother-in-law takes charge of domestic work and child care while she is away, and may, in addition, devote considerable effort and time to domestic sidelines. In other families, the younger woman works in the fields, and also undertakes domestic work and domestic sidelines alongside her mother-in-law (see Appendix 1 for examples).

The number of couples establishing new nuclear families increases as subsequent children are born.[10] For women at this stage in their life cycle the domestic workload is usually heavy, because of the demands of small children and because they are more likely to be living in a nuclear family with less support from female relatives or in-laws. Even where families have divided, however, it is common for children to be cared for during the day by their (usually paternal) grandmother, with their mother or father delivering them in the morning and picking them up in the evening, if necessary. Most women return to paid employment a few months after the birth of a child, but at this stage their employment options may be limited, both because of their heavy domestic work duties, and also because, as will be discussed in Chapter 9, some employers in industry do not hire married women, especially those with small children.

Family planning policies have led to a decrease in the number of children born to each woman. In the Sichuan survey, the women who married between 1961 and 1971 gave birth 3.6 times on average, as compared to 5.9 among the women married between 1939 and 1949.[11] As mentioned in Chapter 3, fewer children is likely to have meant a reduction in the amount of time and effort spent at domestic tasks for some women, but for many this will have been offset by the lack of help from older children with such tasks.

Some women in the middle stage of their life cycle find themselves running a family single-handedly. While they are a minority, the number of women in this position has increased in the 1980s and 1990s. This is, firstly, because more men are moving away from home in search of work than previously, and, secondly, because divorce rates, although still very low, have been increasing.[12]

In the last years of her life a woman most commonly lives in proximity to, or with, a married son and his wife and children. She is largely supported by them, but is likely also to make a significant contribution to the running of the family by caring for her grandchildren, tending domestic livestock and doing other domestic tasks.

FAMILY RELATIONS

Relations between members of a family are characterised by a complexity and variety to which I cannot hope to do justice in this short section. Instead, I will confine myself to a brief examination of three issues which, I believe, are central to an understanding of how gender divisions of labour are maintained and how they affect women's lives. First, I will outline some of the key power dynamics and the roles that women are expected to play in the dyadic relationships likely to dominate an adult woman's life in the family: that is, the relationships between mother- and daughter-in-law, wife and husband, and mother and child. As will become apparent in subsequent chapters, these play an important part in shaping gender divisions of labour outside the family, as well as within it. Second, I will examine decision-making processes in the family and the extent to which women participate in decisions relating to the use of family income; and third, I will discuss the question of whether women are able to control or own land and other property. These last two issues are important for an understanding of the extent to which women benefit from the products of their own labour (and that of other family members).

My discussion of these issues is motivated by the following three key assumptions. First, individual men and women in rural China make decisions about work patterns not in isolation, but in relation to strategies for survival and advancement adopted by their families, which involve cooperation and interdependence between the activities of family members. Second, while these family strategies are the outcome of attempts to maximise economic benefits to the family, they are also shaped by expectations that individual family members will perform certain roles. Third, the decisions families make on how to use the products of their labour are arrived at through processes characterised by both agreement and conflict between individual interests, in which individual family members have different degrees of bargaining power.

These assumptions are neither new nor unusual. Although not spelt out, they are implicit in many anthropological studies of rural China.[13] The first assumption, in fact, is common not just to studies of rural China, but to peasant studies in general.[14]

However, the second and third assumptions suggest a model of the family that is somewhat different from that implied in a large range of studies on the rural economy in China and, more generally, in much of the literature on peasant economies world-wide. Some of these works treat the family or household as a homogeneous unit and concentrate on the relations between the family and larger institutions. Others treat the family as if it were characterised, on the one hand, by a division of labour between its constituent members, but on the other, by either a single decision maker or by a process in which unanimous, 'rational' decisions are taken with the aim of maximising economic benefits to the family.[15] These models have been useful for elucidating many aspects of peasant economies. From the point of view of this study, however, they are unsatisfactory because they obscure power relations and inequalities within the family, and ignore the effects of cultural values and role ascriptions on individuals' behaviour in the family economy. They consequently cast little light on the question of how or why particular gender divisions of labour are maintained, and what impact these divisions have on the lives of individuals.

What may at first seem a major problem for the view of the family suggested in my third assumption, above, is that peasants often seem to think not in terms of their personal or individual interest, but rather in terms of the family interest.

Thus, a Chinese peasant woman when asked about her status or her personal welfare will very often either be completely nonplussed by the question, or will respond in terms of her family's welfare. I would argue, however, that the notion of personal interest is not as foreign to Chinese peasant women as this might suggest. Peasant women have traditionally sought to maximise their own personal interests within, but going against the grain of, a patriarchal system which ignores those interests, by using a range of strategies. These have included maintaining ties with their natal families in the early years after marriage[16] and cultivating and manipulating their relationship with their sons.[17] Most peasants have also, of course, been exposed for the past forty years and more to Communist policies and propaganda aimed in part at developing a greater degree of equality between individuals within the family. Thus, the establishment of the Women's Federation, the promulgation of the Marriage Law, and the recruitment of women into wage labour have all played a role in identifying the interests of women as distinct from those of their family.

Even given that Chinese peasant women do not always recognise their personal interests or welfare as distinct from the interests of their family, 'it is far from obvious', as Amartya Sen points out, in relation to traditional peasant societies generally, 'that the right conclusion to draw from this is the non-viability of the notion of personal welfare'.[18] Sen argues that, on the one hand, 'personal interest and welfare are not just matters of perception . . . For example, the "illfare" associated with morbidity or undernourishment has an immediacy that does not await the person's inclination or willingness to answer detailed questions regarding his or her welfare.'[19]

On the other hand, 'the lack of perception of personal interest combined with a great concern for family welfare is, of course, just the kind of attitude that helps to sustain the traditional inequalities'.[20]

Expanding on these points, I would argue that not only is it analytically useful to counter the model of a unified family, it is also politically desirable, for it is only when Chinese rural women perceive their personal interests and the fact that, as things stand, these are far from always coinciding with family interests as others perceive them, that they will overcome inequalities within the family.[21]

Mothers- and daughters-in-law

Just as before the revolution, it is commonly accepted in rural China today that after her marriage a woman's relationship with her mother-in-law will dominate her life at least to the same extent as, and probably more than, her relationship with her husband.[22] However, expectations about the mother-in-law/daughter-in-law relationship have changed somewhat since 1949. Previously, the ideal daughter-in-law was expected to be subservient to, and to care for, her mother-in-law and to take over from her most of the burden of domestic work. With increasing numbers of young women working in the fields and earning an income after 1949, however, mothers-in-law no longer had as much power over daughters-in-law, and they were expected to do a greater share of the domestic work. Understandably, in the 1950s there was a good deal of resentment amongst middle-aged and older women over these changes in the division of labour and the balance of power between mothers-in-law and daughters-in-law, and much propaganda was directed at improving the behaviour of older women vis a vis their daughters-in-law.[23]

By the 1980s, however, daughters-in-law had become the focus of greater attention in the media and in campaigns run by the Women's Federation. As Honig and Hershatter point out, young women were now expected not only to be subservient to their mother-in-law, as before the revolution, but to take responsibility for maintaining harmonious relations with the older woman.[24]

Woman as wife

While there are obviously exceptions, most relationships between women and their husbands in rural China are characterised, as they have always been, by reserve and distance, in comparison to those in urban China and in western societies.[25] Women now enjoy considerably more equality with their husbands than before the revolution. However, the patrilocal, exogamous nature of most rural marriages continues to bolster the husband's ultimate authority and the wife's relative insecurity. Friendships amongst villagers take a long time to mature, and it is usually some years before villagers stop seeing married women as outsiders. This means that newly married women are relatively isolated and vulnerable within the family, and it also makes it particularly difficult for married women to gain the trust necessary to assume any form of leadership in the 'outside' sphere, whether it be in politics or in the local economy.

Perhaps the most alarming expression of their subordinate position in marriage is violence perpetrated against women by husbands, in-laws and others. Such violence has been reported in the media with increasing frequency in the 1980s and 1990s. This does not necessarily mean that incidences of such violence are increasing – it may simply reflect greater awareness and concern. This is the case, I believe, with rape committed by husbands, reports of which were not discussed in the media until the early 1990s.[26]

Some kinds of violence, however, do seem to be related to the aggravation of problems connected with marriage practices that has stemmed from recent social and political change. In particular, as discussed in Chapter 3, the conflict between the state's one-child family policy and the need felt by peasant families for at least one son to provide labour and support for parents in old age has given rise to a spate of domestic violence, in which husbands and in-laws abuse and beat women following the birth of a girl.

In other cases, high bride-prices are the issue. Traditionally, marriage was accompanied by elaborate rituals. As part of the rituals, the conclusion of the first phase of marriage negotiations was marked by the presentation of a bride-price or betrothal gifts from the young man's family to the woman's family.[27] The prospective groom's family was also obliged to provide a wedding feast for friends and kin. For their part, the prospective bride's family customarily provided a dowry to be taken by the young woman into her new family.

The CCP under Mao discouraged elaborate marriage rituals and prohibited the payment of money and gifts in connection with marriage. It was critical, in particular, of the payment of bride-prices, because it symbolised the procurement of women, which perpetuated both women's low status and class inequalities; the latter because it made it harder for poor men to marry.[28] In the post-Mao era, however, the CCP has adopted a less critical stance toward peasant rituals generally, and in this more relaxed atmosphere there has been an upsurge in elaborate and increasingly costly marriage rituals.

Reports indicate that in most places bride-prices have been considerably higher than dowries, and have risen markedly over the 1980s and 1990s.[29] According to one extensive national survey, bride-price (*caili*) payments increased tenfold between 1980 and 1985, from between 100 and 300 *yuan* (that is, 10 to 40 per cent of the average net income of a rural family), to between 1,000 and 3,000 *yuan* (63 to 189 per cent of average net family income). In addition, in 1985 the families of prospective grooms paid 2,500 to 4,000 *yuan* for new housing for the new couple and also held large wedding feasts. The survey found that most peasants save for five or six years for a wedding, and must also borrow money from friends and relatives.[30]

One of the effects of increased bride-price payment has been, just as the CCP previously feared, the maintenance and reinforcement of the view of women as commodities bought and sold by patrilineal families. This is most starkly illustrated by the abduction and sale of young women as brides. According to one report, almost 10,000 women and children are abducted and sold each year in Sichuan alone.[31]

In other cases reported in the press, the payment of a high bride-price has increased the expectation of a man and his family that a wife will do their bidding, and has resulted in abuse of the woman when the family felt she was not serving them well enough.[32] High bride-price payments also make it more likely that a family will resist a woman who seeks divorce. This they can often do very effectively because they hold more sway amongst local officials, who may well be kin, than a woman who has married in and who is still regarded as an outsider to the village. In addition, a demand that the bride-price be repaid can make divorce very difficult for a woman. In one example reported in *ZGFN*, a man agreed to his wife's request for a divorce on condition that she pay back her bride-price. When she refused to pay the full amount the husband's brothers helped him to beat her up and held her down while he raped her.[33]

While on the one hand officialdom and the media have strongly condemned instances of violence by men against their wives in recent years, on the other hand a shift in the images of model women seen in the media and in campaigns run by the Women's Federation has weakened the cause of equality and undermined the criticism of domestic violence by reinforcing traditional notions that it is a woman's duty, above all else, to serve her husband and her children. To give one example: between 1984 and 1987, *ZGFN* ran a discussion on 'What Chinese society today must expect of women and how today's Chinese women should mould themselves'. The discussion began with a focus on Tao Chun, the main female character in the film '*Xiang Yin*' (usually translated as '*Country Couple*' or '*Local Accent*').[34] Tao Chun was the epitome of the traditional 'virtuous wife and good mother' (*xianqi liangmu*), devoting all her energy to caring for her husband and children, but receiving no acknowledgement from her husband until she was dying from cancer. A lengthy debate ensued over whether or not Tao Chun was a suitable character ideal for women of the 1980s. While one writer praised Tao Chun and saw her undivided attention to her family as thoroughly good and proper,[35] most felt that the traditional Confucian ideal of 'virtuous wife and good mother' had to be given a new meaning to suit the 1980s. In particular they believed that women should not devote themselves *solely* to their family, but should also work outside the home.[36] Most participants in the discussion nevertheless defined the 'ideal woman' as a wife and mother whose primary role was to serve her family. As one writer put it: 'Since nature has decided our sex, we must of course discharge our responsibilities as wives and mothers ... The question is not whether being a virtuous wife and mother is a good thing or not, but whether or not we need a new standard for the virtuous wife and good mother for the 1980s.'[37]

This was in stark contrast to the (equally one-sided) portrayal during the Cultural Revolution of model women such as engineer Wei Fengying who always put politics and production before her family, and who said that 'sometimes in the course of making these [technical innovations in production] we [herself and her husband] forget to put soda in the dough, forget to put salt in our cooking and even forget our meals entirely. But we are happy, family life has not hampered us'.[38]

Woman as mother

As suggested in Chapter 3, in addition to the greater stress on women's role as wife, the role of motherhood has also been given greater emphasis and, despite family planning, the demands on mothers have in some ways increased, for while the CCP is anxious to see the number of children that are born reduced through family planning, it is also vitally concerned that those children that are born be inculcated with values and standards of behaviour conducive to social stability and modernisation. A reaffirmation by the state, via the Women's Federation, of the importance of the family, and especially of women as the key figures in the 'inside' sphere, has been a major element in attempts at achieving these goals.

Thus, Song Qingling, a high ranking member of the Women's Federation, claimed in 1980 that 'Chinese women know well that it is their unshirkable duty to train and educate the children and youngsters so that they might become healthy both physically and mentally ... Let us women set a good example for our children and shoulder the sacred duty of bringing them up in a proper way so they become reliable successors to our cause'.[39]

In women's magazines, such as *ZGFN* and *Nongjianü Baishitong [Rural Women Knowing All]*, numerous articles are devoted to the rearing and educating of children. These clearly illustrate the increasing demands placed on mothers by the Chinese state in its attempts to modernise. One article, for example, praised mothers who study for their child's sake, arguing that

> The amount of learning required to educate a child is very great. In order to educate a child, you must first understand children, you must understand psychology and must grasp the psychological characteristics of children at each age level. When you dress a child, you must be conscious of aesthetics, you must appreciate art, and in order to satisfy your child's thirst for knowledge, you must yourself be learned and able.[40]

Another article claimed that humans today use only five to 30 per cent of their brain's capacity, and that there is enormous potential for the further development of humanity's intellectual resources. In this context, the article argued that many parents, especially in rural areas, neglect the education of their child in the early years, concerning themselves only with feeding the child and keeping him or her warmly dressed. Warning that such neglect was detrimental to the development of a child's intellectual abilities, the teacher urged parents to pay more attention to young children's education.[41]

It is most probable that magazine articles such as these are read by only a minority of peasant women. Nevertheless, I would argue that they do shape the thinking of better educated rural women, especially young women in more developed rural areas who strive to be more like their 'modern', urban counterparts. They also influence the ideas of rural cadres in the Women's Federation, who then apply those ideas in campaigns with peasant women (see Chapter 5).

For rural women, bearing children, especially sons, continues to be one of the most important ways of ensuring respect and security for themselves within their husband's family. Conversely, a woman who does not bear children, or who gives birth only to daughters, runs the risk of being abused or abandoned and, as has already been mentioned, this risk has increased as a result of the conflict between the state's one-child family policy and the production responsibility system.

Apart from ties of affection with both sons and daughters, rural women cultivate their ties with their sons because it is they who will support them in old age, whereas daughters 'belong to someone else'. On the other hand, daughters are desired by women because while they are young, they will help their mothers with the domestic work, whereas a son will not.[42]

CONTROL OVER FAMILY INCOME

How, and by whom, decisions are made about the expenditure of family income is a subject on which we have very little information, and it is likely in any case that there is considerable variation from one family to another. It is possible, however, to construct a rough model and to discern some trends over time. Accounts of pre-1949 China suggest that the head of the family, who was usually the father (at least until his retirement from field labour when a son might take over) had ultimate control over family finances. The most common picture of traditional Chinese families is one in which the father alone decided all matters relating to the family expenditure, without consulting his wife or children. However, Martin Yang suggests that there was substantial consultation between husbands and their wives.[43] Also, Delia Davin claims that it was usual for the older woman in the house to be in charge of small-scale family expenditure, and that, of particular importance in a subsistence economy, it was she who decided what and how much each family member should eat.[44] That it was at least culturally acceptable for women to be the key decision makers on issues such as these is further suggested in the saying 'men rule outside, women rule inside' ('*nan zhu wai, nü zhu nei*').

As mentioned in Chapter 2, with the collectivisation of production in rural China from the 1950s onwards, women's participation in 'outside' work, and the income they earned from this work, helped to improve their bargaining power in family decision making, although it did not give them control over their income, since family members' earnings were usually pooled and the total given to the male head of the family.

Parish and Whyte, in their study of rural families in Guangdong in the early 1970s, found that decision making in the family had become somewhat more democratic, with more women being involved, or at least being consulted, by their husbands. However, in 65 per cent of the villages studied (N = 40), it was still most common for a man to be regarded as head of the family, and for him to control the purse-strings. Generally, the father occupied this role until his retirement from field labour. In some families, as was common before 1949, the father continued to maintain close control over family finances and to demand respect and deference from other family members well after his retirement. It had become more common, though, for fathers to hand over control to their adult sons once the latter became the main income earners in the family.[45]

The interviews I conducted with rural women in 1989 confirmed that, as others have noted for earlier periods,[46] in most rural families the income generated by all members is pooled into a common fund. Cash income is generally kept in a safe in the house or in a single bank account, or both.

Table 4.3 outlines the information on family decision making that was given to me by rural Sichuanese women. My findings suggest that women now play a more active role in family decision making than in the past. They indicate that women are commonly responsible for expenditure on items of basic necessity, such as food and clothing, and that in decisions involving larger expenditure, democracy and equality in family decision making are, at the least, recognised ideals.

Most women I talked to claimed that, apart from those relating to daily consumption, decisions on family expenditure are made through discussion between family members. In only three families did a man appear to dominate all

Table 4.3 *Decision makers on expenditure in rural families in Sichuan (percentages)*

The Main Decision Maker	Expenditure in the Family Economy	Purchase of Expensive Items	Daily Living Expenditure
Husband	13.3	9.7	2.5
Wife	30	9.7	70
No single person	56.7	80.6	27.5
Total no. families	30	31	40

Source: Interviews conducted in Xindu, Jinniu, Wenjiang, Guan and Mianyang counties, October–December 1989.

decision making on issues involving substantial expenditure. Details on the gender divisions of labour in these families are given in Appendix 1 (families nos. 33, 44 and 47).

In another three families (Appendix 1, nos. 27, 32 and 49) most decisions relating to family expenditure are made by a woman. In all three of these families the woman runs a private business of some kind. This finding confirms claims, discussed in detail in Chapter 8, that the expansion of private production has provided an avenue through which at least a small number of women have improved their authority within the family.

Table 4.4 shows the findings relating to family decision making of the *Survey of Women's Status in Contemporary China* undertaken in 1991 by the Institute of Population Studies, the Chinese Academy of Social Sciences. As can be seen from the table, the study confirmed my own findings that in the majority of rural families husbands and wives make decisions on major issues together. The table also suggests that the role of parents in decision making is now much less than that of adult children.[47]

Another approach which may help in constructing a fuller picture of the participation of individuals in family decision-making processes is to examine the factors affecting that participation. The power dynamics and expectations of roles in family relations discussed above are one such factor. In addition, as has long been recognised by Marxists and feminists, gender divisions of labour, the type of work undertaken by adult family members and the way that work is perceived, and the income which each person contributes to the family, are factors of great importance.

Since the introduction of the production responsibility system, and the opening of new opportunities for employment in domestic sidelines and non-agricultural ventures of various kinds, numerous articles in the media have claimed that women are now earning incomes which are higher in relation to those of male family members than previously and that, as a result, their power in the family has increased. As discussed in Chapter 3, however, recent surveys show that rural women continue to be relatively concentrated in the lower income brackets. This aside, the degree to which women's incomes have improved in relation to men's in the family, and the extent to which their incomes have translated into greater power, has varied according to the type of economy practised, and the gender division of labour adopted, within the family.[48] The relationship between different gender divisions of labour and the power of women within the family will be examined from a number of angles in subsequent chapters. Here, I will just summarise my main points.

In families in which both women and men continue to work in agriculture, the removal of the work-point system of remuneration, in which women were

Table 4.4 *Decision makers on specific issues in rural families across China (percentages)*

The Main Decision Maker	Purchasing Cattle, Horses and Other Livestock	Purchasing Production Tools	Building House	Purchasing Household Durable Consumer Goods	Giving Money or Sending Gifts at Festivals	When to Start Children's Education	Whether Children Continue Their Education or Not	Selection of Children's Marriage Partner	Purchasing Sons' Betrothal Gifts	Purchasing Dowry for Daughters
Wife	3.52	3.86	2.28	13.01	10.08	5.94	5.78	9.37	7.19	8.20
Husband	28.56	26.91	17.14	17.83	14.29	9.97	8.94	4.31	5.20	5.34
Both H'band and Wife	57.18	59.78	76.25	66.96	73.35	82.00	81.55	66.58	74.19	73.02
Parents	3.60	2.42	3.11	1.20	1.55	0.27	0.33	0.35	0.63	0.53
Other	7.14	7.03	1.22	1.00	0.73	1.83	3.40	19.39	12.79	12.92

Source: Institute of Population Studies, Chinese Academy of Social Sciences, ed., *Sampling Survey Data of Women's Status in Contemporary China*, International Academic Publishers, Beijing, 1994, pp. 312–316. Survey of 4,524 couples, conducted in 1991.

consistently discriminated against, has enabled women to earn more. At the same time, however, any improvement that this might have made in women's power in the family may well have been cancelled out by the fact that the individual contribution to the family's income made by women is now no longer as clearly identifiable as under the previous system.

In the cases (which are discussed in Chapter 7) where men continue to work in the fields, but women withdraw to the 'inside' sphere to undertake domestic work, it is likely that women's power in the family is relatively weak, both because they earn a lower income than male members of the family, and because of the low status of work in the 'inside' sphere. Many women in this position now also have less contact with people outside the family than in previous years when they worked in the fields, and as a result are more vulnerable within the family.

The role in family decision making of women who have developed lucrative domestic sidelines or who have expanded their domestic sidelines into private enterprises or specialised households, however, has in some cases improved substantially (as, for example, in the families outlined above). This is less often true in families where a man is also involved in the same venture, for he is then most likely to act as the manager of the business, making the major decisions on issues such as investment and marketing, and representing the business to the outside world.[49] However, a small number of women whose husbands work elsewhere run specialised households on their own, and acquire considerable authority in doing so (see Chapter 8).

As will be discussed in Chapter 7, it is becoming increasingly common for men to work for long periods of time away from home, leaving their wives in charge of domestic work and agriculture. Some women in this situation will have gained a good deal of power over family decision making, although this may not always be the case. Studies in other developing countries suggest that in families where the husband works away from home for much of the year and the wife is the apparent head of the family, it is nevertheless common for major decisions relating to family finances to be taken either by other senior male kin or by the husband while he is at home.[50]

In families in which women as well as men work in industry, it is likely that decision making over family finances will be a more democratic process, since each person's contribution to these finances will be clearly identifiable. Given the prevailing occupational segregation in industry, however, it is likely that women's earnings will be less than those of their male kin. Finally, young women who leave home to work as nannies or as temporary workers in urban industry will gain autonomy and at least some control over their individual earnings, although, as will be discussed in Chapter 9, they may well remit a substantial proportion of their earnings to their parents.

LAND AND PROPERTY

Apart from participation in decisions relating to the use of family income, control over land and property is commonly identified in the literature on women and development as a key factor affecting the extent to which women benefit from the products of their own labour and that of other family members.

Before 1949 women in China generally had no right to own or to inherit land or other property. As mentioned in Chapter 2, land reform in the 1940s and early 1950s in theory granted women, as well as men, ownership rights over a piece of land. The Marriage Law of 1950 also stipulated that husband and wife had equal rights in the ownership and management of property. In practice, however, women's land was usually considered the property of her family, and the title deeds were handed to the head of the family who, in most cases, was the woman's father, father-in-law or husband.

The collectivisation of land and the major means of production reduced the significance of inequality in property ownership. However, women continued to be disadvantaged in divorce because they were not accorded the right to independent ownership of property such as housing, consumer durables and savings. As unmarried daughters also, women's rights to a share of their natal family estate were not implemented because, with patrilocal marriage the norm, granting such rights would have meant allowing the woman to take property out of the family upon marriage.[51]

With the introduction of the production responsibility system and the accumulation, in some families, of substantial amounts of property, the consequences for women of this basic inequality have become more serious. Thus, nowadays when a woman divorces she may well be forfeiting considerable capital which she has helped to build up.[52] As a consequence, divorce represents a significant threat to rural women, who then also feel that their bargaining position within the family is weak.

Problems relating to women's lack of ownership rights in land, and the fact that their use-rights are dependent on their relationship to men, have also been exacerbated by the introduction of the production responsibility system. As mentioned in the previous chapter, land is allocated to households according to their population. Rather than adjusting land holdings immediately following any change in the size of a household, however, it has become more common for local governments to adjust the land holdings of all households every few years. This has made the management of land allocation less cumbersome, but has also meant that some women who have just married or who have just divorced have been left without land for a number of years. Media reports claim that in some places other types of land allocation systems, even more problematic for women, have been introduced. In a letter to *NMRB*, for example, a woman complained that in her village in Hunan women were being pressured to conform to particular marriage patterns by a fifteen-year contract system that was introduced in 1985, whereby each member of a family was allocated land according to their age and sex. Males and females under eleven years of age were allocated the same amount of land. From then on, though, land allocated to males increased each year and they could also obtain land for a wife and child in advance of marriage. Females, on the other hand, had land taken from them each year, until by the age of twenty-five they had none, the assumption being that by that age women would have married out of the village. Upon investigation, it was found that this method of allocating land was widespread in Hunan.[53] In another example reported in the press, ten rural women who had married men with urban household registration themselves continued to live in their natal village and to retain their household registration there. However, when land was being divided up in the village, they were considered as having married out and were allocated no land on which to farm or build a house. Later, their children also suffered discrimination, and when they left school were neither assigned land in the village nor given work in local industry.[54]

In 1985 an inheritance law was promulgated for the first time in the PRC. The law reaffirms and draws attention to the rights of women to own and inherit property on an equal basis with male kin. However, as Delia Davin points out, the main purpose of the law is to provide a stable legal system of property ownership and inheritance, as a basis for the new family-based rural economy. Any attempt made to implement women's rights, in the case of divorce, for example, will be regarded as a threat to the family-based economy and is therefore not likely to be supported any more than previously.[55] Furthermore, under Article 13 of the inheritance law, it is stipulated that the rights of heirs who do not support their parents in old age may be less than those of heirs who provide for their parents. This further undermines women's right to inherit property, since the patrilocal marriage system means that most parents are supported primarily by their sons, and less by their daughters.[56]

To conclude, gender divisions of labour, women's work patterns, and the extent to which women benefit from their labour, are determined not solely by factors external to the family, such as the policies of the state or the characteristics of the market. Nor are they the outcome simply of 'rational' responses to these factors made by a homogeneous family unit. They are strongly influenced by the structure and size of the family, by power relations inherent in family structures and processes, and by expectations as to the roles of individuals within the family.

Thus, women's workloads and the type of work they undertake vary from one stage in the family cycle to the next. Before childbirth, for example, a woman's domestic workload is relatively light and there are comparatively few constraints on opportunities to work in the 'outside' sphere, for example in industry. Women with children generally have a heavier domestic workload and are more likely to work solely in the 'inside' sphere.

Women in contemporary rural China now play a more active role in decision-making processes within the family than they did before 1949 and hence have more control over their labour and over the products of their labour. Nevertheless, women's power within the family continues to be seriously undermined by certain structures and practices. In particular, the continuance of patrilocal marriage casts women as temporary members of their family before marriage and as 'outsiders' to the family after marriage. This has a number of serious consequences. As illustrated in this chapter, for example, patrilocal marriage combined with the practice of bride-price payment means that newly-married women are particularly vulnerable to the dictates of their husband and in-laws. Women's lack of power in the family is also reinforced by the difficulty that women have in obtaining divorce, and by their lack of control over land and other property. All of these were important factors in women's subordination before 1949. None were overcome by the CCP, either under Mao Zedong or under Deng Xiaoping.

As discussed in this chapter, certain role expectations also reinforce women's subordination in the family. These include, in particular, the expectation that women should strive to maintain harmonious relations within the family, and that they should place the needs of other family members before their own. The centrality of such notions to popular perceptions of womanhood was challenged to some extent by the CCP under Mao, but in the post-Mao era it has been lent support once more.

Finally, women's subordination within the family both feeds into, and is compounded by, their lower rates of participation in education and in politics. These are topics that will be pursued in the following chapter.

5

Education and Politics

I NOW examine the relationship between rural women's education and their involvement in politics, and the work patterns of women and men. It is evident that both education and political participation (or lack thereof) have a major influence on gender divisions of labour. In dialectical fashion, gender divisions of labour also shape women's involvement in education and politics. The first and second sections of this chapter examine women's participation in education and politics respectively. The third discusses the All-China Women's Federation and the campaigns it has run in rural China in the post-Mao era.

EDUCATION

As is common across the world, rural women in China are on the bottom rung of the ladder when it comes to educational opportunities and attainments. For example, in 1990 approximately 70 per cent of the country's 182 million illiterates aged 15 and above were women. Of these, 84 per cent were rural residents.[1] The higher the level of education, the lower are women's and rural residents' participation rates, so that of all university graduates in 1990 only 30 per cent were women, the vast majority of whom were urban residents.[2]

In addition to the gender inequalities found in educational attainment, males and females are taught different messages about their future roles in society and at, and above, secondary level are often segregated into different areas of specialised education.

In this section, after a brief examination of education policy, I will examine in more detail the question of how rural girls and women have fared in education in the post-Mao era, in terms of access, achievement and the types of education they receive. I will also discuss the relationships between gender inequalities and differences in education and the gender division of labour, arguing that in general the one reinforces the other. Since so few rural women, or for that matter rural men, undertake tertiary education, I will discuss primary and secondary education only.

Education policy

After Mao's death in 1976, Chinese leaders shifted away from the late Maoist approach to education which had promoted structures and teaching practices aimed at expanding basic mass education, inculcating political consciousness and breaking down divisions between knowledge and practice, and mental and manual labour. Instead, the need for a small core of highly educated people to lead the country through modernisation was given most weight, academic standards were raised, political education and manual labour were scaled down, and there was a move toward re-regularisation, 'rationalisation' and the reassertion of central control.

A 'two track' approach to schooling, similar to that of pre-Cultural Revolution years, was adopted. One track in this approach was toward the cultivation of a small group of academically gifted students for entry into university. The second track aimed to provide the majority of the population with a vocationally-oriented basic education. Resources were concentrated in the first track, especially in a few elite 'key point' institutions, and the number of schools, especially of those providing an alternative to full-time academic study, was reduced so as to promote quality.[3]

During the 1980s and 1990s serious problems have emerged in education, particularly in rural areas. These problems stem primarily from a lack of funding and from the aggravation of inequalities through the combination of the reforms undertaken within education itself, with reforms of the economy undertaken at the same time.

In rural areas, as previously, the state expects a large proportion of funding for primary and secondary schooling to be generated locally. As mentioned in Chapter 3, however, the introduction of the production responsibility system made it more difficult for local governments to collect funds for education. Such funds are now being generated, in part, by taxes on local township enterprises. However, local governments often do not see education as a priority, preferring to use the majority of the funds they receive from township enterprises either for lining their own pockets or for further investment in economic ventures which will bring to the collective more immediate profit than education. In any case, though, it is only the wealthier, more developed townships that have enterprises that can afford to provide funds for education.

The scarcity of state or collective funding for education has meant that many schools have closed. In rural areas this has often increased the distance that children must travel to school, which in turn has resulted in declining enrolments and high drop-out rates.[4]

In the case of rural secondary schools, decline in enrolments in the late 1970s and early 1980s was also a result of deliberate policy. In order to make more 'efficient' use of existing resources, and in its concern for quality rather than quantity, the state called for restrictions in secondary enrolments. In rural areas junior secondary school programmes attached to production brigade primary schools were abolished in the late 1970s, and in most places only one junior secondary school was retained in each commune. The senior sections of commune secondary schools were mostly closed, leaving no more than a few complete secondary schools in each county.[5]

Lack of funding has meant, in addition, that many existing school facilities are in abysmally poor condition. Furthermore, because of poor working conditions and because they are very poorly paid, many teachers are leaving the profession.

To make up for the shortfall in collective funding, individual families are being called upon to pay increasingly higher fees for their children's education. Such fees mean that some poorer families cannot afford to send their children to school. Other families, who may be able to afford the direct costs of educating their children, nevertheless decide that they cannot afford the costs of the labour power relinquished as a result. Yet others consider that rural education is of poor quality, and of little practical value, and believe that the family would benefit less from educating all its children than from keeping at least some of them (usually the girls) at home from an early age to look after younger siblings, help with domestic work or be involved in production.

In the mid-1980s the CCP responded to these problems, and to growing criticism of the education system, with a number of reforms. In 1984, for example, local authorities were instructed not to reduce secondary school enrolments any further,[6] and consequently, the decline in secondary school enrolments was slowed (see below).

Legally compulsory education for all children has been extended from six years of primary school to include three years of junior secondary school. The nine-year compulsory education law went into effect in July 1986, but different timetables were set for its full achievement. For one quarter of the population residing in cities and the most economically developed areas, it was expected that junior secondary school education would be made universal by 1990. The same achievement was expected for semi-developed towns and villages, where roughly half of the population lives, by about 1995. For the remaining one quarter of the population residing in the poorest areas, local authorities were simply urged to popularise basic education as much as possible.[7]

As a statement of the CCP's intent to improve basic education, the compulsory education law is symbolically important, but its implementation in rural areas continues to be hampered by lack of funding, declining numbers of schools, shortage of teachers, poor quality and unsuitable courses, and low enrolment and high drop-out rates. Thus, by the mid-1990s, while reports were generally positive about the gains that had been made, it was also acknowledged that some of the poorest rural areas were unlikely to make universal primary, let alone junior secondary, education by the year 2000.[8]

The introduction of the law has, however, been accompanied by campaigns aimed at improving basic education, amongst females and rural residents in particular. For example, the 'Prairie Fire' plan aims to eliminate illiteracy among young and mature adults, to set up a range of cultural and technical educational establishments for rural residents, and to provide students at rural primary and secondary schools with technical training.[9] The 'Hope Project', initiated by the China Youth Development Foundation in 1989, seeks donations nationally and internationally to help school drop-outs in poverty-stricken areas return to school.[10]

At local levels, campaigns have been run in which girls are given preferential treatment in order to encourage them to attend school. Measures include waiving girls' tuition fees and subsidising the costs of their books and stationery, offering scholarships to girls who perform well, and allowing those whose work duties prevent them attending the full school day to come late and leave early.[11] While it is probable that other causal factors are also involved, the fact that the female proportion of enrolments in primary and secondary schools has increased slightly since the second half of the 1980s suggests a degree of success for 'affirmative action' campaigns such as these.[12]

Adult Education Bureaux have also targeted women for short-term classes combining literacy and technical training, and in this they have been joined by other government departments and, in particular, the Women's Federation (see below).

Another set of reforms introduced in the mid-1980s concerned the increase of diversification and vocationalisation of schooling, particularly at the secondary level. The aim has been to provide the majority of the population with schooling which will be vocationally useful, but which will not enable them to proceed to tertiary education. Central to this aim are three categories of vocationally oriented senior secondary schools: Specialised schools (*zhong deng zhuanye xuexiao*), which include technical schools (*zhongdeng jishu xuexiao*) and teacher training schools (*zhongdeng shifan xuexiao*); skilled-worker schools (*jigong xuexiao*); and agricultural and vocational schools (*nongye zhongxue* and *zhiye zhongxue*).[13]

In a directive on rural education published in 1983, primary schools were called upon to orient their curricula to rural life, and junior secondary schools were required to undertake revisions to make 30 per cent of their courses vocational. By 1990 it was expected that at the senior secondary level at least

30 per cent of all courses run in regular rural schools would be vocational, and that there should be at least as many students in vocationally oriented rural schools as in regular rural schools.[14]

Participation rates in rural education

Primary school

As a result of the problems described above, the number of students enrolled in rural primary schools declined from 128.8 million in 1978 to 110.8 million in 1985, and to 89.7 million in 1993.[15]

The rate at which children withdraw from primary school part-way through has also increased. In fact, in the 1980s primary education was dubbed the '9–6–3' system: that is, nine out of ten children are enrolled in primary schools, but only six of them attend the full six years of primary school, three of them with satisfactory results.[16]

The problems of low enrolment and high drop out rates from primary school are particularly serious amongst girls in rural areas, and has led to concern that the proportion of illiterates amongst rural girls may be increasing greatly. A report published by the Fujian Education Commission suggests that the problems are even more serious than official statistics generally reveal. For example, according to statistics from thirty townships in Fujian, the primary school enrolment rate in 1986–87 was about 98 per cent for boys and 95 per cent for girls. These figures, however, were based on birth registration statistics which did not include significant numbers of children, especially girls, who, because they were born outside the plan, were not registered and were not receiving an education. One survey of three villages found that in addition to 656 primary school age children listed in the household registration records, there were 32 not listed. In investigating the retention rates of female students in primary schools, the Commission found that in one district 491 boys and 446 girls were recorded as being enrolled in primary school. Of the 446 girls, however, only 203 or 45.5 per cent were enrolled in full-time primary school, while the remaining 235 were enrolled only in part-time or irregular schools. Furthermore, of the latter, only about 57 per cent were actually attending school. In the first to third grades of the full-time schools, girls comprised only 35 per cent of all students, and in the fourth and fifth grades the figure was 15 per cent.[17]

Aside from the non-registration of girls born out of plan, one of the chief reasons for the large proportion of girls amongst children not attending primary school is the fact that when they marry, women usually leave their natal families, who, as a result, often see education for daughters only as an expense incurred on behalf of other families. In addition, in poor, isolated rural areas it is common for parents to limit their daughters' education in the fear that, having received an education, the girls will be harder to marry off, or they will refuse an arranged marriage from which the parents can obtain a high bride-price.[18]

The other major reason for girls' low rates of participation in primary education is the fact that girls are often expected to undertake a large proportion of their family's domestic work and to care for their younger siblings. Since the introduction of the production responsibility system, the workload of some women has increased as a result of them taking over responsibility for agriculture and expanding domestic sideline production. In order to cope with the extra workload women often transfer more of the burden of domestic work onto their daughters, even at the expense of the girls' schooling, since this is seen as of relatively little benefit to the family.[19] It is much less common for a boy to be withdrawn from primary school to help with work at home because it is believed that a boy's education will benefit the family more in the long term.

Secondary school

In 1978 the number of children enrolled in regular rural secondary schools was 48.2 million. This declined to just under 29 million by 1985 and to 25.6 million by 1993.[20]

For the cleverer and more fortunate students enrolled in urban secondary schools, cutbacks in enrolments in the post-Mao era and the subsequent increase in competition may have resulted in improved educational standards. However, for large numbers of rural children, especially girls, they simply closed off educational advancement. Not only do relatively few rural students pass the examinations into senior secondary school, but many, realising that they have little hope of passing, simply drop out of school beforehand.

Two factors contributing greatly to the high withdrawal rates of rural children from education before or part-way through secondary school are the widespread view that the secondary curriculum is of little benefit or relevance to rural life, and the costs of maintaining children through secondary school. Fees for secondary schooling are generally higher than in primary schools. So too are the opportunity costs of keeping a child in secondary school, because of the recent growth in demand for children aged between roughly 10 and 16 in township- and village-run enterprises, as well as in family-based production, especially in the south-eastern coastal provinces.

In most cases that have been reported, the majority of child labourers and of children withdrawn from education before or part-way through secondary school are girls.[21] Thus, according to an investigation carried out in Jinxiang

78

Township, Wenzhou, 405 out of 483 children in the family workshops in 1985 were girls. Thirty per cent of the children were illiterate and 20 per cent had only had one or two years of schooling.[22]

Patterns such as these are due, not just to the greater value placed by parents on boys' education than on girls', but also to the fact that in secondary school girls' grades are on average lower than boys', as are their pass rates in examinations. In all seven counties in which I collected information on education in 1989 the proportions of girls and boys enrolled in primary school were reported to be roughly equal, but in secondary school, in particular senior secondary school, there was a marked drop in girls' enrolments. Education Bureau officials explained this in terms of girls' greater failure rates in examinations, which they all attributed solely to biological differences between the sexes. In Huairou and Xindu counties the explanation was that girls are not as smart as boys. In primary school this is not apparent, it was said, because the boys play around. In secondary school, however, they knuckle down and then their grades outstrip the girls'. In Jinniu and Wenjiang counties it was claimed that in the earlier years girls' and boys' intellectual abilities are much the same, but that when they reach puberty girls' thinking becomes 'scattered' (*fensan*). Instead of concentrating on their school work, girls start to think about boy-friends and establishing families.[23]

From the media, girls receive somewhat conflicting messages. They are told that they are as clever as boys, but that they need to build up their self-confidence, and that discrimination against them in education and work is a result merely of traditional prejudices, held nowadays only by a minority of people, which can be overcome by those with the will to do so.[24] The intelligence of females and males is described as equal but different. However, as Emily Honig and Gail Hershatter point out, because male characteristics are taken as the desired norm, female 'difference' translates into inferiority in much of the literature.[25] For example, one author claims that males are good at working independently, though they are not always as thorough or careful as they might be. Females, on the other hand, 'often have stronger memory and language ability, and are more diligent and meticulous. But they have one-track minds, do not think dynamically enough, have a rather narrow range of activity, and easily become interested in trivial matters. Their moods fluctuate easily, they are shy, and they don't dare to raise questions boldly'.[26] What could be seen as superior qualities in this list of female traits are glossed over. Instead, the author emphasises females' lack of capacity for independent thinking as the reason for their lower grades in senior secondary school, and urges them to try to overcome their deficiencies by emulating their male classmates.

If media articles such as these give girls the impression that they are not as smart as boys, this message is further reinforced by a lack of female role models in positions requiring relatively high levels of education. The fact that there are fewer female than male teachers, particularly at secondary level and above, does not help here. According to the State Statistical Bureau, in 1993 women comprised 45.2 per cent of all primary school teachers, and only 34 per cent of teachers in regular secondary schools.[27]

From a feminist perspective which seeks to illuminate and focus on the social, rather than the biological, construction of difference and inequality between women and men, one could argue that while there may well be differences between the patterns of thought common in boys and girls, socialisation plays an important role in the formation of these differences. Furthermore, there is no 'natural' or inevitable link between these differences and the inequalities between female and male educational achievements. Females fare relatively poorly in the education system, first because of socially constructed barriers to their participation, such as the patrilocal marriage system, the responsibility for domestic work that is placed on their shoulders, and institutional discrimination, evident, for example, in the requirement for entrance into some secondary schools of a higher examination result for females than for males (which is discussed below). Second, education for females is not valued as highly as it is for males. Third, the patterns of thought and behaviour more common in females are deemed inferior in definitions of educational excellence. And fourth, females internalise the messages that they are not as clever as males which they receive from parents, educators, the media and the lack of female role models.

Some of the points I have made here relating to the social construction of gender inequalities in education are also commonly made in Chinese analyses. Thus, the patrilocal marriage system, traditional prejudices against educating women, and girls' responsibility for domestic work are commonly identified as the key obstacles to improving female participation in basic education (even if little is done to overcome the obstacles). However, when it comes to analyses of females' lower grades and lower enrolment rates in education at senior secondary level and above, social factors largely drop out of sight and 'biology' takes their place as the main obstacle. A corollary of this is that while female participation in basic education is seen as an issue on which social or political action can and should be taken, the same is largely not the case with female participation in higher levels of education.

The relatively low attainments of females in the formal education system and the message that females are not as smart as males clearly reinforce each other, and they also have the effect of strengthening assumptions of female inferiority in aspects of social life other than education.

Lower levels of educational attainment also contribute to more concrete restrictions of women in employment and other aspects of the 'outside' sphere, which in turn reinforce existing divisions of labour. Economic development, especially technological advances and the development of a market economy since 1978, have made this a particularly important issue. As will be discussed in Chapter 8, successful entrepreneurial activity, for example, requires a certain level of education since it entails learning new, more efficient techniques of production and developing an understanding of market dynamics, state regulations and accounting. Partly as a result, most specialised households are run either by men, or by households in which a woman provides most of the labour but her husband is in charge of marketing, sales and other aspects of managing the business. As will be noted in Chapter 9, rural women are also disadvantaged in rural industrial employment because many township enterprises now require a minimum level of formal education (usually junior secondary school) from their workers. Finally, it appears that pressure for better educated cadres may have contributed to an erosion of women's political representation since the late 1970s (see below).

Gender segregation in education

Gender divisions of labour are affected not just by unequal participation rates in education, but also by differences between the kind of education received by males and females. Of particular significance, in this regard, are the shifts toward a greater degree of vocationalisation in education in the 1980s and 1990s.

As Suzanne Pepper argues, the education system at senior secondary level has been 'retracked and streamed in a manner deliberately designed to exploit and reinforce the existing social divisions of labour'.[28] She has in mind here the reinforcement of divisions between the elite and the masses, and between mental and manual labour, which have resulted from the 'two track' system of academic training for tertiary entrance on the one hand and vocationally oriented training on the other. I would argue further that the 'vocationalisation' of a substantial proportion of secondary schooling has also exploited and reinforced existing gender divisions of labour, involving, as it does, a shift from courses in which boys and girls undertake essentially the same academic curriculum, to one in which they spend a substantial proportion of their school time in vocational courses where gender segregation is marked.

No national statistics are available to indicate the gender composition of enrolments in specialised, vocational and agricultural schools according to area of specialisation. Statistics collected by the Women's Federation do, however, indicate the proportion of females enrolled by skilled-worker schools run by the different industrial units and ministries under the State Council. Taken as a whole, these schools enrolled a quota of 30 per cent females in 1988. There was, however, a good deal of variation in enrolments between the schools. For example, there were 2,236 students in schools run by the Ministry of Textile Industries, of whom 41 per cent were females, but in the schools run by the Ministry of Railways there were 31,160 students, of whom only sixteen per cent were female.[29]

To some extent, the differing enrolment rates of males and females in vocationally oriented schools are a result of overt, institutional discrimination. As Beverley Hooper claims, such discrimination is apparent in all types of secondary and tertiary education, but particularly so in vocationally oriented schools which often impose quotas on the proportion of girls enrolled, and enforce those quotas by requiring higher entrance examination results from girls than from boys. One of the chief justifications given for such discrimination is that many employers express a preference for male workers.[30]

On the other hand, some vocational schools enrolling only women (*nüzi zhiye gaoji zhongxue*) have also been set up. The rationale given for the establishment of one such school in the city of Dalian in Liaoning Province was that 'in the sphere of work one must take into consideration the biological differences (*shengli chabie*) between males and females; likewise in education. Only once we have seriously addressed the issue of women's vocational training and devoted major efforts to developing women's intellectual resources (*zhili ziyuan*) will we be able to raise their employment capabilities'.[31] In its first year of operation the school enrolled 500 girls in courses in secretarial and typing skills, tourism, pre-school teaching, and child care.

Apart from these forms of institutionally created gender segregation, the differences between the vocational courses taken by males and females are determined by the choices of the students themselves. These choices are, however, heavily influenced and restricted by social perceptions of biological difference between males and females, and assumptions that these differences should be reflected in certain differences in education and employment. In Jinniu District, for example, I was told by Education Bureau officials that boys do not choose kindergarten teacher training courses because if they were to become kindergarten teachers they would be looked down upon. The officials themselves condoned the choice, however, saying that women are more suited to kindergarten teaching because the bond that small children have with their mothers is stronger than that with their fathers, and because women are more patient, tender and caring than men.[32]

With the vocationalisation of much of secondary schooling, boys and girls are effectively segregated into separate specialised areas of training and work earlier than in the academic education system in which marked differences in the subjects taken by men and women are apparent in university enrolments, but not before. However, this segregation in vocational secondary schools and universities merely develops assumptions of difference between males and females that are already built into education at all levels and are apparent, also, in the media.

Thus, in regular primary and secondary schools girls and boys participate, by and large, in the same curriculum (with some exceptions, for example in sports programmes), but that curriculum teaches very different, and what is more, unequal, roles for males and females. This was strikingly illustrated by an analysis published in *ZGFN* in 1989 of the twelve-volume textbook used for courses in Chinese in full-time six-year primary schools. The analysis found that, in total, the names of only eleven female persons were mentioned, in contrast to 82 male personages. Several tens of male writers were noted, but only three female writers. All the scientists, literary scholars and artists mentioned were men, and there was also a wide range of other roles for men, including many leadership positions in various fields. In contrast, a narrow range of roles for women was included, and most of them were relatively low status workers. Similarly, a wide range of personality traits were described in relation to men, whereas women were characterised by a very narrow range. Deng Yingchao, a veteran of the revolution and, at the time, the most powerful woman in the Communist Party, was portrayed only as a kindly, motherly figure – once giving a raincoat to a guard on duty and once sitting, mending pyjamas with sewing box, scissors and thread laid before her.[33]

Messages, such as those evident in this textbook, about the roles most suited to men and women, have been reinforced since 1978 by a vast body of literature which emphasises that physically, as well as mentally, men and women are different, and which presents the differences in such a way that women continually appear to fall short of the male standard. One article on 'labour and exercise for young women', for example, summed up its comparisons between young women and men by saying that 'whether in functions of the kinetic system, blood, circulation, respiration, and adjustment of body temperature, or in endurance and adaptability in heavy manual labour and physical training, young women cannot match young men of the same age'.[34]

Other articles then take these physical differences as the grounds on which to argue directly for particular divisions of labour. An article published in a women's magazine in 1986 argued, for example, that 'in order to give full play to women's abilities, one must not require them to undertake work that does not suit their special characteristics, but rather develop to the full their superiorities ... Apart from meticulous work such as embroidery, women generally achieve outstanding results in animal husbandry, processing and services'.[35] It is significant that according to articles such as this, the 'superiorities' women apparently enjoy make them most suited to areas of employment which in general are relatively poorly paid and of low status.

In education and the media there is, then, a contrast in attitudes toward the gender division of labour between the late Maoist period and the post-Mao era. In the Cultural Revolution women were urged to become 'Iron Girls' who, in challenging the existing gender division of labour, made superhuman efforts to overcome their 'inferior' biology and become more like men. Since Mao's death, on the other hand, women have been taught to accept that biology is destiny,[36] whether in relation to education or work. A striking similarity between Maoist and post-Mao approaches, however, is the degree to which women's worth is measured in terms of the extent to which they do, or do not, conform to a male standard.

POLITICAL PARTICIPATION[37]

Between the 1950s and the late 1970s, women's involvement in political affairs grew substantially, both through increases in female representation in formal political institutions, and through women's direct involvement in political study groups and public meetings held by production teams to discuss production, work allocation and remuneration, and other local issues. Despite the increases, however, in terms of formal representation women reached nothing like equality with men. For example, women have never made up more than about ten per cent of the full membership of the Central Committee of the CCP. Furthermore, even at the local level, women were usually marginalised in collective debates and most decision making was done by male leaders.

Since the late 1970s the proportion of women occupying leadership positions at all levels of institutional politics has declined. In addition, with a return to family farming and a rejection of Maoist methods of political mobilisation, the active participation of ordinary rural women and men in political debate and action has been reduced. Both trends, to be discussed in more detail in the following paragraphs, have limited the possibilities open to women for affecting changes in gender relations and the position of women in their communities.

As mentioned in Chapter 3, areas of decision making relating to the rural economy and to rural government and administration which were formerly both controlled by officials in the commune structure, were in theory, at least, split in the post-Mao era.

With the introduction of the production responsibility system, much of the decision making relating to production devolved to individual families, so that families now had more freedom to choose for themselves what areas of production to engage in and how to use the products of their labour. To some extent, as Sulamith and Jack Potter argue, in this context 'freedom' 'is essentially a male-centred notion, signifying the men's right, reclaimed from team leaders, following decollectivisation, to direct the economic activities of the women and children of their households. Zengbu women do not have "freedom"; their former subordination to the team leaders who once directed their labour has merely been exchanged for subordination to their husbands'.[38]

As discussed in Chapter 4, this is likely to be the case in those families in which women work in agriculture and sidelines, though for a number of women now running private enterprises or specialised households, or working in industry, the economic reforms may have brought greater autonomy from their husbands. Just as in other societies, however, the 'freedom' of both men and women to decide economic matters is constrained by various external factors over which they have little influence. In contemporary rural China these include central and local government policies relating, for example, to land tenure and usage, labour migration, and taxation; prices and forces of supply and demand; and the recruitment policies of local industries, as well as the decisions on village economic matters now taken by village committees or corporations in the place of production brigades. Interestingly, as Ellen Judd points out, and as will be taken up again in Chapter 8, 'the autonomy gained may be much less than hoped, but the hope itself and the changes in this direction that have come with the reform movement are powerful forces in this cultural field'.[39]

Governmental functions at local levels have been taken over by township governments and village committees. Mass political campaigns have been largely discredited and there has been a decline in the number of collective meetings held. This has led to a decrease in opportunities for direct contact between 'the masses' and representatives of the state.

On the other hand, more indirect or representational forms of political involvement have been encouraged and strengthened: mass organisations, such as the All-China Women's Federation (which is discussed in the following section), have been re-established and urged to be more active in representing their constituents' views, Party and government institutions have been rebuilt, and elections for positions in those institutions have been revived and improved as a channel for the expression of rural people's political views.

In formal institutions of political power, however, women's representation has declined since the end of the 1970s. The proportion of women appointed to full membership of the Central Committee of the CCP declined from 7 per cent in 1977 to 5.2 per cent in 1982 and 6.3 per cent in 1992.[40] At the other end of the scale, women's Party membership has also declined, and in recent years a number of letters complaining about the difficulties women have entering the Party because of prejudice against them has been published.[41]

85

In Yiyang District, Hunan Province, an investigation of nineteen townships in six counties undertaken in 1988 found that of a total of 9,597 Party members, only 731 or 7.6 per cent were women. The highest proportion of women Party members per township was 11.8 per cent. Out of 322 villages, 35 or 10.9 per cent had no female Party members. The average age of women Party members was 42, and 21.1 per cent of townships had no female Party members aged 30 or under. According to the investigation, more than 70 per cent of women Party members joined during the Socialist Education Campaign and the Cultural Revolution. Only 14.2 per cent have joined since 1980; and 31.6 per cent of townships have not had a new female Party member since 1987.[42]

Media reports claim that the lack of women newly joining the Party is contributing to a situation in which the proportion of female cadres is declining at all levels, the average age of female cadres is relatively old, and there are few women newly joining the cadre ranks.[43] Although not a formal necessity, Party membership is, in practice, required for participation in leadership at the township level and above. However, entry to Party membership is usually granted only after a lengthy period of observation, and in this a woman trying to gain membership of the Party is disadvantaged by the patrilocal marriage system. If she does not gain entry between the age of eighteen (the minimum entry age) and the time of her marriage, it will be many years after she has settled into her husband's village before the Party will reconsider her, by which time she may well be too busy with domestic work and production to be involved in politics.[44]

Comprehensive statistics on women's political representation at local levels are not available, but the following reports give some idea of the situation in the 1980s and 1990s. In their work report to the Fifth National Women's Congress in 1984, the Secretariat of the All-China Women's Federation claimed that in the provincial level Party and government departments of 28 provinces, women comprised an average of only 6.5 per cent of leading cadres.[45] Nationally, at county or commune level, the report claimed, only two per cent of all Party Committee Secretaries and Deputy Secretaries were women.[46]

In 1988 the Central Organisation Department of the CCP and the All-China Women's Federation claimed that nationally women comprised 43.6 per cent of the workforce but only 28.8 per cent (8 million) of all cadres. At provincial, district and county levels they comprised about five per cent of leading cadres, and less at township level.[47]

Chen Muhua, Chairperson of the All-China Women's Federation, claimed in 1990 that women account for 7.99 per cent of all officials at county level in the country. She called the ratio 'rather low', and drew the attention of Party committees at all levels to this problem.[48]

The reasons for the low numbers of women in institutional politics in recent years, especially in rural areas, relate to continuing prejudices against women in the 'outside' sphere of politics, and to the fact that most women, especially married women, are too tired after the long hours they put into domestic work and rearing children, as well as production, to be able or to want to become politically active. The patrilocal, exogamous marriage system is also a factor because it means that women are regarded as temporary residents in their natal village and strangers in the village into which they marry, and hence it adds to women's exclusion from the informal networks of power amongst (male) villagers. None of these factors are new, of course, but their effect has been compounded by a withdrawal of the CCP pressure on local leaders to improve women's political representation that characterised the early-to-mid-1970s.

Thus, in the Yiyang district example cited above, the reasons put forward to explain the decline in female Party membership were, firstly, that some township and village Party committees were too demanding of prospective women members, claiming that young women were not eligible because they lacked stability, married women because they were burdened with child care, and older women because their education and health were not good enough. In some cases the regulations governing entry into the Party about age (under 40) and education (upper secondary school) were applied very strictly to women, but not to men. Secondly, many township and villages trained the heads of Village Women's Congresses, but made no effort to train other promising women for Party service. Finally, since the introduction of the production responsibility system, many women (but fewer men) have stopped participating in political activities and have shown little interest in joining the Party.[49]

The decline in the number of women cadres stems also from the poor performance of women in elections for delegates to the People's Congresses. Throughout the 1980s and 1990s, approximately 21 per cent of all delegates to the National People's Congresses were female, but at local levels it was often the case that far fewer women were elected. To give one example, the *Chinese Women's Daily* reported that in Yanshi County, Henan Province, in the county and township elections held in April 1987, none of the eight women candidates was elected. Amongst the 50 township heads and deputy heads newly elected there were no women.[50]

In accordance with the revised Election Law of 1979, direct elections were held for the first time in the 1980s for delegates to the People's Congresses at county level, and in elections at all levels, a requirement that there be more candidates than posts to be filled was introduced. In many rural areas the 1980s was also the first time since the 1950s that direct elections were held at the township level. In theory, villagers were previously supposed to elect the leaders, deputy leaders and management committees of production teams and brigades, but in practice, committee members were usually simply appointed by the leading local cadres.[51] A further change was the removal of quotas. Previously, targets and quotas had commonly been set at the local level to ensure a reasonable proportion of female cadres, but during the 1980s many, though not all, counties dropped the quota system.[52]

These were the immediate causes of the poor showing of women in the elections: now that villagers had some choice in who their leaders would be, and pressure to elect a minimum number of women was reduced or removed, the extent of the obstacles facing women's involvement in politics became fully apparent.

During the late 1980s and 1990s, commentators and officials expressed considerable concern at the low level of female political participation and debated, in particular, the desirability – or otherwise – of a quota system for the election of women to People's Congresses.[53] However, at the national level at least, the debate and rhetoric translated into rather less in the way of practical measures to improve the situation, or to provide standardised guidelines or policy for local level governments. In the process of drafting the 1992 Women's Rights Protection Law, the Women's Federation lobbied for the inclusion of a clause establishing a minimum quota for female delegates to People's Congresses. In the final draft, however, the relevant clause (Article 10, Clause 2) stipulated merely that 'delegates to the National People's Congress and to local People's Congresses at all levels should include an appropriate number of women, and the proportion of female delegates should gradually be increased'.[54]

In my discussion so far, I have lent support to the argument that direct state intervention to improve gender equality is an important factor in increasing women's participation in institutional politics, and that lack of such intervention contributes to lower rates of political participation by women. However, I would argue that in post-Mao China, it has not only been the case that the state has neglected gender issues and hence *allowed* women's rates of political participation to slide. It has also actively, although not necessarily wittingly, promoted that slide.

As discussed in Chapter 3, a reconfiguration of gender relations and gender identities has been a central aspect of change to social and political discourse which the CCP under Deng Xiaoping has encouraged in order to strengthen its reform programme and the legitimacy of its rule. One element in this reconfiguration has been a denigration of women in positions of power. As Marilyn Young writes, 'in dramatic writings about the "ten years of turmoil", women in political roles are universally depicted in the most negative way . . . Evil itself has been feminized, and the message to women is clear: there is something in the natural order of things that does not love a woman exercising public power'.[55] This is connected to the unpopularity, and the state's manipulation of the unpopularity, of Jiang Qing – Mao's wife and a member of the Gang of Four. Because she was a *woman* wielding power, Jiang Qing is now portrayed as a 'white-boned demon', a witch and a prostitute.[56] Ross Terrill goes so far as to say that 'having struggled all her life to transcend the housewife's role, Jiang had been tried in part as a housewife – who exceeded a woman's proper functions and led her husband astray … Jiang Qing was not really guilty of wrong ideas ("counterrevolution"), but of playing the wrong social role'.[57]

The negative images used to portray her have helped to discredit not just Jiang Qing as an individual, but the Gang of Four and the 'ten years of turmoil' in their entirety. At the same time, they have been extended to all women who are active politically.

The effects of the low level of women's political participation on women's work and gender divisions of labour are several. First, it means that at the macro level women have little input or representation in the planning of development strategies, and they have little power to alter existing policies or have new policies adopted so as to protect and further women's interests. Second, at the micro level, many women have little control over the allocation of their own labour, this being in the hands of male heads of families and male leaders in the local economy and government. Third, the lack of women in politics, combined with the negative image of politically active women, reinforces notions that the 'outside' is men's realm. This then strengthens gender divisions of labour between 'outside' and 'inside' work. It also makes it difficult for women to attain positions of leadership in the economy, for example, as enterprise managers, even in industries where the labour is predominantly female.

In China there is no organised women's movement and few groups concerned with improving the position of women that are independent of the state.[58] Within the state system the All-China Women's Federation has been given the task of furthering the interests of women, as well as of mobilising support for Party policy amongst women. As outlined in Chapter 2, the Women's Federation is a mass organisation consisting of a hierarchy of groups extending from the level of National Congress downwards, with indirectly elected representatives at each level of government, down to the village level.

To some extent, the poor representation of women in institutional politics in China generally has been offset by the existence of the All-China Women's Federation. In the following section, therefore, I examine the Federation and address the question as to whether the Women's Federation has played any part in shaping or changing gender relations, in particular, gender divisions of labour, in rural China; and if so, to what extent and in what directions?

THE ALL-CHINA WOMEN'S FEDERATION

Structure and status

Disbanded, along with other mass organisations, at the beginning of the Cultural Revolution because its concern with gender issues was seen as undermining the CCP's overriding emphasis on class struggle, the All-China Women's Federation was rehabilitated at provincial and national level in 1978.

Along with the change in state and Party leadership, the repudiation of the Cultural Revolution and the call for the 'four modernisations', the revival of the Women's Federation was greeted by women across China with an optimism which, however, very quickly turned sour. As one young woman complained in a letter to Deng Yingchao: 'Reports and decisions made at the [4th National Women's] Congress were very encouraging indeed. But three years have passed since then and the record of work among women is very disappointing.'[59]

Throughout the post-Mao era the Women's Federation has continued to be held in low regard by Chinese women. By shifting its emphasis away from political rhetoric toward more concrete help in combating particular instances of discrimination and abuse of women, and in providing advice and training, the Federation has made its work somewhat more relevant and helpful to its constituency. Nevertheless, as I will show, the effectiveness of the Women's Federation as an advocate for women's interests has been severely constrained by lack of resources, lack of autonomy and authority and, perhaps as a result, a failure to challenge the ideological and structural foundations of gender inequality.

During the 1980s there was some official support for the suggestion that the Women's Federation should speak out more boldly and independently in defence of women's interests. In practice, however, the present day Women's Federation is bound, as much as ever, by the dictates of the CCP.[60]

In establishing policies and principles to be handed down as guidelines for all lower level Women's Federations, the national leadership of the Women's Federation is given explicit and detailed directions by the CCP.[61] Lower level women's cadres, particularly those at county and township levels, frequently appear to be less constricted by Party rhetoric in their discussion of women's problems, and show more enthusiasm and initiative in carrying out their work than cadres in the national and provincial Women's Federations. Regardless of their enthusiasm, however, grass-roots women's cadres work under enormous constraints. Their wages and what little additional funding is received by women's organisations from provincial down to village level are determined and provided by local government, rather than through the Women's Federation and, according to the constitution of the Women's Federation, women's organisations at provincial, municipal, county and township levels 'carry out their work under the leadership of the local Party Committee' as well as with the guidance of the Women's Federation just superior to them.[62] Personnel appointments to grass-roots women's organisations must also meet the approval of, and can be changed by, the local Party Committee.

These restrictions on the Women's Federation are compounded by lack of resources, and by the difficulties that the Federation has had in adjusting to the changes brought about by the demise of the commune and the introduction of the production responsibility system. As with cadres in general, with the intro-duction of the production responsibility system, the authority of women's cadres and the relevance of their work came under attack from the general population, who argued that 'now that everyone can participate in production we don't need the Women's Congress; now that responsibility lies with the household, there's no need for cadres' ('*Shengchan jiajia hui, bu yao fudaihui, zeren dao le hu, hebi yao ganbu?*').[63] In the early years of the production responsibility system, a number of communes did in fact remove their women's representatives at pro-duction brigade and team level, in effect doing away with separate representation for women at grass-roots levels entirely.

In response to such pressure, and in attempting to adapt to the new economic and political structures being established in the countryside, the Women's Federation stipulated that women in each village should be represented by a Grass-roots Women's Representative Congress (henceforth Village Women's Congress) (*jiceng funü daibiao hui* or *fudaihui* for short). According to the Women's Federation's 1983 constitution, the executive committee of the Village Women's Congress is to comprise one head, a deputy head and an unspecified number of committee members. Delegates to the Congress are to be elected every two years to represent the different residential areas and types of employment of the women in the village. The constitution stipulates that Women's Congresses are also to be formed at township (*xiang, zhen*), county and provincial levels. At township level these congresses are to meet once every two years, at county level once every three years, and at provincial level once every five years.[64]

In practice, there is some regional variation in the form and extent of women's representation at grass-roots levels. In most of the counties that I visited in Beijing, Shandong and Sichuan in 1989 I was told that Village Women's Congresses usually consist of one woman who may or may not be a full-time cadre, who, in addition to woman-work, usually does most of the education and propaganda for family planning in the village. In addition to the head of Con-gress, most Village Women's Congresses appoint several delegates to represent women from different occupations and residential areas. These representatives may or may not play a significant role in representing women at Women's

Congress meetings, but aside from this they only occasionally undertake tasks assigned to them by the Congress, for which they are compensated for labour-time lost (*wu gong butie*). Township Women's Congresses are generally staffed by one full-time head of Congress doing woman-work, which in some cases includes family planning education and propaganda, and other Party work. Township Women's Congresses generally also have a committee of anywhere between two and nine part-time members. County Women's Congresses are staffed by four to ten full-time cadres, doing mostly woman-work, but also other Party work.[65]

In addition to women's organisations based on residential and governmental structures, the Women's Federation has, since the early 1980s, encouraged the establishment of women's representative groups in different areas of women's employment, especially in township enterprises. As will be discussed in Chapter 9, however, only some township enterprises have set up such groups.

Many Women's Federations have claimed in recent years that at the grass-roots level women's organisations are understaffed and their members overworked. Particular resentment is expressed by some county women's cadres at the fact that township and village women's cadres must spend so much of their time on family planning. Another major source of dissatisfaction among Women's Federations is that their members are poorly paid, and they have little authority or status, either with the local population, or among other cadres.[66]

It is recognised that in some cases women's cadres' lack of status or authority is due to the fact that they are poorly qualified, and, as in Party and government organisations, there have been calls for younger, better educated women's cadres to be appointed, and for women's cadres to undergo training in the theory of the women's movement, legal education and technical skills useful for developing the commodity economy.[67] As one Women's Federation report points out, however, women's cadres are given fewer opportunities to undertake training than their male colleagues, and even when such opportunities are made available, family responsibilities often prevent women's cadres from taking them.[68]

Finally, many Women's Federation leaders express dissatisfaction at the level of funding that their organisations receive. Among the counties that I visited, total funding for the County Women's Federation received from the county government varied from 1,000 *yuan* per year to 10,000 *yuan* per year. Women's Federation cadres at the level of township and below generally did not receive funding above their wages. Funding for training classes and the like generally came from local government departments.[69]

Activities

Despite the many problems besetting the Women's Federation, it is probably fair to say that in the post-Mao era it has been more active in protecting the particular interests of women than at any time in the past, with the exception of the land reform and marriage campaigns of the early 1950s. During this period the Women's Federation has shown greatest concern with the following issues: the protection of the legal rights of women and children, the care and education of young children, women's contribution to the development of 'spiritual civilisation', the improvement of women's 'quality' (*'suzhi'* – which refers to their political consciousness as well as their education and practical skills), and an improvement of women's employment opportunities.

In the 1980s the protection of the legal rights of women and children was a particular focus of the Women's Federation's work. Across the country, women's cadres distributed leaflets and organised classes and consultancy services to educate women as to their legal rights and responsibilities. They also mobilised people to report crimes against women, investigated reports and complaints made to them, and in some cases intervened directly to protect women or to seek redress on their behalf.[70]

Another aspect of the Women's Federation's work in protecting the legal rights of women and children has been their attempts to combat direct discrimination against women in industrial employment. Thus, one of the most vigorous and effective campaigns run by the Women's Federation to date has been the one aimed at combating discrimination against women in the recruitment of workers into industry, the disproportionate retrenchment of women workers, and calls for women to withdraw from employment and 'return to the kitchen'. These forms of discrimination have largely occurred in urban state-run industries, where, in trying to overcome problems of overstaffing, managers have targeted women because they must be paid maternity leave if they give birth, and because of their responsibilities for domestic work and child care.[71]

In rural areas, in addition to trying to improve women's representation in township enterprises, the Women's Federation has drawn attention to the poor working conditions faced by women in many such enterprises, and to instances of unequal pay. In terms of its overall programme, however, the Women's Federation has put relatively little effort into combating these problems, perhaps because there is a general acceptance of the notion that, in the early stages of development in particular, township enterprises cannot afford to meet the same standards of workplace equity and welfare as state-run enterprises.

The Women's Federation's efforts at improving women's legal rights and combating discrimination can be said to have culminated in the promulgation in 1992 of the Women's Rights Protection Law. However, on the whole, the law simply reiterates principles and laws already laid out elsewhere. The main aim of the law appears to have been not so much to provide women greater protection, as to impress upon both the Chinese population and foreign governments the importance accorded to women's rights by the CCP.

In addition to promoting women's rights, Women's Federations have devoted much of their energy, during the early 1980s in particular, to improving family life and young children's education. As mentioned in Chapter 4, for example, a large proportion of articles in *ZGFN* are devoted to the rearing of children. Women's Federations across the country have also worked with other bodies to increase the provision of child care and kindergarten places, to improve the training of nursery and kindergarten teachers, and in some cases to establish classes and schools on good mothering.[72]

As an extension of their responsibility for the upbringing of their children, women are further held responsible for the task of improving family life and furthering 'spiritual civilisation'. One of the Women's Federation's main activities in this area has been the campaign, similar to that of the 1950s, to select and reward 'five good' families (*wu hao jiating*). In 1983 the Chairperson of the Women's Federation, Kang Keqing, laid out the criteria for 'five good' families as follows:

(1) Love the socialist fatherland and the collective and abide by the law.
(2) Work and study hard and fulfil one's duties.
(3) Enact family planning, educate one's children well and be thrifty and industrious in managing the household.
(4) Alter prevailing habits and customs, be civilised and polite and maintain cleanliness and hygiene.
(5) Respect the old and love the young, maintain democracy and harmony in the family and unite with and help one's neighbours. In family life husband and wife must love and respect each other, help each other and yield to each other, carefully rear the next generation together, fulfil their obligations to support the elderly, and oppose the maltreatment of the elderly and of other family members.[73]

It is noteworthy that the 'five good' families campaign is directed primarily at women. Furthermore, although mutual help between husband and wife is included in the criteria, there is a noticeable lack, in the Women's Federation's work, of attempts to change the assumption that domestic work and child care are a woman's responsibility. Thus, the Federation's work in improving family life has reinforced the image of woman as primarily mother and domestic worker, responsible for an 'inside' sphere, which is in turn subordinate to, and in the service of, the nation's economic and social wellbeing. This has undermined the

Women's Federation's own efforts in urban areas to combat calls from employers for women to withdraw from employment to 'return to the kitchen', and in rural areas, to train women so as to improve their participation in agriculture and the commodity economy.

Since the mid-1980s, however, although concern with protecting women's basic legal rights and with children and family life has been maintained, in rural areas it is improvement of women's employment opportunities which has been given the greater emphasis in the Women's Federation's campaigning.

In June 1986 the All-China Women's Federation convened a work conference for heads of Women's Federations of province, autonomous region and municipal levels, at which the Federation's work in rural areas was discussed and its aims and tasks for rural areas in the period of the Seventh Five-Year Plan (1986–1990) were set out.[74]

Women's Federations were called upon, first of all, to raise women's consciousness and improve their understanding of current CCP policies – 'to educate women to liberate themselves from the fetters of traditional concepts of small production and egalitarianism',[75] to improve women's self-confidence, and encourage them to develop commodity production. These were to become the main elements in the ongoing 'four selfs' campaign to develop women's self-respect (*zizun*), self-confidence (*zixin*), independence (*zili*), and strength (*ziqiang*).

The other task given particular emphasis at the work conference was that of providing practical support and training for women to overcome poverty, improve their involvement in the rural market economy, and raise their incomes. In poverty-stricken areas it was argued that the aim should be not merely to provide relief funding and grain, but also to arouse enthusiasm, teach skills, and help with technology and the supply of information. Prosperous areas were to emphasise vocational training and, where appropriate, girls' vocational schools were to be established. Training was to focus on young and middle-aged women, in particular educated young women.

In all areas, it was argued, women were to be encouraged to make full use of their 'particular strengths and abilities' in crop planting and animal husbandry, processing, textiles, services, foodstuffs, electronics and traditional handicrafts. Elsewhere, in a summary of the Women's Federation's work in alleviating poverty made in 1989, the deputy head of the Federation, Huang Qizao, stressed that while local conditions must always be taken into account, 'development of the courtyard economy (that is, small-scale agriculture and non-agricultural production, especially of handicrafts, commerce and services undertaken in the home or courtyard) is an excellent way of alleviating poverty and raising incomes that can be implemented everywhere. It is particularly important given that the

95

area of arable land is decreasing and that women are the dominant labour force in courtyard production'.[76]

Since the mid-1980s, numerous favourable reports have appeared in the Chinese media describing the successes of the Women's Federation's efforts in training and supporting women in the courtyard economy. One newspaper article reported, for example, that in 1986 the Shandong Provincial Women's Federation made plans to train ten million rural women in the Seventh Five-Year Plan period. In that year various levels of the Women's Federation in Shandong ran more than 30 thousand classes (sessions) for women on horticulture, animal husbandry, processing, spinning and weaving and sewing, involving 1.17 million women.[77] Classes run by Women's Federations in conjunction with other departments numbered 20,000 (sessions), and involved more than 800,000 women. According to incomplete figures, in 1986, two million women in Shandong learnt one or more technical skills.[78]

In addition to providing classes locally, the Women's Federation has tried to improve women's participation in various forms of distance education. Since 1993, for example, the journal *Nongjianü Baishitong [Rural Women Knowing All]*, published by the Women's Federation, has joined forces with the Beijing Agricultural University to provide training in four main areas: household management, the home production of handicrafts, animal husbandry and agricultural management. Teaching materials, written by experts from the Agricultural University, are sent to registered students for a small fee, and after one year of study, successful students are awarded a certificate.

Aside from organising technical training classes, the Women's Federation also provides legal advice to women and makes links with other bodies to help women obtain bank loans and to assist them with the supply of raw materials and feed for livestock etc., and with the marketing of their produce.[79]

One of the largest and most successful campaigns to have been undertaken by the Women's Federation in rural areas since 1978 is the campaign to 'study culture, study technology; compete in results, compete in contributions', or 'double study, double compete' ('*shuang xue, shuang bi*') campaign for short. Begun in 1989, the campaign was initially planned to run for five years but was then incorporated into the Five-Year Plan (1991–1996) and the Ten-Year Plan (1991–2001). It is being run by the Women's Federation in conjunction with a number of government ministries. The latter are responsible for the formulation of principles and policies, overall planning and command of production and the provision of services, while the Women's Federations attempt to coordinate the activities of the different government departments, publicise the campaign, and mobilise and organise women to be involved. At the national level the campaign is led by a coordinating committee chaired by the head of the Women's

Federation, Chen Muhua, with the deputy secretary of the State Council, and the heads of the Ministries of Agriculture and Forestry as deputy chairs.[80]

The aim of the campaign is to encourage and help women to improve their skills and productivity in commercial agricultural production (both as part of the courtyard economy and on a larger scale). The focus on agriculture is, according to the deputy chairperson of the Women's Federation, Huang Qizao, both a reflection of the Party's emphasis on the fundamental importance of agriculture to the national economy and – as a result of the rural reforms and ensuing development – of the fact that women are increasingly becoming the major force in agriculture, while more and more men are moving into non-agricultural production.[81]

According to the *People's Daily*, between 1989 and 1994 approximately 120 million women were involved in the campaign. Of these, 90 million received technical training, and 510,000 were awarded certificates as agro-technicians.[82]

There is no doubt that the 'double study, double compete' campaign and other campaigns run by the Women's Federation to improve women's participation in the economy have contributed to the employment opportunities and incomes of rural women, at least to some extent. It is probable, however, that the impact of such campaigns is considerably less than the enthusiastic media reports would suggest; that such enthusiasm is more indicative of CCP policy orientations than of the real situation. Thus, the claim that in 1986 two million women in Shandong learnt one or more technical skills is less impressive in light of the fact that the skills are very basic, having been acquired in sessions lasting usually no more than a few days, and that while two million women is many in absolute terms, they represent only about one per cent of Shandong's rural female labour force.

Furthermore, accounts of the Women's Federation's success in various counties across China may be atypical. I myself found that in Ling County, Shandong, five out of seven women aged between 14 and 45 (excluding cadres and delegates to the Women's Federation) participated in training classes run by the Women's Federation. However, amongst the 42 women in this age group that I interviewed in other counties in Beijing and Sichuan, none participated in training classes run by the Women's Federation, although some had received other forms of short-term training. Most women said they only participated in the Women's Federation's March 8th activities and, at most, one or two other meetings with the Women's Federation each year.

Insofar as the Women's Federation has any impact at all on women's participation in the rural economy, the effect is primarily to reinforce certain gender divisions of labour. As we have seen, its activities in improving family life and 'spiritual civilisation' have resulted in a strengthening of the image of woman as mother and domestic worker. In other areas of work, more directly concerned with improving women's position in the economy, the Women's Federation has hailed the courtyard economy and agriculture as particularly suited to women's 'special strengths and abilities'. In general, in fact, the Women's Federation is one of the strongest advocates of the argument that women and men are biologically different and therefore suited to different types of work.

Gender divisions of labour are also, of course, reinforced by what the Women's Federation does *not* do. Of greatest importance in this regard is that since the late 1970s it has taken no significant action in relation to domestic work; whether it be to lobby for the recognition of the importance of such work to the economy, to argue for its socialisation, or to pressure men to share domestic work with their female family members.

As discussed in this chapter and in Chapter 4, failure to challenge the prevailing patrilocal marriage system also reinforces particular gender divisions of labour. As mentioned in Chapter 2, the 'criticise Lin Biao and Confucius' campaign of the 1970s included moves on the part of the CCP and the Women's Federation to promote matrilocal marriage. Today, however, patrilocal marriage is rarely identified as problematic and there is no longer any significant effort being made to promote matrilocal marriage.

Given that, as a result of family planning, there are now more families with only one child to care for them, the resistance to matrilocal marriage (in which a family relinquishes its son) will be high and it may not, in fact, be a workable strategy to encourage it. An alternative strategy for improving the status of women might be to encourage intra-village marriage so that women can retain contact with their friends and natal family, and also provide support for their parents in old age. Reports do in fact suggest some increase since 1949 in the incidence of intra-village, and also intra-surname, marriage.[83] However, such marriages are also not without their problems. Sulamith and Jack Potter found that one significant reason for the continuing reluctance of families to undertake such marriages in Zengbu is that they do not expand families' social contacts in any useful way. Also, villagers believe that quarrels between a husband and wife who are both locals can too easily escalate into quarrels between two families.[84]

It is clear, then, that any attempt to change existing patrilocal and exogamous marriage practices is extremely difficult because such practices perform important functions in village life. Nevertheless, given their centrality in the subordination of women, the fact that the CCP and the Women's Federation do not attempt to challenge the dominance of such marriage practices suggests that ultimately the issue of subordination is not of primary concern.

This can be said too of the other ways in which the Women's Federation lends support to existing gender divisions of labour. It is important to also understand, however, that there are powerful reasons for the Women's Federation, as for Chinese women generally, to choose to condone, and even strengthen, such divisions. First, a reaction against Maoism is important in this respect, for, as we have seen, the particular ways in which gender divisions of labour were challenged during the Great Leap Forward and the Cultural Revolution caused a number of problems for women: they meant that women's 'inside' work in domestic work and as mothers was devalued or ignored, but not, on the whole, shared or reduced. Women were judged according to how well they met male standards of achievement in the 'outside' spheres of education, employment and politics, yet the social and structural obstacles to their achievement in these areas were not overcome. In addition, the claim that 'what men can do, women can do too' lent justification to some appalling cases of women being overworked and strained beyond their physical capacities. As observed in Chapter 3, women as well as men also supported a return to more traditional gender relations as part of a reaction against the upheaval of the Cultural Revolution and a desire for stability and order.

Second, the Women's Federation believes that the promotion of women's 'natural' dominance in particular areas of work will bring them certain advantages. To take the courtyard economy as an example: in Chapters 7 and 8 I argue that an increasingly strong association is being made between both the courtyard economy and agriculture, and the 'inside' sphere. Not coincidentally, the concentration of women in these areas of employment signifies, in some respects at least, a marginalisation of both women and these types of production. It has been a common dream of the peasantry through the ages to get off the land and off the farm, and now in the 1980s and 1990s, with rapid industrialisation and the development of a market economy, that dream is being fulfilled by more and more rural inhabitants. From this viewpoint, those who work on the land and on the farm are the unlucky ones, and by reinforcing notions that farm work is women's work, the Women's Federation is colluding in a perpetuation of women's lower status. The Women's Federation, however, promotes women's dominance in the courtyard economy, in part because work in this sector can be accommodated relatively easily with a woman's other commitments in domestic work and child care, and in part because it is an area in which a woman can develop a far greater degree of autonomy and control over her own labour power than in industry. Furthermore, as long as the courtyard economy is seen as 'women's work', and as long as the CCP continues to encourage development of the courtyard economy, rural women will have open to them an area of income generation in which they need not compete with, or antagonise, men.

Finally, as I have stressed throughout, gender divisions of labour are constructed and maintained through a formidable web of institutions, power relations, social acts and beliefs. Given this, and given its own limited resources and power, the Women's Federation perhaps feels that the most worthwhile strategy is not to continually challenge the existing divisions of labour, but rather to concentrate on making those divisions work as far as possible to the benefit of women.

The particular nature of women's participation in education and politics has a major impact on gender divisions of labour. For example, women's commonly lower levels of education and high levels of illiteracy disadvantage them in the 'outside' spheres of politics and industrial employment. In addition, the increasing gender segregation of rural education, especially at secondary level, reinforces divisions of labour according to gender in which women are concentrated in 'light' work, or work associated with the 'inside' sphere.

Similarly, divisions of labour along gender lines, in particular between 'inside' and 'outside' spheres, are perpetuated both by the low levels of participation of women in formal politics, and by the particular strategies of the few women in positions of formal political authority, especially those in the Women's Federation, whose brief it is to further the interests of women.

In turn, gender divisions of labour also influence women's education and political representation. Thus, recent trends which make agriculture, domestic sidelines, light industry and services the most likely areas in which rural women will find employment, lead to an emphasis on the skills required for such work in the education of girls, and in the strategy of the Women's Federation for improving rural women's position in society.

In the book so far, I have provided a theoretical and historical framework for an examination of the impact of reform on gender divisions of labour in contemporary rural China. I have also considered a range of factors, from state policies through to family structures and relations, and women's participation in education and politics, which both shape, and are shaped by, shifts in gender divisions of labour occurring in the process of reform. I will now turn to a detailed examination of gender divisions of labour themselves, to the processes through which these divisions, and the meanings associated with them, have been formed or re-formed in recent years, and to the implications of these divisions for women's lives and for gender relations in rural China.

6

Domestic Work

THIS chapter has three main aims: to discuss the meaning of the term 'domestic work', the status of such work and the associations it has, in particular as 'women's work' belonging to an 'inside' sphere, and as something less than 'real work'; then to discuss the implications for women's domestic work, and the meanings associated with it, of rural reforms and modernisation. It also examines the nature of the tasks undertaken as domestic work, the circumstances in which they are undertaken, the division of labour in domestic work, and the time spent by women in such work.

DEFINITIONS AND PERCEPTIONS

The notion that domestic work is in some way oppressive has been central to Chinese Marxist approaches to women's liberation. Yet for all the centrality of this idea there has been little rigorous discussion of why this is so. Furthermore, what exactly is meant by 'domestic work' is almost never spelt out. It is taken for granted that we all know what it is.[1] I would argue, however, that one of the most important steps to take in order to understand the part domestic work plays in maintaining women's subordination is to recognise that definitions of domestic work are both arbitrary and constantly changing. In this chapter, therefore, we need to examine the particular ways in which certain tasks are defined as domestic work and the changing meanings associated with that term, as well as changes in the content of domestic work and the way it is organised.

In my interviews with peasant women the activities discussed as domestic work (*jiawu laodong*) were the preparation of food for family consumption, cleaning the house, washing family members' clothes, family shopping and tending domestic livestock. Private child care and the sewing and mending of clothes for family members were also considered either as domestic work or as closely associated with it.

Interviews with peasants and rural cadres suggested to me that they associate domestic work tasks most strongly with three attributes: first, they are 'women's work'. Second, they are not as important as other work, or they are not 'real' work, in part because they are 'unproductive' and unremunerated; and third, they are 'inside' tasks, conducted within the boundaries of the family house or compound.

To take these attributes, either separately or together, as a definition of domestic work is highly problematic. On the one hand, some of the individual tasks known as domestic work display only some of these attributes. On the other hand, some of the attributes can also be used to describe tasks not usually recognised as domestic work. For example, certain aspects of domestic work, such as collecting firewood and water, shopping, and even washing, can involve long periods of time at considerable distance away from the house. As well, some 'inside' tasks, such as repairing the house or family furniture, are not considered to be 'domestic work', and are done more commonly by men than by women. Similarly, it is not always possible in practice to make a distinction between one activity termed 'unproductive' domestic work and another termed productive. The care of domestic livestock is a case in point. While livestock is kept partly for family consumption, pigs and eggs, for example, are often sold. Yet the care of domestic livestock is considered domestic work.[2]

These characterisations of domestic work are inexact and arbitrary. For the purposes of understanding how certain gender divisions of labour are perpetuated or changed, and what links exist between gender divisions of labour and other aspects of gender relations in contemporary rural China, however, it is important *not* to attempt to impose a new, more exact or rational definition. Rather, it must be recognised that these characterisations have formed the framework for local evaluations of domestic work and the people who do such work. Therefore, in the following paragraphs I want to explore in more detail the attributes accorded to domestic work and the ways in which they contribute to evaluations of domestic work, relative to other types of work.

The notion that domestic work is women's work is very strongly held by Chinese peasants. This was brought home to me in the field by the laughter that commonly greeted my question as to who – of a couple – did most of the domestic work, and the response that it was the wife, *of course*.

This assumption has remained fairly constant since 1949, being unaffected by either state policy or modernisation. As discussed in Chapter 2, the effects of the attempts made by local authorities during the 'criticise Lin Biao and Confucius' campaign to persuade men to share domestic work with their wives were limited and short-lived. Since then, the attempt has not been revived on any significant scale and, as mentioned in Chapter 5, Women's Federation officials in rural areas nowadays do not regard the gender division of labour in domestic work as an issue of concern. Nor is there any sign that this division and the assumption that domestic work is 'women's work' have been altered as an indirect result of the massive rural industrialisation, rise in peasant incomes, or other changes that have followed the introduction of reforms since 1978.

The majority of the rural women I interviewed in 1989 either shared domestic work with other women in the family, or were responsible for all domestic work (see Appendix 1). In only 16 out of 58 families (27.6 per cent) was there any mention of a male in the family doing any domestic work. Of the 16, almost all played a subsidiary role, doing no more than about one-third as much as the main female domestic worker in the family. Of the men who did some domestic work, all except one were husbands of women aged between 28 and 51, most of whom had no other women in the family to help them with domestic work. Whereas girls and unmarried women were commonly reported as sharing domestic work with their mothers, there was no mention of unmarried sons doing such work.

The assumption that domestic work is not 'real work' is apparent at a number of different levels. In Chapters 1 and 2 I traced the origins of this perception and lower evaluation of domestic work to the adoption of the Marxist paradigm of a dichotomy between production and 'unproductive' domestic work. This dichotomy was further reinforced in rural China through collectivisation, which instituted a clear separation between remunerated work undertaken for the collective, and domestic work and domestic sidelines undertaken 'for the family'.

One consequence of this dichotomy for the ways in which domestic work has been perceived in rural China since the 1950s is that officially it is regarded as petty drudgery: a burden, rather than work.

As discussed in Chapter 2, during the Great Leap Forward child care centres, laundries and other services were set up in an attempt to 'transform most household work from petty irksome drudgery into socially run large-scale undertakings',[3] so as to enable women to contribute more to production. These services may indeed have benefited women but, apart from the child care centres, they were short-lived in all but the wealthiest communes. A more lasting effect of their establishment, though, was a reinforcement of the perception of domestic work as mere toil, that ideally *should* be relieved.

The view of domestic work as a burden, hampering women from contributing more to society, was given further reinforcement during the Cultural Revolution by stories, such as that cited in Chapter 4, of the model woman engineer, Wei Fengying, who neglected the cooking for the sake of making a greater contribution to production. The Cultural Revolution slogan 'What men can do, women can do too' is also revealing in this regard. It has never been claimed that what women can do (domestic work) men can do too.

In 1978, in her speech to the Fourth National Congress of the All China Women's Federation, the chairperson of the Federation, Kang Keqing, called, once more, for the socialisation of domestic work. The Women's Federations, she argued, 'must actively assist and support relevant departments, and take effective measures to gradually convert all petty domestic work into a large-scale socialist economy'.[4] However, apart from child care services, there has been no sign of such public services being established in rural China. In urban areas 'domestic service companies' and nannies have been performing similar functions, but as yet these have not reached most of the countryside. As during the Great Leap Forward, the dominant effect of the Women's Federation's rhetoric has been, I would argue, not to reduce women's domestic workload, which does of course hamper women in 'production'. Instead, it has reinforced the notion that domestic work is 'petty' and, as a corollary, the notion that to the extent that they are engaged in domestic work, women are contributing less to society than men.

Yet at times there have also been official attempts to challenge the view of domestic work as being less of a contribution to society than other activities. However, these attempts have, I argue, been framed by, and themselves reproduce, another problematic dichotomy: that between 'work' and 'family concerns'.

Thus, in the 1980s, as discussed in Chapters 4 and 5, the 'five good' family campaign of the 1950s was revived, and numerous other attempts to give greater importance to the roles of women as domestic workers were made. Readers' letters to *ZGFN*, discussed in Chapter 4, suggest that these attempts both reflect, and have an important impact on, notions of femininity. They reinforce an image of the ideal woman as an attentive, care-giving daughter-in-law, wife and mother. However, this discourse does not enable recognition or acknowledgement of the fact that what women do in this role is *work* – it is regarded as care, love, duty to the family, perhaps self-sacrifice, but not work. At the same time, nevertheless, the emphasis on women's domestic roles has altered and heightened expectations and pressures on women in domestic work. It is not so much that women are expected to do more, or devote more time to, domestic work, but that they are required to take on more responsibility for the psychological, emotional and moral, as well as physical, wellbeing of other family members. Thus, for example, media articles and the 'five good' family campaign exhort young women to take responsibility for maintaining harmonious relations with their mothers-in-law and husbands, *ZGFN* runs articles on the need for mothers to gain an understanding of child psychology, and schools and classes are being established by the Women's Federation to teach women how to be better mothers (see Chapter 5).

Peasant women themselves express a number of different attitudes towards the value or importance of the domestic work they do. Some of these attitudes were apparent in the responses made by Sichuan women to my question 'In your family, whose labour is most important, in your view?' (*'ni juede shei de laodong shi zui zhongyao de?'*). Amongst a total of thirty-one women, only eight said that their husband's labour was more important than their own. Two reasons were given; that his was the heaviest work, or that he was the income earner. Ten women said that their own labour was most important. They justified this claim in terms of their longer working hours or by saying that they did the domestic work in addition to other work. Some of the thirteen women who claimed that their own and their husband's labour were equally important cited their labour in domestic work as being their contribution, while his work in the fields was his contribution.[5] Others said that the man's work was heavier, but their own was more time-consuming. One woman claimed that her own and her husband's labour were equally important, but that while she could manage on her own, he could not manage without her because he could not wash clothes. Margery Wolf quotes a Jiangsu peasant woman as saying, in similar fashion, that 'among farmers, women are more capable. They can do everything – both indoors and outdoors – but men can only do outdoor things. For example, they can't sew or mend the winter clothes. They are very dependent on women. Without women they couldn't live because they couldn't take care of themselves, but women can'.[6]

These responses suggest a widespread recognition amongst women themselves of the importance of their domestic work within the family economy. On the other hand, though, it is noteworthy that grandmothers commonly say that the 'only' work they do is look after their grandchildren, feed the pigs and chickens, and do the cooking and cleaning. Also revealing is that women often trivialise and underestimate the total amount of time they spend each day doing domestic work.

The association made between domestic work and confinement to an 'inside' sphere that limits a woman's activities 'outside', in terms of movement as well as time, is indirectly apparent in a number of contexts, and has important consequences for women's involvement in other areas of work and social life. For example, there are two aspects of rural reforms that peasant women point to as being most welcome: the devolution of production management to the family, and the expansion of domestic sidelines. Together, women claim, these reforms have enabled them to organise their own time and labour so as to accommodate best productive tasks to their domestic work responsibilities. Underlying this is, of course, the assumption that domestic work is a woman's primary responsibility and that this responsibility limits her in certain ways.

As will be discussed in Chapter 7, the limitations that their responsibility for domestic work impose on women also mean that fewer women than men travel away from home in search of non-agricultural employment, although this is also related to the relatively high status of non-agricultural work and a shift in the responsibility for agriculture onto women.

THE IMPACT OF REFORM

I have argued that the gender division of labour in domestic work and the assumption that domestic work is 'women's work' have been essentially the same in the 1980s and 1990s as they had been decades previously. Reform policies and economic growth have, however, wrought important changes both on the content of domestic work and on the context in which it is undertaken. Before I turn to the types of domestic work tasks undertaken by women in rural China today, and how particular domestic work tasks are changing as a result of economic growth, I wish to reflect, in more general terms, upon the effects that reform and economic growth are having on domestic work in rural China. In so doing, I will be summarising some of the points already made, as well as foreshadowing the discussion to come.

One effect of economic growth and of a general improvement in peasant incomes and living standards since 1949, and in particular since the reforms of the late 1970s, has been a reduction in domestic workloads. As I will discuss in the following section, the greater availability on the market of, for example, ready-made clothes and shoes, the provision of electricity and running water, and the use of appliances, especially washing machines, have reduced, for better-off women, the amount of time and effort spent in domestic work.

Clearly, in the less developed areas of rural China and in poorer families, there is much potential for domestic workloads to be further reduced through an improvement of basic amenities. It is questionable, however, whether in better-off areas even further reductions in workloads will result from the use of a wider range of consumer items and domestic appliances than is now available. Studies from the US have shown that domestic appliances have not reduced the time women spend on domestic work in recent decades. Rather, they have simply altered the type of work performed and have resulted in expectations of higher standards.[7]

While the domestic workloads of many women have been reduced since the 1970s, some reports suggest that at the same time the total number of women engaged *solely* in domestic work may have increased. An article published in *ZGFN*[8] and debated at some length in the press[9] claimed, for example, that in Daqiu Village, near Tianjin, before the Third Plenum of the Eleventh Central Committee (December 1978) 95 per cent of women had participated in collective labour. Among these, there were approximately 100 women over 60 years old who had engaged in part-time or full-time employment. Following the Third Plenum, however, all the women over 60 retired from collective labour and 525, or 84 per cent, of married women under the age of 45 withdrew from employment and became full-time housewives.

The two main factors the authors put forward to explain this withdrawal of women from the paid labour force were, first, that the pace of work in industry is very fast, there is much heavy work and hours are long. They claim that this type of work 'not only repels women, it is also very stressful for men',[10] and it makes life easier if the women can stay home to do the domestic work for their husbands. Second, wages in Daqiu are now high enough that couples are able to live on just one person's salary and can afford to have the spouse stay at home.[11]

The authors of this article, and of others on Daqiu Village, stress that the women of this village were not retrenched or discriminated against in the paid labour force, and that they became full-time housewives of their own accord. I am somewhat suspicious of this claim, given certain remarks made by the manager of the Daqiu Village Corporation which strongly suggest that he may have pressured women into withdrawing from employment. He said first, that it is not a bad thing if, after marriage and especially during and after pregnancy, women stop working. Second, he felt that educated women should participate in employment but their hours should be shortened to, say, six hours a day to enable them to look after their families. Third, he felt that all women over fifty years of age should not participate in employment.[12] It should also be noted that the reports on Daqiu Village have been used for a particular purpose in the media: to support and condone the pressure that has been applied on women in urban, state-run industry to withdraw from employment and 'return to the kitchen' (*huigui guotai*) in response to unemployment problems and the attempts of employers to 'streamline' their workforces.[13]

Aside from these suspicions, I would argue against the suggestion that a voluntary withdrawal of women from employment into full-time domestic labour has been, or will in the near future become, a common trend, or that it is 'an inevitable transition phase in the development of productive forces in the initial stage of socialism'.[14] There are two aspects of Daqiu's economy which may have contributed to women's withdrawal from paid labour. First, incomes are high enough for it to be feasible for a married woman to depend on her husband's wage and not be employed herself. It is understandable that this might be an attractive proposition to some, especially given the strength of the assumption that women are responsible for domestic work, and the demands of such work. Second, Daqiu's agricultural labour force is now very small, there is no private sector, and the majority of the newly established industries are heavy industries. This probably contributes to a low employment rate for women because the prevailing gender divisions of labour in employment in rural China are such that women are engaged primarily in agriculture, the private courtyard economy and light industry. Both these factors are, however, highly unusual. In most rural (and urban) areas incomes are such that the majority of women at present, and for the near future, will feel it necessary to have some form of remunerated employment. In addition, agriculture continues to be a mainstay of rural employment, while in the more developed provinces along the eastern seaboard an important aspect of reform has been the development of light industries and of the private sector, both of which employ relatively large numbers of women.

There are other reports which suggest, though, that in some areas the number of women engaged solely or primarily in domestic work increased during the 1980s and 1990s as a result of somewhat different trends. In a 1986 study of rural families in six counties in Sichuan, Wang Shuhui, a member of the Sichuan Provincial Women's Federation, found that a relatively high proportion of women were spending more time in domestic work than 'productive' work.[15] She reported that 23.4 per cent of all rural women surveyed undertook domestic work as their sole or primary occupation. This included 63.1 per cent of women over the age of 55, 16.0 per cent of middle-aged women and 20.9 per cent of young women. In contrast, she claimed that before the introduction of the production responsibility system, amongst all women except the elderly and the weak, domestic work was subsidiary to collective work.[16]

Wang Shuhui suggests that the increase in the number of women in rural Sichuan undertaking solely or primarily domestic work is related to the appearance of a large amount of surplus labour in agriculture in some areas, and the lack of alternative employment.[17]

Other media reports support the notion that in some places surplus workers in agriculture have been unable to find alternative employment, and that most such workers are women. This trend will be discussed in more detail in the following chapter. For now, however, I will just point out that while it appears that this was a serious issue in the early stages of reform, and is likely to continue to be important in less developed areas, the general thrust of rural reform has been toward an expansion of employment opportunities outside agriculture which has been eagerly embraced by both women and men.

A number of Marxists and feminists have argued that in the west, modernisation, or more specifically, industrialisation and the maturation of capitalism, resulted in a sharper split between domestic work and commodity production, and that this split altered and intensified women's subordination. For example, Jill Matthews, in her work on the construction of femininity in twentieth-century Australia, has written that until the 1890s small family farms, on which whole families worked to produce goods for both the market and household consumption, were common in Australia. In the following decades, however, such family farms, while continuing to produce some basic goods for household consumption, also became increasingly dependent upon money to buy a wider range of goods in the public market. Matthews argues that the importance of the small family farm for women had been that its work could be accommodated to the patterns and demands of domestic work, which was regarded as the primary responsibility of married women. However, as the command economy took over local production, it became increasingly difficult for women to combine paid and domestic work. Consequently, some women became full-time housewives and suffered the effects of isolation and demoralisation that later became known as 'suburban neurosis'. Others, attempting to do both paid and domestic work, struggled with a heavy double burden.[18]

At the same time, Matthews shows how various processes contributed to a downgrading of women's work. Thus, whereas before 1891 the entire range of women's work 'had been acknowledged as valuable and part of the productive activity of the nation',[19] in the 1891 census a new distinction was drawn between 'breadwinners' and 'dependents'. Women working in the sphere of the household were defined as dependents, or non-workers. On the other hand, women who worked outside the home in remunerated employment received lower rates of pay than men, this being justified with the assumption that men were family breadwinners and therefore needed a 'family wage', whilst women were either single and working merely to fill in time before marriage, or were married and supported by their husbands, and therefore required a lower income.[20]

How then does the situation regarding domestic work in rural China, following decollectivisation, the growth of markets, massive industrialisation and growth in incomes, compare with this scenario? In one respect, the impact of modernisation in rural China has so far been very different. As I will discuss shortly, the growth of a commodity economy has meant that more items consumed by peasant families are now bought, rather than produced at home. However, this has not resulted in a greater division between domestic and other types of work.

I have argued that one consequence of collectivisation in the 1950s was a greater division between domestic work and 'production' than had hitherto existed, and associated with this, a devaluation of women's domestic work. However, decollectivisation and the diversification of the rural economy from the late 1970s onwards meant that the commonly perceived distinctions between domestic work and other work shifted and were blurred once more. One aspect of this was that with the introduction of land contracts for individual families, a distinction between agricultural labour for the collective and labour spent tending a private plot of land was no longer meaningful. Consequently, whereas before the introduction of the contract system tending the private plot was regarded as a domestic work responsibility, nowadays this task is subsumed under that of agriculture.[21]

As a result of decollectivisation, each person's time is now no longer clearly divided between a full work day in the fields and after-hours at home. As mentioned above, many women cite this as a benefit of the reforms, since it means that they are free to organise their own time between domestic work and other tasks in a more integrated and efficient manner.

In addition, with the expansion of markets and of small-scale commodity production many women have become involved in profitable domestic sidelines, such as making handicrafts or growing cash crops inside the home or in the courtyard. While such activities had also been undertaken under the communes, they were then done on a smaller scale and were less profitable. Women's work in these sidelines tended to be 'invisible' – often their income was not recognised and their work was linked with 'mere' domestic work. In practice, there is considerable overlap between domestic work tasks and those involved in domestic sidelines, especially in the case of animal husbandry, but an improvement in the status of domestic sidelines has not led also to any significant re-evaluation of domestic work. On the contrary, in the 1980s, as will be discussed in Chapter 8, the state's attempts to encourage women's involvement in domestic sidelines involved an ideological dissociation of those sidelines with the negative attributes accorded to domestic work. Thus, the income earning potential of domestic sidelines was stressed, both in terms of its contribution to society and its liberating effects for women. In addition, 'domestic sidelines' were renamed with the somewhat more important-sounding title 'courtyard economy', or in cases where such activities generated a large proportion of total family income, they were termed 'specialised household' production.

Rural reforms have resulted not just in an expansion of opportunities for income generating work within the courtyard, however. As mentioned, whilst the early stages of reform were characterised by underemployment and unemployment, the longer-term trend has been toward an expansion of employment opportunities in the 'outside' sphere. Thus, in more developed areas the reforms have resulted in the development of rural industries and in a large movement of labour into urban industry, construction and transport work. This has not had any significant impact on the perception or valuation of domestic work or on the distinction between domestic and non-domestic work. It has, however, resulted in a redefinition of the dichotomy between 'inside' and 'outside' work, and has in some respects made that dichotomy a more salient aspect of gender divisions of labour than the domestic/non-domestic dichotomy. The newly emerging dichotomy is one between women's work on the farm, which includes not just domestic work but also domestic sidelines and agriculture, and men's work in industry or other non-agricultural work away from the home village. Just how this dichotomy has emerged, how it has been legitimated, and its effects on gender relations are topics to be taken up in the following chapter.

TIME SPENT IN DOMESTIC TASKS

The time spent by peasants in domestic work, and the nature of that work, is a topic on which we have very little information.[22] One of the few published studies which addresses this topic is a report of a survey undertaken by Elisabeth Croll in rural Shanghai and rural Beijing in the summer of 1980. During the survey, Croll collected statistics on the time spent in particular domestic work tasks related to the procurement and processing of food. Her findings are summarised in Table 6.1.

Table 6.2 is a summary of the information given to me by peasant women in rural Beijing, Shandong and Sichuan in 1989, on the time they spent each day in preparing meals, cleaning the house, washing clothes, tending domestic livestock, and shopping.[23] The time women said they spent at these domestic work tasks varied from no time at all, in the case of one 73-year-old woman whose

Table 6.1 *Procuring and processing food in rural Shanghai and rural Beijing (average daily hours)*

	Average no. of Persons in Household	Cooking	Shopping	Livestock Care	Private plot
Rural Shanghai (N = 23)	4.0	1.8	0.3	1.0	0.6
Rural Beijing (N = 17)	4.4	2.2	0.13	0.74	0.1

N = number of households

Source: Elisabeth Croll, *The Family Rice Bowl: Food and the Domestic Economy in China*, United Nations Research Institute for Social Development, Geneva, 1982, pp. 298, 300. (Survey conducted China's Summer 1980.)

Table 6.2 *Time spent by women at domestic work tasks (average daily hours)*

Average no. of Persons in Household	Meal prep- aration	Cleaning	Washing	Livestock Care (a)	Shopping	Total Domestic (b)	Primary Non- domestic
4.7	2.9	0.8	0.7	1.7	0.3	3.5	5.7
N = 50	N = 38	N = 21	N = 33	N = 12	N = 6	N = 17	N = 31

N = number of households

(a) This does not include 15 families that did not keep domestic animals or whose domestic animals were the main source of family income.

(b) This refers to the length of time reported by the interviewee for all her domestic work, rather than to the sum of hours she spent in individual tasks.

Source: Interviews with rural women in Beijing, Shandong and Sichuan, August–December 1989.

daughter-in-law did all the domestic work of the family (see Appendix 1, family no. 36), to nine hours a day in the case of a 51-year-old woman who did most of the domestic work for herself, her husband, four children, a daughter-in-law and a grandchild (family no. 46).

In general terms, although we have no detailed statistics on this issue, it can be expected that women's domestic workloads vary according to their own and their families' life cycles. As discussed in Chapter 4, upon marriage women commonly live with their husband's family. Their domestic workload is likely to be considerably heavier than before marriage, but will be shared, in most cases, with their mother-in-law. The domestic workload is generally heaviest for women in the middle stage of their life cycle: as a result of the demands of small children and the fact that by then husband-and-wife couples are more likely to be living in their own separate household. This means that they receive much less help with domestic tasks from their mother-in-law, although it is common for the latter to take a primary role in the care of her grandchildren. In their later years, most women live near or with a married son and his wife and children, and share domestic work tasks with the daughter-in-law.

Meal preparation

In her 1980 survey, Elisabeth Croll found that in rural Shanghai the number of hours spent each day preparing meals ranged from one to three, with an average of 1.8 hours (N = 23). In rural Beijing the preparation of meals took longer, mainly, Croll suggests, because of the time spent preparing flour products. The times spent ranged from 0.3 to 6 hours, with an average of 2.2 hours.[24] The times women spent in meal preparation that I recorded in 1989 were similar to these latter figures, ranging from 1.5 hours to 6 hours, with an average of 2.9 hours (N = 38). This did not in all cases refer to the time spent continuously working at preparing meals: many women said that while the rice was cooking they did other tasks, especially feeding domestic livestock and sweeping the house. Nevertheless, during this time they had to remain close to the kitchen, and hence the range of other activities they could undertake was restricted.

Rural women commonly prepare three meals a day. In central and south China rice is the staple, eaten with vegetables and small amounts of eggs, meat or fish. In northern China the staple consists of both rice and other grains and flour products such as noodles, steamed bread, buns and dumplings, which are more time-consuming to prepare than rice. In both north and south the preparation of vegetable and meat dishes involves a good deal of chopping, so as to cut down on the use of fuel for cooking.[25]

In most of the families that I visited the stoves were fuelled with either coal or dried rice or wheat stalks. Using the latter fuel, women had to bend down frequently to feed fuel into an opening in the front of the stove, in order to keep it hot.

In many families another particularly time-consuming and laborious aspect of preparing meals is collecting water. There are still many areas in China where women must travel up to a kilometre to collect water from a well or stream and carry it back in pails weighing forty kilograms, balanced from shoulder poles.[26] A World Bank study in 1984 found that in rural areas clean water in sufficient quantity was available to 40 per cent of the population, of whom fifteen per cent received piped water and the rest used wells and hand pumps. They estimated that approximately 40 million people suffered from water shortage and at least 500 million required an improved water supply, including 150 million who drank untreated surface water.[27] Since then there have been major improvements, however. One report from the Xinhua News Agency noted that, as a result of a heavy investment in the construction of rural public facilities during the Seventh Five-Year Plan period (1986–1990), tap water was available in 50 per cent of towns in 1990.[28] In Sichuan most of the families that I visited in 1989 had hand water pumps in their courtyards. Women said they drew water once or twice a day, taking 20 minutes each time. In rural Beijing some families had internal water taps.

Cleaning and washing

The women I interviewed claimed they spent from a few minutes to two hours a day cleaning. As I have mentioned above, many did at least some of the cleaning while meals were cooking. For many women in the Chinese countryside, cleaning may have become easier in recent years with the building of large numbers of new houses with floors of concrete instead of earth. It is possible, however, that such improvements in living standards may also have been accompanied by increased standards of cleanliness, and hence more work. This is suggested by the claim made by Anita Chan and her co-researchers that in Chen Village in the 1970s 'with the animals penned outside, and with cement replacing the earth flooring, the peasants began to make vigorous efforts to keep their homes, belongings, and selves clean'.[29]

In the families that I visited clothes washing took an average of 42 minutes a day (N = 33). Those who washed by hand commonly spent more than twice as much time on it as those who used a washing machine. Moreover, whilst washing clothes by hand required constant, heavy work, the use of a washing machine enabled women to do other things while the clothes were being washed. Women who did not have a washing machine commonly spent half a day once or twice a week scrubbing and pounding clothes by hand. They generally worked outside, in the company of other women, by a pump or squatting by a nearby river or, as I saw in Sichuan, by an irrigation channel.

Using a washing machine means that washing clothes becomes much more of a private or 'inside' activity, rather than a time for interacting with other women in the village. On the other hand, it cuts down enormously the amount of work involved in washing clothes, although in most places I visited in my fieldwork houses did not have interior water taps. The washing machine had to be filled manually from a hand pump outside. In addition, of course, the clothes still had to be manually hung out to dry.

Most of the women I talked to who had washing machines were pleased with them because they cut down their workload. One woman, however, said that the machine did not wash the clothes properly; another said that she rarely used her machine because the electricity was too expensive. One woman who did not own a washing machine said that the reason was that the supply of water was too limited.

It should be noted that in terms of washing machine ownership, my sample is highly unrepresentative. Amongst the families that I interviewed, 81 per cent (N = 57) owned washing machines (many of which had been purchased only within the last five years). According to the State Statistical Yearbook, however, across the whole of China only about eight per cent of rural families owned a washing machine at the end of 1989, and 13.8 per cent at the end of 1993.[30]

The production of consumer durables has increased dramatically in the post-Mao era. However, it is probable that for some time to come the purchase of larger items, such as washing machines, will be limited to families in cities and suburbs and the wealthier families in rural counties. This is not just because of the high cost of the items themselves, but also, and equally importantly, because not all rural areas yet have access to, or can afford frequent use of, electricity. In 1989 the energy ministry estimated that 29 counties and 25 per cent of rural families were without electricity.[31] In the case of washing machines, the lack of piped water discussed above is also, of course, a severe limitation.

Care of domestic livestock

Most rural families keep domestic livestock; usually at least a few chickens and one or two pigs. Both are an important source of fertiliser. Apart from this, I found in my survey that pigs were generally kept to be sold at market and the eggs and meat of most chickens were consumed by the family. Caring for these domestic livestock is regarded as a domestic work task and is done by women at the same time, or in between, other domestic tasks. It involves cleaning the area in which the animals are kept and preparing and distributing feed. Some feed is bought, some is grown, and some is household waste. Green feed for pigs is often chopped and cooked – a time-consuming task.

In my survey the times reported for tending domestic livestock ranged from half an hour to four hours a day. These times refer only to the tending of domestic livestock where this did not constitute the main source of income for the family.

My results were somewhat higher than those reported by Elisabeth Croll in 1980. Croll found that in rural Beijing families spent between 0.3 hours and 2 hours a day tending domestic livestock, with an average of 0.74 hours per day (N = 17), and in rural Shanghai they spent 0.5 to 1.5 hours a day, with an average of 1.0 hour a day (N = 22).[32] The differences appear to relate to the number of animals kept. Croll reports that fewer animals were kept in rural Beijing than rural Shanghai. In the latter location, families kept an average of 3.6 pigs and 9.6 chickens.[33] In my survey, the families with domestic animals kept an average of 3.9 pigs and generally between 10 and 20 chickens or other poultry.

Shopping

Elisabeth Croll reports that in rural Shanghai in 1980, shopping was usually undertaken three or four times a week in the nearby town five minutes' walk away, and took an average of 18 minutes a day.[34] This is similar to my findings in 1989 that shopping for groceries was commonly done locally between one and four times a week, taking from an hour to an hour and a half each time, with an average of about 18 minutes a day. Croll reports that in rural Beijing, however, shopping took an average of only eight minutes a day once or twice a week. The shops were further away, but the shoppers usually travelled by bicycle.[35]

There are a number of opposing trends which in recent years may have influenced the time spent by peasants in shopping. On the one hand, with the growth of a commodity economy, peasants are now buying, rather than themselves producing, more goods for consumption than previously. Thus, whereas in 1978 only 24 per cent of peasant household consumption of food (measured in *yuan*) was of bought items, this had increased to 52 per cent by the end of 1989. This then declined again to 44 per cent by the end of 1993. For clothing, the proportion of total consumption that was of bought, rather than home-made, items increased from 89 per cent in 1978 to 98 per cent in 1989 and 99 per cent in 1993.[36] These factors may have led peasants to devote more time to shopping than previously.

On the other hand, the increase in the number of shops and markets may, for some, have reduced the time spent travelling to do the family shopping. For a very small number of rural families food shopping time will also have been reduced by storing food in a refrigerator. At the end of 1989, 0.9 per cent of rural families across China owned refrigerators. This had increased to 3.05 per cent by the end of 1993.[37]

Sewing and mending

Rural women nowadays spend relatively little time sewing, as most family clothing is bought. In addition, many families own a sewing machine which reduces the time spent in sewing and mending. In my survey, the women who did not own sewing machines said it was because they did not know how to sew. According to the State Statistical Yearbook, 54 per cent of rural families in China owned sewing machines at the end of 1989, and 61.3 per cent at the end of 1993.[38]

This picture is in stark contrast to that of earlier periods, when most clothes were made at home and sewing and mending were time-consuming and arduous tasks. In *Report from a Chinese Village*, an account of life in Liu Ling, Shaanxi, in the 1960s, Jan Myrdal recorded the timetable of a 29-year-old woman, Li Yangqing. Sewing took up a very large proportion of her time. Throughout the year she spent most of her evenings, and in winter much of the afternoon, sewing. She did not own a sewing machine, and in fact at that time only one person in the village did. In January and February each year her primary task was to make clothes and cloth shoes for the family. She made all the family's clothes – a new or remade quilted coat, an unquilted coat, and one pair of quilted and one pair of unquilted trousers for each person each year. She also made all the family's shoes – ten pairs for each person, each pair taking about ten days to make.[39]

By the mid-1970s Delia Davin reported that most women bought factory-made, plastic soled shoes, but they still sewed most of their families' clothes.[40]

116

Child care

The care of infants and small children is generally undertaken by mothers and, most importantly, grandmothers. The *Sample Survey on the Status of Women in Contemporary China* found that in 52 per cent of rural families the first child is cared for by his or her grandmother during the first three years. In 35 per cent of families the mother is the primary care-giver.[41] In my interviews, women often complained of how tiring it is to look after children, citing this as a reason why they would not want more than one or two. Child care is generally not considered a separate task, however, and women found it very hard to say how much time they spent at it, since it was spread through the day and undertaken at the same time as cleaning, cooking, and other domestic work.

In most villages, nursery care for small children is either not available or is seen as less preferable to care within the family. It is more common for older children to go to kindergarten but, again, this social service is not always available. As mentioned in Chapter 3, the introduction of the production responsibility system resulted, at least initially, in a widespread decline in rural welfare services, including child care centres. According to the State Statistical Bureau, between 1976 and 1984 the proportion of kindergartens situated in rural areas declined from 94.8 per cent to 73.3 per cent. In 1985 some 34.4 per cent of urban children in the relevant age group were in kindergartens, as compared to only six per cent of rural children.[42] A letter published in *ZGFN* in 1981 claimed that in one commune in Guangdong, following the introduction of the production responsibility system, half the production brigades closed down their kindergartens.[43] Another letter from a rural county outside Shanghai complained that brigade leaders did not provide enough funds for kindergartens. The buildings were small, the tables and chairs broken and there were few toys for the children to play with. The teachers were untrained and treated the children badly, so that the older ones ran away and the younger ones were unhappy. Yet if women took their children with them to the fields instead of leaving them in the kindergarten they were told that they would have work-points deducted.[44]

Penny Kane suggests that the decline in the provision of collective welfare services was short-lived and that greater prosperity helped to strengthen collective welfare in later years.[45] Undoubtedly, some townships do now provide better social child-care facilities than ever before. In particular, where reforms were followed by the large-scale development of township enterprises, local governments have controlled a large proportion of enterprise profits and in some cases have used part of these profits to provide child care and other social services for the local population. Some local governments, for example, stipulate that 30 per cent of the after tax profit of a township- or village-run enterprise be used to subsidise local agriculture and welfare.[46] However, in poorer areas, where township enterprises are less well developed, little revenue is available to local governments for social welfare. Furthermore, even where revenue is available, local officials are, as I have mentioned, often reluctant to spend it on social services or welfare.

In most places in the post-Mao era child care has been high on the agenda of the Women's Federation, and some of the grass-roots women's representatives that I interviewed devoted considerable effort to pressuring for the establishment of child-care services and to the training of child-care staff. The Women's Federation, however, has relatively little power and no money. While it can pressure village officials, the provision of child care is ultimately dependent not on the Federation, but on the will of the village government leaders who are usually male and who may not attach much weight to such matters.

In the counties that I visited in 1989, children up to the age of two or three were looked after largely by their mothers or their grandmothers. Children between the ages of two and six were looked after by mothers or grandmothers or were sent to kindergarten. In most of the counties that I visited the majority of villages had kindergartens. Some of the wealthier ones also had nurseries for younger children. For example, in Huairou county, Beijing, there were 250 nurseries and kindergartens for 293 villages. They admitted 80 to 90 per cent of small children. In Jinniu, Sichuan, there were 200 kindergartens for 2–6 year olds, run either by townships or villages. Wenjiang and Guan counties, Sichuan, both had kindergartens in each village. In Mianyang county, Sichuan, 89 per cent of villages had kindergartens for 3–6 year olds. There were 394 kindergartens altogether, taking 13,000 children, or 76 per cent of the total.

Recent media reports suggest, though, that women in many, if not most, other villages are considerably less fortunate with regard to the availability of socialised child-care facilities. A 1987 article claimed, for example, that in Jilin province many villages had no child-care facilities and during the busy agricultural season parents were forced to leave their children at home alone or to take them to the fields.[47] Even in Shandong, where there had been a 64 per cent increase in the number of year-round child-care centres run by villages, the admittance rate of children over the age of three was still only 56.5 per cent in 1987.[48] An extensive nationwide study undertaken by the Central Institute of Education Research revealed that in 1991 only 20 per cent of rural children aged between four and six attended nurseries or kindergartens.[49]

As a point of comparison, Marina Thorborg estimates that in early 1959 during the Great Leap Forward, which represents the peak in Maoist attempts at providing public welfare services, 53 to 73 per cent of pre-school children of women working in agriculture were taken care of by child-care stations.[50]

To conclude this chapter, in contemporary rural China domestic work tasks are undertaken almost entirely by women. This is an important element in women's subordination; not so much because of the work itself but because, firstly, it is, in a number of ways, devalued in relation to other work; secondly, women are expected to undertake such work in addition to other work and hence suffer a double burden; and finally, due to the above two factors, it has certain negative consequences for women's involvement in other types of work.

Reform policies introduced since the late 1970s, and the consequent economic growth, have had a major impact on the nature of domestic work tasks undertaken in rural families, and the time spent in such tasks. In particular, the improvement of basic amenities and the greater availability of consumer goods on the market have reduced the amount of time and effort spent in domestic work.

The form of economic development that has occurred in rural China in the post-Mao era, involving, in particular, decollectivisation and a large increase in rural non-agricultural employment, has also had important consequences for the relations between domestic and other forms of work. On the one hand, the devolution of economic management to individual families, combined with the expansion in small-scale commodity production, has blurred the distinctions between 'inside' domestic work and 'outside' production that had been so clearly delineated under the commune system.

On the other hand, in more developed areas, the employment of large numbers of men in non-agricultural work which takes them away from home for much of the year and the subsequent 'feminisation' of agriculture have been accompanied by a devaluation of agricultural work and the formation of a new conceptual dichotomy between women's 'inside' work, which now includes not just domestic work and domestic sidelines, but also agriculture, and men's 'outside' work in non-agricultural employment away from home.

Rural reform has not, however, resulted in any change to the division of labour in domestic work, or to the value attached to such work. Domestic work continues to be women's work and to be regarded less as work, contributing to the economy, than as a petty burden, and the time and effort spent by women in domestic work tasks tends to be invisible to peasant women and men, officials, and researchers.

7

Agriculture

REFORM in the post-Mao era has resulted in significant changes to the type of agricultural work undertaken by rural people, the organisation of that work, gender divisions of labour in agricultural work and between agriculture and other work, and the way in which agriculture is perceived and valued in comparison to other activities.

This chapter is not a detailed empirical study of the work of women and men in agriculture. Instead it seeks to outline gender divisions of labour within agriculture, and then to discuss two key trends relating to divisions of labour between agriculture and other forms of remunerated work that have emerged in the 1980s and 1990s. The first of these is a withdrawal of women from agriculture in areas where there is a surplus of agricultural labour, but a lack of alternative employment. The second is a contrasting trend in which responsibility for agriculture has been taken over by women, whilst larger numbers of men have been absorbed into non-agricultural employment.

GENDER DIVISIONS OF LABOUR IN AGRICULTURE

On the eve of reforms in the late 1970s the majority of both men and women in rural areas worked in some form of agricultural labour. There were, however, significant differences in their patterns of employment. These differences relate, first of all, to a division between an 'inside' sphere of work, dominated by women and comprising those activities undertaken within the family house or compound for family consumption or cash income, and an 'outside' sphere dominated by men, comprising labour allocated by the production team and undertaken for the collective. Thus, as already noted, the care of domestic livestock and maintenance of the private plot were regarded as domestic work or domestic sidelines and were commonly carried out by women,[1] but collective agriculture was dominated by men. Women's participation rate in collective agriculture was about 70 per cent and women formed between 40 and 50 per cent of the collective agricultural labour force.[2] However, only one-third of women working in collective agriculture (that is, about 23 per cent of all working-age women) worked full-time, defined as more than 250 days per year, while two-thirds worked part-time or less than 150 days per year. In contrast, one-third of the men worked part-time and two-thirds worked full-time.[3]

Within collective agriculture there were further divisions of labour. As was the case before the revolution, it was generally expected that men would undertake the 'heavier' tasks while women would do the 'lighter work'. Consequently, ploughing, for example, was considered 'men's work' while the picking of tea was done mostly by women.

It appears that in some instances, however, the categorisation of certain tasks as 'heavy' men's work or 'light' women's work was as much a result of previous local negotiations and struggle over work remuneration, as of actual differences in physical demands. As mentioned in Chapter 2, under the work-point remuneration system, the principle of equal pay for equal work prevailed in theory, but rural men strongly resisted attempts on the part of cadres to remunerate women for agricultural work at the same rate as them. In some places work-points were allocated on the basis of an evaluation of the *labourer*, in which case lower rates for women were justified on the grounds that they were not as physically strong as men. More common, however, was a system based on the evaluation of the *task* performed. Under this system, the basis for the commonly lower rates of pay for women was a gender division of labour in which the tasks usually done by women were rewarded at a rate lower than that for tasks done by men, on the grounds that they were 'lighter', or that they required less skill. In some places the gender division of labour in agriculture was the same as, or was an extension of, the division that existed before liberation. However, it appears that a division of labour between 'heavy' 'men's work' and 'lighter' and lower paid 'women's work' was in some places newly created or made more rigid than previously. Isabel and David Crook report, for example, that in Yangyi Commune men acknowledged that women were better at certain jobs, such as pruning, but argued that men were better at heavier work, such as ploughing and contouring. They proposed that certain jobs be assigned to women only, and paid at women's (lower) rates, whilst other jobs be assigned to men only, and paid at men's rates.[4]

Margery Wolf, in her survey conducted in 1980, pointed to a number of variations and inconsistencies in the categorisations of tasks as 'heavy' men's work or 'light' women's work. These inconsistencies suggest, once more, that contrary to local claims that gender divisions of labour between 'heavy' and 'light' work are 'natural', they are in fact sites of conflict and negotiation. In this negotiation women have generally been disadvantaged, both by their lack of authority in the community and by the ability of men to manipulate claims as to the 'naturalness' of particular divisions. Thus, Wolf reports that at a field site in

Fujian province, managing a water buffalo pulling the ploughs through the paddy fields was regarded as too heavy a task for women, 'so instead the women carried fifty-pound sacks of chemical fertiliser to the fields while the men trailed along after the water buffalo'.[5] In Shandong Wolf was told that wooden barrows were too heavy for women to manage. In collective work only men used them and they were paid at a rate higher than average. However, one woman, when asked if she could use such a barrow, said, 'Of course. With my husband away in the army I would be in a bad spot if I couldn't, wouldn't I?'[6]

Wolf reports also that where machinery was used it was monopolised by men, and that this frequently made nonsense of the supposed distinction between 'heavy' men's work and 'light' women's work. For example, in one instance, Wolf's assistant came across three people working in the fields. One was a man whose task it was to turn the switch to a water pump on and off. As a technician, he earned 10.5 work-points a day. The other two were women in their thirties 'who were rushing back and forth ditching and damming to keep the water moving evenly through the fields. Although the evening was cool, they were sweating with the effort it took to move the heavy waterlogged earth onto the banks of the ditches. They were unskilled workers and earned 6.5 workpoints for their day's labor'.[7]

Other reports suggest that through the 1980s and 1990s, in villages in which agriculture continued to be collectively managed, divisions of labour and inequalities in remuneration, such as those cited by Wolf, persisted. In one production team in the vicinity of Shanghai, for example, a researcher learnt that amongst those working in agricultural sidelines, women's annual income was some 700 *yuan* less than men's, the rationale being that men did 'heavy' work, whilst women did 'light' work. Observing the situation at the chicken farm, however, the researcher felt that the women's work was far from being lighter than the men's. Men were responsible for carrying bags of feed on their shoulders, and for using a crushing machine to break up the feed. Meanwhile, it was the women's task to mix the feed and give it to the chickens and to collect the eggs. Each day each woman had to collect 1,680 eggs, a task which the researcher estimated would involve them bending down some 280 times a day.[8]

Tables 7.1 and 7.2 summarise the findings of two recent studies on gender divisions of labour in agriculture.[9] These suggest patterns in the post-Mao era similar to those found in earlier years.

The first study was undertaken in 1983 in two separate production teams in the vicinity of Shanghai. The first production team consisted of 82 families, of which 41 drew a part of their income from agriculture. In each of these families one adult worked full time in agriculture. Nine raised pigs or ducks on specialised contracts. The others were all involved in producing vegetables,

Table 7.1   *Agricultural occupations in two production teams in rural Shanghai (number of persons)*

Production Team	Agricultural Occupation	Male	Female	Total
Xinfeng	Vegetable cultivation	0	18	18
	Nursery work (growing seedlings)	1	5	6
	Pig raising	3	3	6
	Duck raising	1	2	3
	Administration/transport	6	0	6
	Machinery operation	2	0	2
	TOTAL	13	28	41
Wanxi	Field work	12	24	36
	Mushroom cultivation	5	2	7
	Pig raising	1	1	2
	Tending the team's 2 water buffalo	1	1	2
	Responsibility for irrigation	1	0	1
	Responsibility for machinery	1	0	1
	Total	21	28	49

Source: Rodolphe De Koninck, '*La réhabilitation de l'agriculture familiale en République Populaire de Chine: quelques intérrogations*' ['The rehabilitation of family-based agriculture in the People's Republic of China: some questions'], *TRAVAIL, Capital et Société* [*LABOUR, Capital and Society*], vol. 18, no. 1, 1985, pp. 56, 59. Survey conducted September–November 1983.

mainly for the Shanghai market. In the second production team, 49 of the 84 working adults were engaged in agriculture, mainly growing grain. In both teams the study found that women were concentrated in field work, while technical tasks, transport and administration were undertaken by men. It will be noted that in contrast to most earlier surveys, this study found that the majority of agricultural labourers in both production teams were women. This pattern, which has become increasingly common in the 1980s and 1990s, will be discussed shortly.

The second study was undertaken in 1992 in Ningjin County, Hebei Province. During the study 50 men and 50 women from separate families selected at random were interviewed. Table 7.2 shows that in terms of crop production in Ningjin County, women contribute most to cotton growing, an activity in which they have traditionally played a major role, and vegetable growing, which in Ningjin County is considered part of the domestic sideline, or courtyard, economy. In more general terms, ploughing and marketing are two tasks largely

Table 7.2 (a) *Gender division of labour in crop production (percentage of average time spent annually)*

Crop		Ploughing	Planting	Day-to-day Management	Harvesting	Marketing	Total Production Process
Fruit	Women	18	21	37	36	18	26
	Men	82	79	63	64	82	74
Wheat	Women	11	19	57	42	14	29
	Men	78	70	43	54	86	66
	Machinery*	11	11	0	4	0	5
Corn	Women	11	28	59	50	17	33
	Men	81	67	41	48	83	64
	Machinery*	8	5	0	2	0	3
Vegetables	Women	37	42	47	54	0	36
	Men	63	58	53	46	100	64
Cotton	Women	13	69	69	72	42	45
	Men	87	31	31	28	58	55

* Gender of operator not specified.

Source: Li Xiaoyun, Lin Zhibin, Liu Yonggong and Li Ou (unpub.), 'The contribution of women to agricultural and household activities in rural areas. A case study in Ningjin County', Centre for Integrated Agricultural Development, Beijing Agricultural University, 1992, pp. 4–6. Survey conducted amongst 100 families in Ningjin County, Hebei Province, 1992.

Table 7.2 (b) *Gender Division of labour in livestock production (percentage of average time spent annually)*

		Buying Young Animals	Feeding	Disease Management	Marketing	Total Production Process
Chickens	Women	96	96	85	88	91
	Men	4	4	15	12	9
Pigs	Women	38	90	51	26	51
	Men	62	10	49	74	49
Large	Women	6	32	25	10	18
livestock*	Men	94	68	75	90	82

* Cattle, horses and donkeys

Source: As for Table 7.2 (a), to left, page 124.

done by men. Planting is also dominated by men, except in the case of cotton. Harvesting and day-to-day field work is fairly evenly distributed between men and women, except, again, in the case of cotton production, in which women play a larger role. In livestock production women play a dominant role in rearing chickens and pigs. This is undertaken mainly for family consumption. They play a lesser role in rearing other livestock which are sold on the market.

THE WITHDRAWAL OF WOMEN FROM AGRICULTURE

As mentioned in Chapter 3, one important effect of the reforms initiated in rural areas in the late 1970s has been to improve agricultural productivity. This, in turn, has made apparent previously concealed underemployment and surplus labour in agriculture.

The problem of 'too many people, too little land' ['*ren duo, di shao*'], and correspondingly high levels of rural underemployment, have always been issues of concern to the CCP. Under Mao Zedong, these issues were addressed by increasing the labour intensity of crop production, by recruiting rural labour during the winter months for the construction of irrigation canals and other forms of rural infrastructure, by developing small-scale rural industry, and by recruiting rural labour for temporary work in urban industry.[10] Until the late 1970s western analysts largely believed that these measures had successfully overcome the problems of rural underemployment. However, such beliefs were brought seriously into question by reports published in the 1980s suggesting that between one-quarter and one-third of all rural labour was surplus to requirements.[11]

Explanations for this high level of rural underemployment generally point to the fact that, under the collective system, far more labour was employed in the fields than was necessary. The work-point system of remuneration was such that all labour was remunerated, regardless of its marginal contribution to output.[12] After the introduction of the production responsibility system, however, it was no longer profitable for labour that was surplus to requirements to be kept employed in the fields, hence the 'emergence' of large numbers of surplus workers, especially out of grain growing, in which roughly 89 per cent of agricultural labour was concentrated in the early 1980s.[13]

The 'emergence' or 'release' of this surplus labour from grain growing has, from one point of view, enabled the development of more profitable forms of agriculture and of non-agricultural enterprises and hence has been a most important step toward modernisation and the improvement of rural incomes and livelihood. From a slightly different perspective, however, it has also resulted in enormous strains on the Chinese economy and society. Thus, one report estimates that by the year 2000 the number of surplus rural workers may have grown to 250 million, and claims that 'hundreds of millions of such workers will in the long run be unemployed. This is not merely an economic problem; it is capable of becoming a serious social and political problem, as well'.[14]

As it turns out, by the late 1980s and early 1990s in more developed rural areas, especially on the southeastern seaboard, the pressure of surplus agricultural labour had been greatly reduced, with rural people taking up employment in a wide range of agricultural and non-agricultural ventures. As will be discussed shortly, these areas are also now absorbing immigrant labour from poorer areas across China, where employment is scarce.

However, in the early stages of reform and still today in numerous less developed areas, not all the surplus workers from agriculture are able to find alternative forms of employment. One report claimed, for example, that in Huairen County, Shandong, shortly after the introduction of the production responsibility system (but before 1983, when new lines of production were developed), one-third of all labourers were no longer needed in agriculture and the majority of women had no paid work.[15] Similarly, a survey carried out in 1986 in Heze prefecture, a very poor region also in Shandong, found that local enterprises were developing very slowly and there were no outlets for surplus female labour. Women were keen to earn money, but lack of funds, skills, avenues for work and sales outlets thwarted their enthusiasm.[16]

In areas inland and far from large cities, in particular, markets, services and transport are all relatively underdeveloped. Many such areas still have few local industries and those that exist often employ workers on only a part-time, temporary basis. In addition, peasants in these areas lack the capital and the skills necessary for work outside agriculture. All this makes it difficult for peasants in less-developed areas to find non-agricultural employment, either in their home county or elsewhere, or to start up their own non-agricultural ventures. Nevertheless, many peasant families have found it advantageous to withdraw surplus workers from full-time agriculture (rather than have that person be underemployed in the fields, as would have happened under the commune system) so that they can do the family's domestic work.

In such circumstances, as the above examples suggest, women have been the first to be withdrawn from agricultural work. This illustrates a continued identification of women primarily as 'inside' domestic workers and only secondarily as workers 'outside' in agriculture. Thus, on the one hand it is assumed that since women already carry responsibility for domestic work, it is most efficient for them to concentrate on such work, while the man or men of the family work in the fields.

At the same time, women's withdrawal from agriculture also stems from the perception that women are less capable of agricultural work than men, since they lack technical skills and are not as strong physically. Some reports suggest, furthermore, that mechanisation has not only resulted in changes in women's work in agriculture, as suggested above, but in some cases has led to women being pushed out of agriculture altogether.[17]

Such reports confirm for rural China a trend similar to that found in other developing countries in which the use of new agricultural machinery is monopolised by men, and women are either marginalised in the most tiring and monotonous manual work in agriculture or are pushed out of employment.[18]

In rural China, however, the impact of mechanisation on women's employment in agriculture was an issue of greater concern before the introduction of rural reforms in the late 1970s than it has been since. This is because the introduction of the production responsibility system has fragmented land holdings, making it difficult to use large machinery. Furthermore, the machinery that is used is usually shared between a number of families since it is too expensive for most peasant families to afford on their own. In the post-Mao era, rather than mechanisation resulting in a withdrawal of women from agriculture, it appears that *lack* of mechanisation may be contributing to another very different trend, which will be discussed in the following paragraphs. As William Hinton has suggested, 'the women are going to be left farming the land by primitive methods and the men are going to go off and do anything but farming and earn a decent livelihood'.[19]

THE FEMINISATION OF AGRICULTURE

Where opportunities for non-agricultural employment have become available, men have been the first to leave agriculture to take up such employment, and agriculture has increasingly become the responsibility of women, especially married women. As will be discussed in Chapter 9, women are also employed in industry, but in smaller numbers than men, and there are significant differences between their occupations.

According to census data, nationally men still outnumber women in agricultural work. Nevertheless, in 1982 women already comprised 46 per cent of the agricultural labour force, and by 1990 this had increased to 47.4 per cent.[20] By the mid-1990s, one report claimed, 60 per cent of all agricultural labour was performed by women.[21] Furthermore, while 70 per cent of the total male labour force was engaged in agriculture in 1982 and 69 per cent was so engaged in 1990, 78 per cent of the female labour force was engaged in agriculture in 1982 and 76 per cent in 1990.[22]

In some areas it became apparent as early as the mid-1980s that agricultural work, once undertaken primarily by men, had been taken over almost entirely by women. South China led the way in this 'feminisation' (*'funühua'*) of agriculture. Philip Huang claims, for example, that by the mid-1980s in the majority of villages in the Yangzi Delta farming was being done by what was jokingly referred to as the 'Three Eight Team' (*sanba duiwu*) – a reference to March 8, Women's Day, and off-farm employment was dominated by men.[23]

Similar trends have also been reported for other parts of China. For example, in an article published in 1984 it was claimed that following the introduction of the production responsibility system in Xinjin County in Sichuan, a large proportion of men went to work outside the county. Women now perform 60 per cent of work in agriculture and more than 80 per cent of work in domestic sidelines.[24] In 1988 a survey of 4,700 members of 1,110 families in three townships in Fugou County, Henan, found that 70 per cent of the male labour force was occupied in communications, transport or handicraft production, or had migrated elsewhere to work, and women provided the bulk of agricultural labour.[25]

In her survey of two villages in Shandong, conducted in 1986 and 1987–8, Ellen Judd also found that as non-agricultural production expanded, agriculture became largely the responsibility of women, or, more particularly, married women. The processes through which this occurred differed somewhat between the two villages, however.

The first village, Qianrulin, was unusual in that it had not been decollectivised. Agricultural tasks were regarded by villagers as the least desirable form of work, but nevertheless still had to be performed. They were assigned by the village's male leadership to married women, who were generally regarded as non-working 'housewives'.

In the second village studied by Judd, Zhangjiachedao, the economy had been decollectivised, at least formally, although there was still a strong village government. Rural industry was well developed, and there were plenty of opportunities for non-agricultural employment for both men and women in the village. In the early 1980s agricultural work was done by families that undertook to specialise in that area. These families, however, received less income than those engaged in non-agricultural production, and so, in an attempt to reduce inequalities between families, the village government replaced this system by one in which each family was allocated a small amount of land and made responsible for its cultivation. Villagers employed full time in local industry commonly also participated in their family's agricultural work after hours. Only ten men in the village were engaged primarily in agriculture; all of them were elderly, had poor health or work records and some combined agriculture with commerce or craft work. In contrast, however, in a number of families agriculture was undertaken largely by an older married woman, for whom this was the primary form of employment. Judd reports that although women usually preferred to work in the better-paying village enterprises, where domestic conditions made it difficult for all women in a household to undertake such work, it was common for one woman to undertake agricultural work in combination with domestic and child-care responsibilities instead.[26]

As Judd concludes, then, in these two villages 'women are distinctly more concentrated than men in agricultural labour, for reasons connected both with local policy decisions and with household configurations, although the results are not uniform either between communities or within them'.[27]

My own fieldwork confirmed many of the patterns that have been outlined in these examples. In Ling County, Shandong, and in Wenjiang and Guan Counties in Sichuan, for example, officials in the Agricultural Bureaux claimed that in a large proportion of couples the husband works in a township enterprise whilst the wife works primarily in agriculture. The reverse division of labour is much rarer. In Wenjiang County officials talked explicitly of a feminisation and ageing (*laohua*) of the agricultural labour force. During the busy seasons (one month in May–June and one month in September–October) all those in the villages help with agriculture,[28] but otherwise it is managed largely by women and older men. Of a total rural labour force of 119,565, some 19.1 per cent are employed in township enterprises. Of these, however, only 23 per cent are women.[29]

Table 7.3 summarises information on the division of labour between agricultural and non-agricultural employment in the sixty families that I visited in 1989. It gives a clear illustration of the feminisation of agriculture. In total, in twelve of these families (20 per cent) both the interviewee and her husband were engaged primarily in agriculture. There were no families in which the woman interviewed was engaged in non-agricultural production, whilst her husband undertook agriculture. In contrast, there were twenty-three families (38 per cent) in which agriculture was undertaken by the woman interviewed (either as a primary or secondary occupation), whilst her husband was engaged in non-agricultural work. There were five families (8 per cent) in which both the interviewee and her husband were engaged primarily in non-agricultural work, but also undertook agriculture. In eight families (13 per cent) neither the woman interviewed, nor her husband, were engaged in agriculture. In two of these, agriculture was undertaken by other members of the family, and in six families either workers were hired to do agriculture or land had been given or sub-contracted to a relative or a neighbouring family.[30]

By the beginning of the 1990s a dominance of women in Chinese agriculture was widely taken for granted by Chinese commentators. A case study of women's contribution to recent rural development claimed, for example, that

Table 7.3 *The division of labour between agriculture and other remunerated work in 60 families in rural Beijing, Shandong and Sichuan*

Families in which the interviewee and her husband are both engaged primarily in agriculture	12
Families in which the interviewee is engaged primarily in agriculture and her husband is engaged primarily in non-agricultural work	15
Families in which the interviewee is engaged primarily in non-agricultural work and her husband is engaged primarily in agriculture	0
Families in which both the interviewee and her husband are engaged primarily in non-agricultural work but also undertake agriculture	5
Families in which the interviewee is engaged primarily in non-agricultural work but also undertakes agriculture, whilst her husband is engaged solely in non-agricultural work	8
Families in which the interviewee is engaged solely in non-agricultural work, whilst her husband is engaged primarily in non-agricultural work but also undertakes agriculture	0
Families in which neither the interviewee nor her husband are engaged in agriculture, but other family members are	2
Families in which no members are engaged in agriculture	6
Other	12

Source: Interviews with rural women, August–December 1989.

women are the most important labour force in agricultural production in rural China, comparing their contribution to agriculture to that of women in Africa.[31] The report made no mention of the fact that while Africa has been described as traditionally 'the region of female farming *par excellence*',[32] in China before 1949, women's contribution to agricultural production was minimal and, in fact, according to most analyses, continued to be significantly less than men's until the late 1970s.

The feminisation of agriculture is a trend that has been reported in many other countries as a corollary of industrialisation. Ester Boserup, in her ground-breaking study of women's role in economic development, noted, for example, that in the 1960s there were more women than men in Japan's agricultural labour force, and that in the United States a decrease in the agricultural labour force was accompanied by an increase in the proportion of women in it.[33] Similarly, Barbara Jancar reported in 1978 that women predominated in farming in all the countries of eastern Europe and the Soviet Union, and that the feminisation of agriculture was a central concern of eastern European regimes.[34]

Nor is the feminisation of agriculture in rural China in the post-Mao era without precedent in China itself. As was noted in Chapter 2, the development strategy adopted during the Great Leap Forward involved the recruitment of women into agricultural labour to replace men who were then employed in rural industry and capital construction projects. In later years, this pattern was repeated and, in the late 1960s, as Marina Thorborg has pointed out, it was promoted as a national model in Daqing. There, the men and some young women worked in the oilfields, while the majority of the women were given the responsibility of agriculture.[35]

Yet it remains true that the dominance of women in agricultural work across much of rural China is a very recent phenomenon and represents a radical shift in work patterns. Given this, the questions that must be asked are, firstly, what have been the processes contributing to the feminisation of agriculture in the post-Mao era, and how has such a trend been legitimated and made to appear ordinary? Secondly, what are the consequences for gender relations and for women's lives of such a trend?

The greater rate of absorption of rural male labour into non-agricultural employment and the feminisation of agriculture must first of all be seen in the context of long-standing peasant desires to leave both the land and the village on the one hand, and restrictions on the mobility of rural men, and especially women, on the other. In comparison with work in industry, agricultural work is widely seen as arduous, tiring and 'bitter' (*ku*), and rural/urban inequalities are such that rural residents suffer not just lower living standards, but lesser access to services, education and entertainment than urbanites. In addition, and associated with these inequalities, peasants have for centuries been looked down upon by city dwellers; a stigma that has persisted despite Maoist attempts at levelling distinctions between urban and rural dwellers.[36]

It is only in the post-Mao era, however, that any more than a tiny minority of peasants have been able to improve their status. Until the late 1970s opportunities for non-agricultural employment in rural areas were relatively scarce, and the household registration system strictly limited labour movement, especially that from rural to urban areas. Under this system, introduced in the mid-1950s, primarily as a way of keeping labour in agriculture and of preventing excessive strain on urban resources, all Chinese are registered at birth as belonging either to a 'rural agricultural household' (*nongye hukou*) or an 'urban resident household' (*chengshi jumin hukou*). One of the defining characteristics of the latter is that it entitles the holder to subsidised grain from the state. Peasants, on the other hand, must produce their own grain, or buy it at a higher price on the market.

Household registration is inherited from the mother. Only in exceptional circumstances can a rural agricultural household registration be converted to an urban one. Sometimes, however, in suburban counties, adjacent to a town or city, expanding state enterprises will appropriate peasants' land and in return provide employment or award them a cash payment (or both), new housing and urban household registration.[37] Since 1984, in an attempt to encourage rural non-agricultural employment, the state has also allowed some peasants working in rural enterprises and private businesses in small towns to settle there permanently. These peasants are given 'self-supplier household' status (*zili hukou*), that is, they are treated as urban residents, except that they are not entitled to state-subsidised grain.[38] In addition, urban male workers married to women with rural registration have, in some cases, been permitted to transfer their job and household registration to one of their children, providing that they themselves have been reclassified as rural residents.[39]

Otherwise, a small number of (mainly male) peasants are able to obtain urban registration as a result of entrance into university, or by rising through the ranks of the Communist Party. In addition, in the Maoist period those who joined the army were, after demobilisation, given preference when peasants were recruited for employment in industry.[40]

These avenues for status improvement are largely beyond the reach of peasant women. However, marriage is one further strategy that peasant women are able to use to improve their status. As William Lavely has discussed, peasant women and their families frequently try to improve their living standards and their status by marrying into a family of higher standing than their own.[41]

Not surprisingly, given their higher status and often higher incomes, amongst the most sought-after husbands for peasant women are those with urban household registration.[42] A woman marrying a man with urban household registration will not, however, have her own registration changed. She might live with her husband in an urban area, but this is relatively rare because she would have difficulty finding a secure, long-term job and would not be entitled to the subsidies given to urban workers. It is more common, therefore, for women in such marriages to remain in the village of their husband's family, working in agriculture or in township enterprises, or in both. This, then, helps to explain one particular manifestation of the 'feminisation' of agriculture most apparent in suburban counties, that is the prevalence of couples in which the man is an industrial or administrative worker with urban registration, while his wife is primarily an agricultural labourer with rural registration (see Appendix 1 for examples).

Outside suburban counties, families with split household registration are relatively rare, and the benefits of urban registration, or even of association with someone with urban registration, are out of reach for the majority of peasants. Apart from the introduction of the 'self-supplier household' category in 1984, economic reforms introduced since the late 1970s have not greatly altered this picture. However, as will be discussed in more detail in Chapter 9, they have resulted in a large expansion of opportunities, indeed demand, for temporary employment of rural labour in urban industry, construction and services, and for a range of non-agricultural forms of employment in villages and townships.

At the same time, though, there is a number of pressures on rural families to continue to undertake some farming, so that even where the opportunity for all members of a family to give up farm work and undertake non-agricultural employment is available, it is not always taken up. Thus, it is usual for rural families to continue, at the least, to cultivate grain to meet the state's tax requirements and to grow vegetables and grain for their own consumption, rather than buying it at higher prices on the market. As mentioned in Chapter 3, land is also an important source of security for Chinese peasants and, while it is often less profitable, agriculture provides a more stable source of income than work in private entrepreneurial activities, township enterprises or urban industry. Many families therefore continue to engage one or more members in farming as a way of balancing the risks involved in other forms of employment.

The reasons for the concentration of *women*, in particular married women, in agriculture are related both to local policy decisions and to the strategies of families and individual women themselves. One reason why it is women, rather than men, who continue to work the land is that women's right to land (and other property) is tenuous, and is likely to be lost if the land is not used. As discussed in Chapter 4, under the prevailing patrilocal marriage system when a woman marries she loses the right to land in her natal village and is in time allocated land in her husband's village. As a relative outsider, however, her rights in her husband's village are tenuous. If she divorces, or if her husband dies, a woman's right to land in the village comes under question, and might be withdrawn, particularly if it is contested by a relative of her husband. However, if she has been farming that land, she will have a much stronger claim on it than if she has not. In contrast, a man who leaves the land and even the village for many years will still retain the right to return to it.

The 'feminisation' of agriculture relates also to the comparatively low cost of keeping women, especially married women, in farm work, due to the lesser opportunities available to them in industry. As will be discussed in Chapter 9, in the township enterprise sector, for example, fewer women than men are employed, in part because the recruitment policies of some industries, especially heavy industries, discriminate against them. Some township enterprises also do not employ women after they have married or had a child. Furthermore, women have fewer chances for promotion than men in township enterprises and their wages tend to be lower. On the other hand, women are often able to supplement their incomes from agriculture with earnings generated through non-agricultural production in domestic sidelines.

Finally, the predominance of women in agriculture is related to the strong identification of women with an 'inside' sphere of work in child care and other domestic work, and domestic sidelines. This tie has meant that it is largely only unmarried women who leave home to work, for example in the urban service sector, and the assumption is that they will return to the village after a few years to get married, have children and take over domestic duties and agriculture. As Margery Wolf found in her survey conducted in 1980, their responsibility for domestic work also leads many married women, especially those with children, to prefer farm work, or a combination of farm work and part-time work in a local factory, to full-time work in a factory. As one woman in Jiangsu explained, 'During harvest or planting you might have to put in long hours, but you can catch up with the household work in the slack season. Also women do most of the work on sideline products. It would be hard to keep factory hours and do the rest of the work after'.[43]

These then, are the chief reasons for the 'feminisation' of agriculture, and the reasons why women themselves often choose to work in agriculture rather than industry. Chinese officials and economists at times express concern that the 'feminisation' of agriculture is causing a decline in agricultural productivity.[44] However, it is important to note that the trend is at the same time being supported and bolstered by the state, in particular through the Women's Federation. In an article published in *ZGFN* in 1991, for example, the feminisation of agriculture was hailed as a 'quiet revolution' for women, and the benefits of being close to the land were extolled (without those benefits being elaborated or explained, however).[45] In more concrete terms, the Women's Federation's support for the feminisation of agriculture is manifested in the campaigns it runs to improve rural women's technical skills, these being focused, by and large, on developing skills in agriculture and the courtyard economy (see Chapter 5).

In official explanations and legitimations of the 'feminisation' of agriculture, women's responsibility for domestic work is commonly cited as an important factor. For example, in the article just mentioned it was claimed that 'with the growth of township and village enterprises, large numbers of men "left the land but not the area" (*li tu bu li xiang*) but women could not leave the family, and hence they could not leave the land'.[46]

It is interesting to note that the identification of women with the family and domestic work functions here very differently from the way it functions in other contexts. Thus, where demand for agricultural employment cannot be fully satisfied, women's domestic responsibilities are used as a legitimation for keeping women *off* the land. Where, on the other hand, a maintenance of labour in agriculture is of more concern, women's domestic responsibilities are used as a legitimation for keeping women *on* the land.

Other attempts to explain and legitimate the predominance of women in agriculture invert arguments about male and female physiology. As discussed above, before the availability to many peasants of work in industry, a restriction of women's participation in agriculture was justified by claims that such work was too heavy for women. Now that possibilities for more desirable, non-agricultural work are opening up, however, new claims are being made. The author of one article published in 1986 said, for example, that when industries were developed, 'in determining who did what work within the family, not only levels of skills but also biological characteristics had to be taken into account, so it was natural that women, the young and the old should stay on the land and young, fit men should go into industry'.[47]

The view as to the 'naturalness' of women's dominance in agriculture is not held by all officials and researchers. An interesting article written by Shi Chenglin claimed that in 1987 rural China had entered a second period of movement of labour out of agriculture into other forms of production (the first period was 1979–1986) and proposed that in this second period women should be the driving force. Shi claimed that since agriculture still requires heavy manual labour, leaving it to women is 'hard on women and detrimental to agriculture. On the other hand, if the majority of women were to move out of agriculture, old members of the household could take over domestic work or else the women could move into industry nearby and still do some domestic work after their eight hours in industry'.[48]

This is, however, the only example I have come across of a challenge to the rationale behind the feminisation of agriculture. The question that remains, then, is: How is it that the feminisation of agriculture is generally taken for granted; why are the inversions of accepted values and perceptions that it involves not challenged or questioned on a wider scale?

The key to answering this question is, I suggest, indicated in a survey report published in 1987 in which the author, Wang Shuhui, describes the dominance of women in agriculture in rural Sichuan in terms of a new form of the traditional gender division of labour exemplified in the phrases 'Men plough, women

136

weave' ('*nan geng, nü zhi*') and 'Men rule outside, women rule inside' ('*nan zhu wai, nü zhu nei*'): nowadays women's 'inside' work includes not just domestic workand domestic sidelines but also work in agriculture. Men's 'outside' work involves leaving the land and going to work in industry or in other non-agricultural activities such as transport or construction.[49]

In Chapter 6 I showed that although reform and modernisation have reduced the burden of domestic work on individual women, the assumption that such work is women's responsibility has not been altered and, indeed, it has been strengthened by the state in a number of ways. As has been made apparent in this chapter, the subsequent reinforcement of a division of labour between women's 'inside' sphere and men's 'outside' sphere has contributed to a concentration of women in agriculture – the area of remunerated work with lowest status. Other chapters show that this division also plays a major part in the perpetuation of other aspects of women's subordination.

Wang Shuhui's article cited above suggests, however, that equally important in the maintenance or re-formation of women's subordination has been a shift in the perception of what constitutes 'inside' and 'outside' spheres of work. Thus, under the commune system, as mentioned, the care of domestic livestock and maintenance of the private plot were considered as belonging to the 'inside' sphere of work, as domestic tasks or tasks closely associated with domestic work, but other agricultural tasks were seen as 'outside' work. In the post-Mao era, however, the downgrading of agricultural work and its corresponding feminisation has occurred, and has been accepted as ordinary, both by peasants themselves and by officials and researchers, because of a conceptual shift of the *whole* of agriculture from the 'outside' sphere to the 'inside' sphere of work, and a closer association made between agriculture and domestic work.[50]

In preceding paragraphs I have outlined the lower status of agricultural work compared to other work, but what are the material effects on women's lives of the feminisation of agriculture? Some reports suggest that a corollary of a decline in agricultural productivity is that women in agriculture are overworked. A letter from Shaanxi, published in *ZGFN* in 1982, claimed, for example, that one production team organised its 70 male workers to work outside the area, leaving 50 women in charge of agricultural production. The women were allocated too much land and their workload was more than they could manage. The local Women's Federation was concerned that their health would be damaged, but was powerless to rectify the situation.[51]

Comments from some of my interviewees suggested that they were able to adjust their work in such a way that they were not overburdened. For example, a woman in Ling County, Shandong,[52] who was responsible for her family's agricultural production, said that she did not grow grain because that entailed

137

too much work for one woman to manage. It may be, however, that in some villages or production teams where production management is still relatively centralised, women are not able to make such decisions themselves. Even where families have more autonomy, individual women may be under considerable pressure from other family members to take on a heavy workload in agriculture and domestic work, so as to relieve others working full time in industry, for example, or simply to maximise family income. As mentioned in Chapter 5, reports suggest that some women in this situation manage by transferring a portion of their domestic work onto their daughters' shoulders, even if this means withdrawing them from school at an early age.

With regard to income, the removal of the work-point system of remuneration will have helped to equalise the earnings of women and men working in agriculture. However, in families in which the women work in agriculture and the men work in non-agricultural employment, it is most likely that the women's income will, once more, be considerably less than the men's.

In some areas the income to be earned from agriculture is similar to, or even higher than, that earned in local industry. This is the case, for example, in parts of south China.[53] In other areas where the average income earned in agriculture is considerably lower than industrial wages, there are nevertheless a few women running households specialising in agriculture who are able to earn incomes significantly higher than those of their husbands and most other villagers (see Chapter 8).

More usually, however, non-agricultural employment generates higher incomes than agricultural work (this being one reason why it is sought after). One survey conducted in Sichuan in 1986 found, for example, that the daily individual gross income earned in crop production was 4.9 *yuan*, and in animal husbandry it was 4.4 *yuan*. In contrast, the processing of agricultural by-products and engagement in commerce or catering earned daily incomes of 8.4 *yuan* and 8.6 *yuan* respectively. Industrial processing and transport earned a daily income of 15 *yuan*.[54] Thus, the feminisation of agriculture involves a concentration of women in the lowest-paid areas of work. This is likely to have a negative impact on women's power and involvement in decision making within families, especially as in many families a large proportion of agricultural produce is consumed, hence the income earned is not as easily reckoned as the cash income earned from employment in industry, for example.

On the other hand, as I have discussed, one reason why women themselves choose to work in agriculture is that it gives them a degree of flexibility in combining their various responsibilities. In addition, numerous media stories show women taking over full control of agricultural production, and in the process gaining a good deal more control over their labour and the products of their labour than they would have had under the commune system, or than they would have working in local industry.[55]

As I will discuss in Chapter 8, however, my own fieldwork shows that even in families where a woman runs a specialised household, whether it be in agricultural or non-agricultural production, it is often the case that her husband is in charge of business matters, arranging bank loans, seeking customers, making decisions on investments, and keeping accounts. It may be that a woman is more likely to assume greater responsibility and control over resources in families in which the man or men work away from home for most of the year. This argument is strongly put by Meng Xianfan. Meng claims that a woman in this situation must, perforce, take charge of agricultural production, including such things as the purchase of fertilisers and other inputs, and arranging for relatives and friends to help her in the busy season, and will also have to make decisions on household expenditure, children's education, and other family matters. In the process, Meng argues, the woman will learn new skills and become more independent, and both her self-esteem and her status in the eyes of her family and amongst other villagers will improve.[56] Some reports suggest, also, that women take on a greater role in formal politics in places where a large proportion of men have left to take up work elsewhere.[57]

Reports from other developing countries suggest, however, that male out-migration does not always leave women with greater power or control over resources. A UNESCO study covering Bangladesh, India, the Republic of Korea, the Philippines and Thailand, found, in fact, that in families in which the men migrated temporarily to the city, leaving women in the village, patterns of family authority changed very little. Final decisions on major issues continued to be made by the husband on visits home, or through letters, and women also deferred to other senior male members of the family. More generally, the study found that 'migration and exposure to modernity have served to cement the bonds of kinship and to reinforce tradition. It is through the network of kinship that people move into the city; it is in the kinship and village circle that they move; and back home the degree of dependence on kinsmen increases with the departure of the male to the town'.[58]

FURTHER TRENDS

So far I have discussed a withdrawal of women from agriculture and a 'feminisation' of agriculture as contrasting trends occurring in response to different stages or different types of development following the introduction of rural reforms. These were the most important trends relating to gender divisions of labour between agriculture and non-agricultural employment in the 1980s and 1990s. However, by no means all families conformed to these patterns.

Furthermore, these patterns will not necessarily remain dominant in the future. They may remain important in some areas but not in others. Indeed, it appears that as early as the mid-1980s, in many villages of south and southeast China, the feminisation of agriculture had already been superseded by further developments, whilst in central China it remained the most dominant trend through the 1990s.

These regional variations are well illustrated by a survey of two villages undertaken by Meng Xianfan in 1992.[59] The first village of Dingjiagou is situated in a mountainous area of Hebei province in central China, some 130 kilometres from Beijing. In this village in 1992, incomes were somewhat lower than the national average and there was very little in the way of industrial employment. Nevertheless, only one household was engaged solely in crop planting. Forestry was an important source of income, as was employment in industries in Beijing and the town of Rongcheng, some 50 kilometres away. Indeed, amongst ten young, unmarried men and eight young, unmarried women, only one man did not work as a temporary labourer in outside industry. The majority of married men, also, worked in outside industry. However, for married women the situation was very different. All worked in Dingjiagou, and the majority were farmers or forestry workers, with just one woman making carpets and three others engaged in making plastic bags. Consequently, amongst all males in the village, 67.2 per cent listed industry as their primary occupation and 32.8 per cent listed agriculture (including forestry). Amongst the women, however, only 18.7 per cent listed industry as their primary occupation, whilst 75 per cent listed agriculture.

The second village of Nanyang is in the southeastern province of Zhejiang. This is a relatively prosperous village, benefiting from a fertile agricultural base, and from its proximity to the city of Ningbo. Industry is well developed in this region, and in 1992 the overwhelming majority of families in Nanyang, men and women, married and unmarried, worked either in private businesses or in village and township enterprises located in, or in the close vicinity of, the village. No longer was agriculture the primary responsibility of married women. Instead, it had been sidelined yet further, and was undertaken on only a small scale after-hours. In Nanyang, then, 79.4 per cent of men and 82.5 per cent of women worked primarily in industry, whilst only 15.9 per cent of men and 14.3 per cent of women listed agriculture as their primary occupation.

The Nanyang pattern is typical of many villages in south and southeast China.[60] In others, however, yet another set of trends has emerged. Anita Chan and her co-researchers note that by the mid-1980s most of the farming in Chen village and neighbouring villages was being done by immigrant labour. Usually this was on a share-cropping basis. Families living in their employers' storage sheds would undertake to pay the state grain levy and to provide their hosts with rice for home consumption in return for the right to cultivate land and reap the profit. In addition, some people in Chen village rented their land to Hong Kong capitalists who developed large agro-businesses growing vegetables for the Hong Kong market, using immigrants as wage labourers.

Few local people in Chen village worked in the fields themselves. As the authors report, 'during the 1980s a prejudice had rapidly developed in Chen village against agricultural labour, even though farming one's own land could net about the same amount of pay as factory work. But farmwork had come to be seen as "backward" and physically onerous, unlike the "modern" and thus more high-status factory labour'.[61]

In the 1980s a large proportion of young men in the village did no work at all, preferring instead to depend on their relatives in Hong Kong. Young local women were generally more willing to work than their husbands and brothers, but they too shunned agricultural labour, preferring to work in the factories of Shenzhen or in local township enterprises.[62]

I have argued in this chapter that distinctions between 'inside' and 'outside', 'light' and 'heavy' and 'unskilled' and 'skilled' work have played a major role in organising and legitimating divisions of labour within agriculture, and between agriculture and other forms of remunerated work, that have marginalised or disadvantaged women in a number of ways. I have demonstrated, however, that while claims as to the naturalness of such distinctions have been used to legitimate particular gender divisions of labour, the meanings of these distinctions have in fact been shaped as much by local negotiations and economic and social change as by 'nature', and that they have changed markedly from one context to another.

Under the work-point system of remuneration women were concentrated in 'light' work, which was remunerated at a lower rate than 'heavy' work. Where machinery was introduced and made work less physically demanding, however, it was monopolised by men and was remunerated at a higher rate than women's heavier, but 'unskilled', manual work. Following the introduction of the production responsibility system, in areas where there was a shortage of employment opportunities, women were withdrawn from agriculture to concentrate on domestic work. This occurred both through a reassertion that women cannot do agricultural work as well as men because it is too 'heavy' and they lack the necessary technical skills, and through the strengthening of the association between women and the 'inside' sphere of work. In contrast to this trend, however, where industrial employment has become available as an alternative to agricultural work, men have taken up such work in disproportionate numbers while women, especially married women, have been relatively concentrated in agriculture. This has occurred through a submergence of the idea that agricultural work is too heavy and technically skilled for women, and a re-characterisation of agriculture as 'inside' work undertaken alongside domestic tasks, as opposed to industrial work 'outside'.

In the 1980s and 1990s, in more developed regions of rural China, the most important trend relating to gender divisions of labour between agriculture and other remunerated work has been the 'feminisation' of agriculture. It is no coincidence that this shift in work patterns has coincided with a re-conceptualisation of agriculture as 'inside work', associated with domestic work, which as we have seen in Chapter 6 is held in low regard relative to other types of work, and that both these changes have followed the downgrading of the status of agricultural work as a result of the expansion of other employment opportunities. Yet the feminisation of agriculture cannot be understood solely in terms of conspiracy or discrimination against women, whether it be by the state or at any other level of society. As I have shown here, this trend is primarily a result both of social structures and attitudes which constrain women in particular ways, and of decisions that women themselves make to concentrate on agriculture because, for all its drawbacks, it offers them advantages not possible in 'outside' industrial employment.

8

Entrepreneurs on the Farm

IN the last chapter I discussed the feminisation of agriculture, that is, a trend in which women are increasingly taking charge of agriculture, while more and more men move into off-farm non-agricultural work. This chapter and the following one add a further degree of complexity to this picture, discussing trends which are occurring within or alongside this one.

Here I wish to focus first of all on the recent development of domestic sidelines and the courtyard economy; areas of work dominated by women. Second, I shall look at the emergence of specialised households (*zhuanyehu*) and private enterprises (*getihu* and *siying qiye*) run by women as an extension of, or specialisation in, activities in the courtyard economy. This chapter analyses the development of women's work in the courtyard economy in terms of the motives of both the state and women themselves, and undertakes a critical examination of the Women's Federation's emphasis on the courtyard economy as a key element in a strategy for improving the economic and social position of rural women.

It will become clear that what distinguishes the areas of work considered below is not so much their content, as their organisation and their perceived location, both physically and in the economy. Thus, while domestic sidelines and the courtyard economy include work defined as domestic work and as agriculture, they are also regarded as a separate set of activities by Chinese peasants, officials and researchers, defined in terms of their location in an 'inside' sphere, their income-earning potential, but also their lesser importance in comparison to the main income-generating activities of the family.

Similarly, whilst (non-agricultural) specialised households and rural private enterprises are a subset of rural township enterprises, they are also considered separately, as small-scale, family-based ventures, many of which are direct extensions of the courtyard economy. In this chapter they are discussed in terms of their significance as ventures developed and managed by rural women on the farm, and from within the 'inside' sphere. In the next chapter they are included in a discussion of sources of off-farm non-agricultural employment, from the viewpoint of women employees.

143

DOMESTIC SIDELINES AND THE COURTYARD ECONOMY

In the simplest terms, the expression 'domestic sidelines' (*jiating fuye*) refers to those areas of production engaged in by peasant families as a supplement to their main productive activity, either for consumption or for cash profit. In China this has included four main types of production: (1) the cultivation of crops, fruit trees and vegetables on land around a peasant's house, on private plots, in between the chief crops or on land not suitable for the chief crops; (2) the rearing of domestic livestock and poultry on land as above or in courtyards; (3) the gathering of medicinal herbs and berries, hunting and fishing; and (4) the home production of handicrafts, including weaving, sewing and embroidery, the home processing of foodstuffs and the home production and repair of farm tools and other implements. Obviously, however, the types and extent of domestic sidelines engaged in by families vary according to their different material and labour resources. Furthermore, the relation of this type of production to others has varied over time with changes to the overall relations of production. The most marked changes have been brought about by the shifts from a family economy to a collective economy in the 1950s and back to a new form of family economy in the 1980s.

As outlined in Chapter 2, following the collectivisation of agriculture and rural industry in the 1950s, peasants' chief occupation became their work in collective production, whilst the term 'domestic sidelines' referred to production undertaken by members of a family not employed in collective production or by others outside their collective work hours. These sidelines were undertaken using small farm tools, scattered fruit trees and domestic livestock which peasants still owned themselves, in the home or courtyard or on the private plot, as noted above. The most important domestic sidelines in the Maoist period were the cultivation of vegetables and fruit trees, and the rearing of domestic livestock, especially pigs and chickens.[1] The private production of handicrafts declined somewhat in this period, relative to pre-revolution years, in part due to the nationalisation of textiles in the 1950s and in part to the centralisation of commerce and restrictions on rural markets.

In terms of gender divisions of labour, the Women's Federation now claims that domestic sidelines have always been women's work. This is not entirely true – for example, hunting and fishing have commonly been done by men, and in the Maoist period men, children and the old all contributed, at least to some extent, to work on the private plot.[2] However, handicrafts, sewing and the day-to-day care of domestic livestock have been undertaken mainly by women, especially older women. As discussed in Chapter 6, these activities are intertwined with domestic tasks. It is common, for example, for a woman to feed the chickens in the yard whilst the rice is cooking.

As a consequence of the association with domestic work, and the fact that they are considered 'women's work', domestic sidelines have, until recently, suffered a kind of invisibility. Despite their importance for the food intake of the family and also for the cash income they bring in, domestic sidelines have tended to be omitted in peasants' accounts of their productive activities, and women's work in this area has often not been recognised, by themselves or others, as a contribution to the family economy. Elisabeth Croll gives an example of an elderly woman who described herself as 'too old to work in the fields' and as 'only able to do her bit by cooking the meals, taking care of the grandsons and raising two pigs and some chickens'. What she did not say was that the sale of the pigs, chickens and eggs amounted to just under half of the total annual cash income of the family.[3] I also found, even in 1989, that small numbers of domestic livestock were commonly not included in peasant accounts of family sources of income.

Whilst work in domestic sidelines has had a low status or a degree of invisibility because of the associations with the 'inside' sphere and with 'unproductive' domestic work, as mentioned in Chapter 2, it was also regarded with suspicion by the CCP under Mao Zedong, ironically, because it was in fact productive and was part of a private market economy which could potentially detract from or threaten the commune economy.

Consequently, while domestic sidelines were generally recognised by the state as an important source of supplementary foodstuffs and cash income, at times, most notably during the Great Leap Forward and the years following the Cultural Revolution, they were suppressed. Under the Gang of Four, in some areas cadres confiscated private plots, rural markets were closed, and in some cases women engaging in domestic sidelines were severely criticised. Domestic sidelines and rural fairs were variously described as 'hot beds breeding capitalism', 'the soil that generates capitalism' and 'capitalist tails'.[4]

As discussed in Chapter 4, the right of commune members to engage in domestic sidelines was reaffirmed at the Third Plenum in 1978. Following this, domestic sidelines were further promoted as a means of diversifying the rural economy, and their development was enhanced by the devolution of economic management to individual families, price adjustments, and the development of free markets. Domestic sidelines have thus taken on a new role in the rural economy, and perceptions of them have changed. As Philip Huang has written,

[I]t is interesting to note how the term 'sidelines' is taking on new connotations. Rural cadres today boast about the climbing share of sidelines and industry in total rural output. For them a 'sideline' is no longer a low return activity that is secondary to agriculture, but a pursuit that, like industry ranks above crop planting.[5]

Since about 1984, the term 'domestic sidelines' has itself increasingly been displaced in the media by the term 'the courtyard economy' (*xiao yuan jingji* or *tingyuan jingji*). The two terms do not refer to exactly the same activities, however. The latter term is used in reference to vegetable and fruit growing, animal husbandry, handicraft production and services (including commerce and small-scale tourism) undertaken in the home or courtyard, but it does not usually include hunting, fishing or gathering.[6] The significance of the change of name is twofold. Firstly, the new term stresses the physical location of certain activities in the home or courtyard. Secondly, it removes the sense that such activities are less important than collectively organised activities. By giving them the title 'economy', the state has accorded these activities a greater value than was perhaps possible using the older term 'domestic sidelines', given the connotations of the latter, as outlined above.

Enthusiasm for domestic sidelines and the courtyard economy is part of a general enthusiasm for commercialisation and industrialisation in the rural economy. In this respect, the courtyard economy is seen as belonging to the same category as more specialised, larger-scale and more capitalised forms of rural industry. Part of the importance of the courtyard economy for the state is that it is seen as being transitional to, and acting as a springboard for, developing these other more capitalised forms of production. And, indeed, as will be discussed in the second section of this chapter, it is the case that many specialised households started off engaging in agriculture and sidelines, for example, and then, finding the sidelines to be more profitable, have made these their main form of production.

However, the courtyard economy is important to the state not only as a transitional stage on the way toward more capitalised development. It is also valued in its own right, as a set of subsidiary occupations existing in between primary agriculture and industry, that requires little capital investment and that can make use of 'surplus' or 'auxiliary' labour, time and resources, to produce goods at very low cost.

Two examples may help to illustrate the role which the state sees domestic sidelines and the courtyard economy as playing. In an article published in 1986 the head of the Rural Policy Research Office of the Central Committee Secretariat stressed the importance of small-scale, family-based animal husbandry, crop planting, handicrafts, sewing and services as sources of employment for surplus labour. He stressed, in particular, the importance of such work for the numerous women who are 'clever and dextrous', yet underemployed.[7]

Another article published in 1988 claimed that in Pingyuan County, Shandong, one hundred thousand women participated in the courtyard economy. It said:

> [I]n rural commodity production the county government found that because of women's physiological, psychological and biological characteristics, their abilities were not being given full play. In order that this group might also contribute to commodity production, the county government called on women to develop the courtyard economy, this being particularly suited to their special characteristics.[8]

The article does not explain the features of the courtyard economy that make it 'particularly suited to (women's) special characteristics'. The usual meaning attributed to this phrase, however, is that the work is 'light' or not as physically demanding as other work, or that it is related in some way to women's roles as mothers or domestic workers, or both.

That it is recommended as an area of work particularly suited to women is, I would argue, an integral aspect of the state's encouragement of the courtyard economy. This is partly related to the fact that, as discussed in the previous chapter, the problem of surplus agricultural labour is chiefly a problem of female surplus labour. Thus, the courtyard economy has been encouraged by the state, in part, as a way of relieving unemployment and discontent amongst women who have lost their jobs in agriculture.

More recently, and in particular in more developed areas, where a large shift of labour into non-agricultural occupations has occurred, the courtyard economy has served to boost the incomes of women 'left behind' in agriculture and domestic work. This has, in turn, helped both to keep agricultural production going and to relieve pressure on the state and collective sector to provide non-agricultural employment. From the state's point of view there are further advantages of the courtyard economy which relate to its particular relationship to other parts of the economy, to its 'subsidiary' nature, and its location, both physically and conceptually, in an 'inside' sphere.

In some cases the subsidiary aspect of the courtyard economy means that women are relatively more keen to undertake the production of specialist commodities that other business people and enterprises avoid because of the high risks involved. Production in the courtyard economy can prove very lucrative in the short term, but it is also very risky. This is illustrated by the experience of one woman from Ningyang County in Shandong. In 1990, in order to supplement her family's low income, she began a scorpion farm with a loan of 5,000 *yuan*. She had misjudged market demand, though, and was not able to sell the scorpions she raised. Then she heard that there were good prospects for raising frogs, so she borrowed another 2,000 *yuan*. This time, the water in her courtyard pond became polluted, and within two days all the frogs were dead. These experiences, apart from incurring severe financial loss, won her only scorn from her friends and complaints from her family, and severely dampened her spirits. She nevertheless persisted, taking out subscriptions to ten different newspapers, in order to be better informed about the market situation. She went on to develop other lines of production in the courtyard economy, and this time made high profits.[9]

A further characteristic of the courtyard economy is that, in general, no one line of production in this sector is highly profitable for very long. Those who initiate production of a novel or much sought-after item will be able to command high prices for a time, but they will find that their success will quickly attract other producers, and prices will be pressed downwards. As Philip Huang explains, however, it is relatively easy for a farming household to adapt to such fluctuations:

> The shocks are cushioned by the fact that the production is only a sideline, so that the household can move out of the activity without devastating consequences to its fundamental livelihood. At the same time, its low-cost and spare-time nature enables the household to move back into production rapidly once the market shifts.[10]

Another advantage of the courtyard economy is that it makes full use of the family's existing material resources, including building space, water and electricity (where it is available), sewing machines and other tools. In addition, the existence of women working in the courtyard economy whilst simultaneously minding children and doing domestic work obviates the need for larger-scale collective enterprises to provide child-care facilities and reduces the domestic workload of workers in those larger enterprises. The fact that most families retain at least one woman on the land, combining crop growing with work in the courtyard economy, also means that families produce much of their own food and, consequently, factory employers do not have to pay their peasant workers wages sufficient to cover the total cost of reproducing their labour.[11]

Finally, by subcontracting tasks to women working at home, both local and international capitalists have taken direct advantage of the old link between unproductive domestic work and domestic sidelines, and the belief that what women earn in the courtyard economy is merely a secondary addition to the primary income of the family, to keep down workers' incomes, and hence to maximise profit.[12] Indeed, anecdotal evidence suggests that a large proportion of women's work in home-based sewing, weaving and handicraft production is tied in with the rest of the economy in this way. In Ling County, Shandong, for example, one large carpet factory in the county town subcontracts work to factories at the township level. These, in turn, subcontract much of the weaving to women who work as individuals in their own homes or in small village workshops. One township enterprise I visited employed 150 women (including apprentices) in the factory, and another 350 working at home or in village workshops, on looms owned either privately or by the village.[13] In Xindu County, Sichuan, 10,000 women undertake embroidery and another 10,000 women do basketwork, all in their own homes. The finished products are collected by the County Foreign Trade Company for export.[14]

Writers such as Maria Mies have shown that in India and other developing countries women's work in household-based handicraft production has been encouraged as a way of tying them into an international market economy that thrives on their exploitation. Mies' study of the lace makers of Narsapur is a good example of this. In Narsapur, Andhra Pradesh, India, poor rural Christian and Hindu women produce lace doilies at home. These are then sold through an extensive network of male agents, traders and exporters. Lace production contributes about 90 per cent of the state's handicraft export earnings and has become very profitable for the male traders. But the women who make the lace earn appallingly low wages, and in spite of a 6–8-hour day at lace work, on top of seven hours of other productive work and domestic work, they are not considered 'workers' but rather 'housewives'. The women originally took up lace making as a spare-time activity in order to supplement their husbands' insufficient incomes. As Mies says, 'as they are defined as housewives, this production does not upset the patriarchal reproduction relations within the family and it prevents the women at the same time from demanding a just wage'.[15] Mies goes on to argue that 'the domestication of women and the propagation of the ideology that women are *basically housewives* is not merely a means to keep their wages below the subsistence level but also to keep women totally atomised and disorganised as workers'.[16]

As far as I know, the degree of exploitation of the lace makers of Narsapur is worse than anything yet occurring in China. Yet, the structures through which such exploitation occurs in rural India are also in place in rural China, and it is possible that in the future women working in the Chinese courtyard economy will be exploited in the same way and to the same extent as in India. On the other hand, if rural development in China continues to expand the range of employment opportunities available to rural women, this will increase their power to demand higher incomes in the courtyard economy as well as in other sectors. Another important factor in determining the degree of exploitation of women in the courtyard economy will be the extent to which the women are able to work together to defend their interests, and the extent to which their interests are supported by the state and local government. In this regard, as I will argue shortly, the role of the Women's Federation and of successful women entrepreneurs will be of great importance.

So far, I have focused on the state's interests in promoting women's work in the courtyard economy as a way of maximising the use of a flexible and cheap source of labour. Yet the expansion of the courtyard economy cannot be understood solely as the top-down manipulation or exploitation of passive women. We must also take into consideration the fact that families and women themselves see important benefits to working in this sector. Moreover, it is usually peasant women who take the initiative to develop production in the courtyard economy, with local officials providing support and encouragement only after they have judged that such production will be viable in the longer term.

Some reports suggest, in fact, that especially in the late 1970s and early 1980s, when private entrepreneurial activities were still viewed with suspicion by many officials, permission to expand production in the courtyard economy came only after considerable pressure was applied on local leaders by women who had lost their jobs in agriculture and had no alternative employment.[17]

Other reports show the courtyard economy being developed largely through the initiative of one particularly enterprising woman, who then employs, or passes on her skills, to other women in the village. One article describes, for example, the efforts of a university graduate who was sent down to the countryside in Hebei Province during the Cultural Revolution and settled there. In 1982 she sought work in a factory in Beijing embroidering sweaters. The factory was so impressed with her embroidery that they signed a contract with her to embroider sweaters at home. Upon returning to her village, the woman began recruiting students. In 1983 alone she taught 300 students and together they earned 47,000 *yuan* producing embroidery for the Beijing factory.[18]

In the majority of rural families, one or more women are engaged in the courtyard economy, at least to the extent of raising one or two pigs and a few chickens to provide fertiliser, eggs for home consumption and a supplementary cash income. As I have suggested, women sometimes seek more substantial work in the courtyard economy as a result of underemployment or unemployment in agriculture and the lack of alternative forms of work. In other cases, women, especially older women, choose to work in the courtyard economy as a way of supplementing their income from agriculture. The limitations on opportunities for female employment in industry are often a factor in their decision to work in these sectors (see Chapter 9).

Sometimes, however, women choose to work in the courtyard economy in preference to employment in industry. Sulamith and Jack Potter claim, for example, that in Zengbu in the early 1980s young rural women were eager to work in the factories being established as joint ventures with Hong Kong capitalists. However, where work in the courtyard economy which paid well was available, it was preferred to work in a factory. In Pondside, for example, the young women chose to work at home making the bamboo sticks used in the production of fireworks, rather than work in local factories. Undertaking such work, they were able to earn more money than they could in the joint-run factories. They also said: 'We like the freedom of working at home at our own speed; if we work for ourselves we don't have to add shifts or work all night.'[19]

The benefits of the courtyard economy most commonly cited by rural women are its income earning potential, the flexibility of the work, and the autonomy it affords them.

The range of incomes that can be earned from the courtyard economy is enormous – from very little to more than half the family income in the case of specialised households. For most women, the income earned from work in the courtyard economy is a welcome supplement to the main family income, but is well below the average rural income. Thus, in 1983 a national survey of rural household income and expenditure covering 22,700 rural households found that average per capita net income from domestic sidelines reached 102.8 *yuan*.[20] This was about one-third of the average per capita net income in rural areas at that time. Other, smaller-scale surveys confirm that the average per capita net income earned in domestic sidelines or the courtyard economy amounts to roughly one-third of the average.[21] As Delia Davin points out, 'much sideline production is monotonous, isolated, undercapitalized and, even by Chinese standards, poorly remunerated. Only exceptionally are large amounts of money made'.[22]

A minority of women working in the courtyard economy have, however, earned very high incomes, usually by engaging in a new and novel line of production, and/or by specialising in one line of production and developing it into a specialised household or private enterprise. The successes of such women have been given a good deal of publicity. For example, after her initial losses, the Shandong woman mentioned earlier took out another loan of 8,000 *yuan* and signed a five-year contract with the local foreign trade department to supply marmots for export. That year, she paid back the loan and made a further profit of 32,000 *yuan*. In the second year she made a net profit of 56,000 *yuan*. In 1993 she took out another 2,000 *yuan* loan in order to start raising ants for use in traditional Chinese medicine. Within nine months she had paid off that loan and made a profit of 29,000 *yuan*. During this nine-month period, her two ventures earned her a total profit of 117,000 *yuan*. Her achievements also earned her special awards from the local county government, and her story was written up in the national media. In addition, in 1994 she was elected as a delegate to the county People's Congress.[23]

It is, in part, examples such as these that attract women to the courtyard economy. Discussions with peasant women and reports in the media, suggest, however, that two other equally important factors drawing women to work in the courtyard economy are firstly, the work's flexibility – the fact that it can be done at any time and can easily be fitted in with women's domestic work – and secondly, the autonomy and control over their own time and labour that women have in this sector. This is contrasted favourably with employment in the fields under the commune system, when women's labour was managed by production team cadres, and (as the quotation about Pondside above indicates) with employment today in township enterprises, where few women attain management positions and female employees have little freedom or control over the production process.

These positive statements should not, however, blind us to the ways in which women's power and autonomy in the family are constrained, and may indeed have become more so as a result of a return to family farming. By shifting the management of labour allocation and income distribution from the production team back to the family, the introduction of the production responsibility system has once more strengthened the authority of the male head of the family – an authority that continues to be underpinned by women's relative insecurity in the family due to the patrilocal marriage system.

In addition, in some cases women's work in the courtyard economy has itself further reinforced men's authority. This is partly because of the strong associations between domestic sidelines and domestic work, which tends to render the former invisible. Thus where, as in the past, women's work in the courtyard economy consists of raising a small number of domestic livestock, the strong associations between such work and domestic work, combined with the relatively low cash income from such work, may render its contribution to the family economy invisible, consequently maintaining the lower status of the women who do such work. However, with the newer and more lucrative sidelines, high income and public prestige is likely to translate into greater authority for women in the family.

Pointing to a more concrete problem of the 'inside' nature of the courtyard economy, Delia Davin has suggested that under the commune system the majority of women worked in the fields with women and men from other families, but under the new system women working in the courtyard economy have fewer opportunities to communicate with people outside their family, and hence are more vulnerable to the dictates of parents, husbands and in-laws.[24]

This is indeed true of women whose work in the courtyard economy is solely for family consumption. An important part of the reform programme has been, however, to encourage once more the commercialisation of production in the courtyard economy. As a result, the situation regarding women's interaction with people outside the family has become more complicated. Some women now take their produce to market and interact with numerous people there.[25] In addition, in some cases women's work in the courtyard economy involves them negotiating loans and arranging business deals, as well as marketing. On the other hand, as mentioned, much of the work that women undertake in activities such as weaving and handicraft production is subcontracted, and in these cases women are not involved in the business side of the work and have little interaction with people outside the family. Furthermore, even where work in the courtyard economy is not subcontracted in this way, it is more common for women not to be involved in business transactions with non-family members. As in pre-1949 China, such activities are considered to belong to the male 'outside' sphere, and are commonly undertaken by the woman's husband, even though he may not be involved in the production itself.

Finally, in more general terms, the increased autonomy that peasants associate with a return to a household-based economy may be somewhat illusory, and their enthusiasm and willingness to work harder for that autonomy might even be considered a form of self-exploitation. Nevertheless, however illusory, autonomy has been a powerful motivation behind peasant choices and behaviour in the post-Mao era.[26]

In this section I have argued that the expansion of women's work in the courtyard economy since the late 1970s has occurred as a consequence of the advantages seen by both the state and women themselves regarding work in this sector. For women, work in the courtyard economy is seen to offer the *potential* for generating substantial incomes and for providing them with a degree of autonomy and flexibility not possible in larger-scale industry. I have argued, however, that just as there is the potential for the courtyard economy to bring important benefits to women, there is also the potential for women working in this sector to be severely constrained and exploited. Both the potentially negative and positive aspects of the courtyard economy relate to its 'inside' and subsidiary nature. Thus, while the fact that the work is undertaken by women at home gives them more flexibility than employment in industry, it also leaves women vulnerable to the demands of husbands and other relatives and to exploitation by capitalists, both Chinese and foreign.

In the final section of this chapter I will examine the activities of the Women's Federation in encouraging women in the courtyard economy and will ask whether, or to what extent, the Federation is helping women to maximise the benefits to be gained in this sector and to minimise the potential for exploitation.

First, however, I wish to discuss the position of the small number of women entrepreneurs who have developed their activities in the courtyard economy into specialised households and private enterprises, for it appears that these women have been able to develop the potential of the courtyard economy to the full, and consequently are amongst those to have benefited most from rural reform.

WOMEN RUNNING SPECIALISED HOUSEHOLDS AND PRIVATE ENTERPRISES

Private enterprises include *getihu* and *siying qiye*.[27] *Getihu* are mainly family-based enterprises engaged in small-scale non-agricultural production, commerce and services, and employing no more than seven people. Between 1984 and 1988 the number of *getihu* registered in rural China increased from approximately 3.3 million to 16.1 million. Political insecurity resulting from the Tiananmen massacre of 1989 resulted in a small decline in the number of *getihu* registered, but by the end of 1991 numbers had increased again to about 16.8 million.[28] *Siying qiye*, formally recognised only since 1988, are non-agricultural enterprises that employ eight or more people (and this can include hundreds of employees). Some originated as *getihu* and then expanded. Others were collectively owned enterprises that were taken over by individuals. Most are engaged in industry, mining, transport or construction. In 1988 the Bureau of Industry and Commerce estimated that there were 225,000 *siying qiye* across urban and rural China.[29]

Specialised households (*zhuanyehu*) are high-earning rural households which derive most of their income from just one area of production or services, whether it be agricultural or non-agricultural. One report claimed that in 1984 there were ten million specialised households in China.[30] With a tightening of standards, estimations of the number of specialised households were, however, subsequently revised downwards. A report published in 1988 estimated that there were approximately four million specialised households.[31]

Amongst the women involved in running agricultural specialised households that I interviewed in 1989, one was engaged in grain production, one in growing medicinal fungi, and one in growing bonsai and flowers. One woman was involved in raising cows, two raised pigs, and four raised chickens.[32] The women involved in non-agricultural specialised households or private businesses included three involved in some form of food processing, two involved in running hotels, two who ran tailoring schools, one who ran a grocery shop and recreation

154

room, one who ran a business machine-knitting jumpers, and two who under-took sewing.[33]

Unfortunately, little survey data is available on the characteristics of the people running private enterprises in rural areas. Therefore, the following discussion is limited to the women who run specialised households. It is likely, however, that much of this discussion could apply equally well to women running *getihu*, since the distinction between non-agricultural specialised households and *getihu* is largely only an administrative one, with little significance in practice. It should be noted, however, that given the more general patterns discussed in Chapter 7, according to which men are the first to move into non-agricultural occupations whilst women remain working in agriculture and domestic sidelines, it is likely that the proportion of women running non-agricultural specialised households and *getihu* is lower than the proportion of women running agricultural specialised households. It is also likely that there are considerably fewer women running large *siying qiye* than smaller private enterprises, firstly, because the former requires greater accounting and management skills, in which women are disadvantaged because of their lower education levels (see Chapter 5). Secondly, the managers of larger enterprises are also more dependent on political contacts to ensure such things as security, the supply of inputs and sales outlets. In this, women are again disadvantaged by their marginalisation in local politics (see Chapter 5). Finally, women are less likely to manage large enterprises, employing non-family members, because of a still powerful cultural resistance against women leading, or having authority over, men outside the family sphere.

According to an investigation carried out by the Women's Federation in fourteen regions across China, specialised households run by women (*funü wei zhu de zhuanyehu*) comprise 35 to 40 per cent of all specialised households and in some developed regions the figure is as high as 55 per cent.[34] County officials told me in 1989 that the proportion of specialised households run by women was highest amongst those engaged in animal husbandry. For example, as illustrated in Table 8.1, in Huairou County, Beijing, there were no women running specialised households in transport, but 67 per cent of such households engaged in animal husbandry were run by women.[35]

In comparison with the tiny proportion of collective industries with women in management positions (see Chapter 9), the proportion of specialised households run by women is high. This may be because, firstly, specialised households are family-based and usually employ no more than a few non-family members, if any. A woman running a specialised household is, therefore, more acceptable in terms of the view that women's work should be confined to the 'inside' sphere. Secondly, the majority of specialised households have evolved from domestic sideline production, which, as we have seen, is dominated by women.[36] The fact

Table 8.1   *Specialised households in Huairou County, Beijing*

Speciality	No. of Households	Percentage run by Women	Average Net Income (*yuan*/year)
Crop Growing	612	36	1,700
Animal husbandry	1,200	67	1,800
Forestry	n.a.	n.a.	2,000
Commerce	500	57	1,800
Processing	5,633	45	2,600
Transport	n.a.	0	2,800

n.a. = not available

Source: Interview with members of the Huairou County Agricultural Work Department and the Huairou County Women's Federation, September 1989.

that there are not more women running specialised households suggests, however, that once a woman's activities in the courtyard economy reach a certain scale and become more profitable than other productive activities available to the family, their management is often taken over by the male head of the family.

In an investigation of 403 specialised households run by women conducted in Huairou County, Beijing, in 1988 it was found that 65 per cent of the women earned incomes higher than their husbands and in 80 per cent of the households the women managed all financial matters.[37] Other examples cited in the media show women running specialised households in control of most aspects of the production process, including contracting with other bodies, taking out loans and being responsible for investments and the sale of produce. In addition, some women running specialised households achieve positions of considerable status in their village by employing other people, by teaching others their skills or by helping them to set up their own businesses, and by joining the Party or receiving 'labour model' status.[38]

It might be supposed, then, that women running specialised households have a high degree of authority in their own family, and that they are also breaking down the inside/outside division of labour, or, to put it another way, that they are successfully using their work in the 'inside' courtyard economy as a launching pad from which to enter the 'outside' male preserve of business and of public prestige.

There are a number of caveats to be made to this proposition, however. In the first place, there are considerable variations in meaning attached to the term 'running a specialised household' and in the powers and responsibilities a woman in this position has. Thus, some of the women running specialised households that I interviewed did seem to be in control of their line of production. Others, however, did most of the work and it was they who had the technical skills required, for example, to raise chickens, but husbands were also involved in the venture, and, in keeping with the traditional inside/outside gender division of labour, it was the husband who arranged loans, signed contracts, sought business, and in general was the family representative to the outside world. In Jinniu County an official that I interviewed in the Township Enterprise Bureau confirmed that in the private sector generally, it is common for men to do the 'outside' work; that is buying, selling and making business deals. Women often sell goods in the market, but where produce is sold to a company, or in cases where business negotiations are involved, this task is undertaken by men. The reason this official gave for such a division of labour was that 'women can't smoke or drink, so they can't discuss business'.[39]

Researchers in Chengdu told me that in other cases, where the husband works in another line of business, the fact that a woman runs a specialised household tells one very little about her status, for the man might still be the household's business representative and major decision maker. It does not even necessarily mean that her income is higher than her husband's. Often specialised households are defined locally in terms of a standard of output. For example, 5,000 chickens might be the standard set for a chicken-raising specialised household, but in any one household the income from this number of chickens might in fact be less than the man's income in another line of production.[40]

It must also be recognised that the people who run specialised households are a privileged minority among peasants. Such people are commonly set apart from others by a number of characteristics. Their families tend, first of all, to be larger and to contain more able-bodied labourers than the average, allowing for the greater and more efficient deployment of family labour and reducing the need to hire outside workers. A survey conducted in rural Sichuan, for example, found that specialised households contained, on average, 6.1 members, whilst other rural households contained an average of only 4.5 people. Amongst the specialised households only 10.9 per cent contained fewer than two able-bodied labourers, whilst 56.9 per cent included more than three. In contrast, 31.6 per cent of ordinary rural households contained less than three able-bodied labourers, and only 8.5 per cent contained more than three.[41]

People who run specialised households also tend to have above-average levels of education. In the Sichuan survey just cited, it was found that in most specialised households, members had received an average education of between four and six years (that is, primary or junior secondary level). This compares with an average education of between 0 and four years amongst members of ordinary rural households.[42] Similarly, an investigation of 212 specialised households run by women in Huaide County, Jilin Province, found that 38 per cent of the women had junior or senior secondary school education and 95 per cent had upper primary school education. Among all women in the county aged 18 to 45, however, 57 per cent were illiterate or had junior primary school education.[43]

Lack of education is likely to limit any increase in the number of women running specialised households, both in terms of absolute numbers and as a proportion of the total. As discussed in Chapter 5, approximately 70 per cent of all illiterates are women, and drop-out rates amongst girls in rural primary and secondary schools are high.

Last, but by no means least, many of the people who run specialised households are able to do so because they have contacts with cadres who give them preferential treatment in terms of securing credit and arranging contracts, for example, or because they themselves are cadres. Thus, in a survey of over 20,000 specialised households conducted in 1984, it was found that 43 per cent were run by production brigade or team leaders, or former cadres.[44]

To conclude this section, some rural women have been able to greatly increase their incomes and their authority, both in the family and in the 'outside' sphere, by expanding their activities into specialised households and private enterprises. The proportion of such ventures run by women is larger than in collective industry. However, it must be recognised that in some cases in which it is claimed that a woman runs a specialised household, it is in fact her husband or another male relative who is in charge of the business side of the enterprise, whilst the woman does most of the production work. Furthermore, women managers of specialised households and private enterprises are an elite minority. There are formidable obstacles to a woman's developing her courtyard activities into a more specialised business, and even when she does, once the business develops to a certain size and becomes particularly profitable, it is often taken over by the male head of the family.

DEVELOPMENT OF THE COURTYARD ECONOMY AS A STRATEGY FOR
IMPROVING THE POSITION OF RURAL WOMEN

In light of the somewhat ambivalent picture drawn here of women's work in the courtyard economy, and as managers of specialised households and private enterprises, what are we to make of the Women's Federation's efforts to support and encourage women in these areas, and the centrality of such efforts to the Federation's work with rural women?

As discussed in Chapter 5, a large proportion of the Women's Federation's work in rural China takes the form of short-term classes designed to provide women with technical skills for use in the courtyard economy. The Federation also helps women in the courtyard economy and those running specialised households and private enterprises by providing legal advice, helping to arrange bank loans, and assisting with the supply of raw materials and the sale of produce.

The Federation justifies this focus in terms of both the overall importance of developing the commodity economy, and of the advantages for women that it perceives in this sector. For example, in an article published in 1984, one county Women's Federation in Shanxi province explained that it became involved in promoting the courtyard economy in response to the large numbers of women surplus to the needs of agriculture, with no alternative employment, and upon observing that some women had become wealthy by working in the courtyard economy. It cited the following advantages to work in this sector: first, the work is flexible, and can be accommodated with women's domestic work responsibilities. Second, it arouses women's enthusiasm for studying science and technology and trains a large number of women managers. Third, it provides women with an income and hence raises their economic status and helps to protect their legal rights; and finally, it advances the development of the commodity economy.[45]

In Shanxi, this article implies, the courtyard economy was encouraged by the Women's Federation in a situation in which large numbers of women were unemployed or underemployed and had no income. In this context, I would argue, support for women in developing the courtyard economy is indeed initially an expedient way of providing women with an income, and hence of improving their status and self-respect. Yet women are being encouraged to develop the courtyard economy, not just in the poorer, less developed parts of rural China where there are few alternatives for employment, but also in the most economically developed regions. The question here becomes, does work in the courtyard economy enhance women's opportunities for income generation, personal development and status improvement, in a way that is comparable with work in other areas of the economy, or is the encouragement of women in this sector merely supporting a marginalisation and exploitation of women in a 'dead-end' part of the economy? In considering this it is worth reflecting both on Maria Mies' discussion of 'housewifisation' and on Ester Boserup's warning that 'training in crafts and home industries is frequently offered to women as a sort of compensation for the refusal to give them jobs in the modern sector and as a deliberate method of reducing the number of women competing with men for employment in the modern sector'.[46]

On the other hand, in China, as we have seen, the courtyard economy is a dynamic and growing aspect of the rural economy, which provides the potential, at least, for earning high incomes and improving a woman's authority and status in the family and in the wider society. Furthermore, echoing claims made by peasant women themselves, Women's Federation officials point out that the most attractive alternative to work in the courtyard economy generally available to rural women, that is employment in larger-scale rural industry, offers them less autonomy and scope for self-development than the courtyard economy, and management of such industries is overwhelmingly male.[47]

In light of these factors, I would suggest that in China, support for women in the courtyard economy *is* a viable strategy for enhancing women's social and economic position. I would nevertheless argue that such support cannot be effective without including certain elements.

First of all, in view of the fact that the market for goods from the courtyard economy is constantly in flux and no one line of production in this sector seems to be highly profitable for very long, what is most required in terms of training for the courtyard economy is basic literacy and numeracy, a grounding in generally applicable technical skills and some knowledge of accounting and of the workings of the market. These are also the types of skills that will enable women either to move out of the courtyard economy, if it ceases to be a viable form of production, or to move on to something bigger and better.

Second, in order to avoid exploitation and to help women retain control over their labour and the products of their labour, some training in accounting, legal matters and management skills is also required. As I have suggested, there is a further need for women working in this sector to be organised to defend their interests, and for support from the state to protect them against excessive exploitation by subcontractors, for example.

Looking, then, at the efforts of the Women's Federation to support women in the courtyard economy, I would argue that in terms of training, there needs to be a shift away from the current emphasis on short-term classes in specialised technical skills towards more effort directed at improving basic education and developing skills in accounting and management.

The prevention of exploitation is not a major focus of the Women's Federation's current work in the courtyard economy. Nevertheless, it does play a useful role in liaising with other bodies – for example, local government, banks and contractors – on women's behalf. It also encourages solidarity amongst women in the courtyard economy by organising meetings for women in this sector to exchange their experiences and by urging successful women entrepreneurs to pass on their skills and lend support to others starting up ventures in the courtyard economy.[48] Finally, although it has few resources, and its reputation amongst women is poor, the Women's Federation has shown in recent years that it can act as an important lobby group to defend women against the worst forms of exploitation, discrimination and abuse.[49]

I began this chapter with a discussion of domestic sidelines and the courtyard economy as areas of production generally characterised as 'light' work belonging to the 'inside' sphere, as subsidiary to other productive activities, and as particularly suited to women. These characterisations have, I argue, been integral to the state's encouragement of the courtyard economy in the post-Mao era. Thus, the characterisation of the courtyard economy as 'light', 'inside' work, particularly suitable for women, has been important in the use of the courtyard economy for the absorption of the mostly female surplus labour from agriculture. In addition, its 'inside' and 'subsidiary' nature has meant that production in the courtyard economy has required little investment from the state and employers, and women have been willing to undertake work in this sector that is most commonly either poorly paid or is highly profitable for only a brief period. From one perspective, then, the characterisations of the courtyard economy as 'light', 'inside', 'subsidiary' work suitable for women have been manipulated by the state in order to exploit women's labour. From this perspective, the Women's Federation's encouragement of women's work in the courtyard economy looks like either co-option or an attempt to make the best of a rather gloomy situation.

At the same time, though, its 'inside' nature means that there are certain important advantages for women to work in the courtyard economy. Most importantly, the work is flexible and allows for a degree of autonomy not possible in larger-scale industry. Furthermore, some women entrepreneurs have been able to expand their activities in the courtyard economy into specialised households and private enterprises, earning substantial incomes, and gaining authority and prestige, both in the family and in the 'outside', 'male' sphere of business, in the process.

In view of this more positive perspective on the courtyard economy, I have argued that the Women's Federation's encouragement of women in this sector could well be a viable strategy for improving the social and economic position of rural women. This is, however, on condition that measures be taken to protect these women from exploitation, and that women are given a broad education covering literacy, numeracy, a range of basic technical skills, and skills in accounting, legal matters and business management. This would enable them to make the most of the potential benefits of work in the courtyard economy, while at the same time not limiting them to this area of employment.

9

Industry

I HAVE focused so far on the construction and legitimation of gender divisions of labour in which the majority of rural women are concentrated in the home and on the farm. As has been indicated, relatively few women, compared with men, are employed in non-agricultural work off the farm. Such work is, however, becoming an increasingly important source of employment for women, especially young unmarried women, as the economy develops.

This chapter, then, discusses rural women's work in off-farm non-agricultural employment. The first section discusses the overall development of such employment in the post-Mao era, and the second the gender divisions of labour apparent in this area of work. The third and fourth sections examine the ways in which these gender divisions of labour shape rural women's experience of non- · agricultural employment, in urban industries and services, and in rural township enterprises, respectively.

THE DEVELOPMENT OF RURAL OFF-FARM NON-AGRICULTURAL EMPLOYMENT

As mentioned in Chapter 3, moves toward a new rural development strategy made by the CCP at the end of the 1970s included encouragement of greater investment in rural industry. Then, in March 1984 the CCP, in line with the changes in administrative structures that had occurred, renamed commune and brigade enterprises 'township enterprises'. It also urged local governments to support and encourage the development of township enterprises, including those run privately and by cooperatives.[1]

Meanwhile, a number of other changes were occurring which made a shift to off-farm non-agricultural employment both feasible and attractive to peasants and local governments. Increases in the productivity of agricultural labour led to increases in peasant incomes and savings which then provided the necessary capital base with which to develop non-agricultural ventures of various types. The increases in the productivity of agricultural labour also enabled a surplus of labour in agriculture to be drawn both into newly established local industries and into employment in urban industry and services.

Township enterprises

Most people drawn into off-farm non-agricultural employment work in township enterprises in their own village or in a nearby county town. 'Township enterprise' (*xiangzhen qiye*) is a term used in Chinese statistics to refer to various economic entities in rural areas and small towns operating outside the state plan. They include undertakings in all sectors of the economy, including agriculture, industry, construction, transport, commerce and services. The proportion involved in agriculture is small, however.[2]

Township enterprises include both collective and private ventures. They may be run by local government at the levels of town (*zhen*), township (*xiang*), district (*qu*) and village (*cun*), or by peasants in cooperation with their village, as partnerships (*lianheti*) or as individuals.[3]

As a result of economic reforms, between 1978 and 1993 the total number of township enterprises increased from about 1.5 million to about 24.5 million, and the total labour force employed in township enterprises increased by some 95 million people, from 28.3 million in 1978 to 123.5 million in 1993.[4]

The growth of township enterprises has been rather uneven, both temporally and geographically, however. Thus, between 1978 and 1983 township enterprise employment grew at an average annual rate of about 2.5 per cent, but between 1985 and 1988 it soared to an average of about 11 per cent.[5] A credit squeeze imposed by the government between late 1988 and mid-1990 resulted in a decline in township enterprise employment of approximately three million people. By the end of 1991, however, the figures had once more increased to greater than those for 1988, and between 1992 and 1993 township enterprise employment grew by 13.4 per cent.[6]

The sectoral composition of township enterprise employment has also changed. In particular, the proportion of people employed in agricultural township enterprises has declined, while the proportion employed in commerce and in food and service industries has increased.

In geographical terms, township enterprise employment is greatest in areas around large cities and in the coastal provinces. According to a World Bank study published in 1990, in the provinces of Liaoning, Hebei (including Beijing and Tianjin), Shandong, Jiangsu (including Shanghai), Zhejiang, Guangdong, and Shanxi, where township enterprises are most developed, the rural labour force accounts for about 38 per cent of the national total, but township enterprise employment makes up about 57 per cent of national township enterprise employment. In the provinces of Henan, Hubei, Fujian, Jiangxi, Hunan, Anhui, Shaanxi, Heilongjiang, Jilin and Sichuan, the rural labour force accounts for 46.1 per cent of the national total and the labour force in township enterprises comprises 40.7 per cent of the national total. In the provinces where township enterprises are least developed, that is, Nei Monggol, Ningxia, Gansu, Qinghai, Xinjiang, Guangxi, Yunnan, Guizhou and Xizang, the rural labour force accounts for 16.2 per cent of the total, while the township enterprise labour force accounts for only eight per cent of the total.[7]

Differences in the availability of natural resources and in overall levels of economic development determine that there are marked regional differences in the type of activity undertaken by township enterprises. In the provinces where township enterprises are least developed, for example, the construction industry (which, incidentally, employs few women) is more dominant than in other regions. In areas with a relatively well developed township enterprise sector, on the other hand, a larger proportion of enterprises are engaged in industrial production. Finally, there are also regional differences in the composition of the industrial sector of township enterprises, such that, generally speaking, light industries, which employ larger proportions of women, become more dominant as one moves from the northwest to the coastal areas in the southeast.[8]

Employment in urban areas

In addition to the growth in local township enterprise employment, the 1980s and 1990s have also seen an unprecedented movement of rural labour into towns and cities and between regions. Moves toward a more decentralised and market-oriented economy have created pressures for increased labour mobility and flexibility, among both employers and rural inhabitants seeking work. In the urban state sector, for example, the implementation of a type of 'responsibility system', involving contracts for managers linked to enterprise profitability, has led to pressure on managers to employ rural residents as contract workers (*hetong gong*) or temporary workers (*linshi gong*), since such workers can be hired more cheaply, can be made to work in conditions that urban workers will not tolerate, and can be more readily retrenched than the latter (for details, see below).

Rural residents are nevertheless attracted to such employment because the wages are still higher than can usually be earned in agriculture. Large numbers of peasants have also been flooding into cities to sell their produce or to engage in other forms of business. Peasants moving from rural to urban areas, or between urban areas, form the majority of what is known as the 'floating population' (*liudong renkou*), that is, people who do not live in their place of household registration. They continue to be registered as rural residents, but come into the cities either on temporary work permits, or illegally. They are able to manage in the cities because they can now buy grain and other goods on the free market, and so are not as limited by their rural registration as they would have been previously. Today the floating population numbers upwards of a hundred million people.[9]

One of the most recent large-scale surveys of the floating population was undertaken in eleven large cities in 1989–1990 by the Chinese Academy of Social Sciences. According to this survey, the floating population in Beijing numbered roughly 1.3 million, or about 22 per cent of that city's permanent non-agricultural population. In Chengdu they numbered 426,000, or about 25 per cent of the permanent non-agricultural population, and in Hangzhou the floating population reached 500,000, or the equivalent of roughly 46 per cent of the permanent non-agricultural population.[10]

The survey found that, nationwide, some 72 per cent of the floating population in large cities was male, and 59 per cent came from the countryside. Roughly half were aged between 18 and 35. Approximately 48 per cent came to the city in search of work or on business. Some 62 per cent stayed in the city for one month or more, and 29 per cent stayed a year or more.[11]

GENDER DIVISIONS OF LABOUR IN OFF-FARM NON-AGRICULTURAL EMPLOYMENT

In Chapters 7 and 8 I argued that changing interpretations of gendered dichotomies between 'inside' and 'outside', 'light' and 'heavy', and 'manual' and 'technical' have been central in the creation of a new set of assumptions in which agriculture and the courtyard economy are considered to be women's work, whilst women's lower rates of off-farm non-agricultural employment are seen as natural. Equally importantly, however, within the sphere of off-farm non-agricultural employment, similar assumptions have also contributed to major differences between the work patterns of women and men. Thus, women in off-farm non-agricultural employment are more highly concentrated in local industries close to home, and those who work away from home are mostly young and unmarried and do so for only for a few years at most.[12] Furthermore, while men tend to be involved in heavy industry, construction or transport work, women are concentrated in light industry and in employment which is seen as a flow-on from their domestic roles as wives and mothers (for example, as nannies or in other service occupations). And finally, within particular industries women are concentrated in the most 'unskilled', poorly paid areas of work.

Township enterprises

Nationally, women form somewhere between 30 and 40 per cent of the labour force employed in township enterprises.[13] However, in light industry and in commerce, catering and services, the proportion of women is somewhat higher. One report estimates, for example, that in Guangdong 90 per cent of the labour force working in township enterprises engaged in wool spinning, clothes making, handicrafts, toys and electronics is women.[14] A survey of 90 township enterprises in Zhejiang, Hebei and Shaanxi, conducted in 1991 by the Rural Development Research Institute of the Chinese Academy of Social Sciences and the Chinese Economy Research Unit at the University of Adelaide (hereafter RDRI/CERU), found that women comprised 64 per cent of workers in textiles, but only 20 per cent in other industries.[15]

Table 9.1 and Appendix 2 show the number of women employed in the township enterprises in the counties in Beijing, Shandong and Sichuan that I visited in 1989. The proportion of women in township enterprise employment ranged from 22.8 per cent in Wenjiang County, Sichuan, to 50.0 per cent in Ling County, Shandong. In some individual textile enterprises, however, women comprised as much as 98 per cent of the labour force.

The majority of women working in township enterprises are fairly young. Duan Daohuai and co-authors claim that nationally 60 per cent of the women working in township enterprises (of all types, including private enterprises and non-agricultural specialised households) are aged between 18 and 25, 30 per cent are aged between 26 and 36 and 10 per cent are more than 36 years old.[16] The 1991 RDRI/CERU survey mentioned above found that 65.6 per cent of female employees in township enterprises were aged between 17 and 29, and 24.7 per cent were aged between 30 and 39.[17]

Because of assumptions that they are responsible for agriculture and for child care, it is generally considered that for women, and especially married women with children, employment in a local township enterprise is a far more viable proposition than work away from home. As Duan Daohuai and colleagues argue, women who work in nearby enterprises 'are able to adjust their working hours in the factory to suit the seasonality of farmwork. They are also able to work on the farms after their shift in the factory. In addition, the daily life of their families is not significantly affected as would be the case if rural–urban migration occurred'.[18]

In at least some places, however, women's employment in township- and village-run enterprises also terminates after either marriage or childbirth. I was told, for example, that in Ling County only 20 per cent of female workers of township- and village-run enterprises return to their factory after the birth of

Table 9.1 *Township enterprise employment in sample counties in Beijing, Shandong and Sichuan*

County	No. of Township Enterprises	No. of Township Enterprise Workers	Percentage of Female Workers in Township Enterprises	Percentage of Rural Labour Force Employed in Township Enterprises
Huairou (b)	700	40,000	37.50	44.40
Ling	3,827	32,438	50.00	n.a. (a)
Jinniu	25,828	168,675	38.50	70.00
Wenjiang	5,275	22,837	22.80	19.10
Xindu	13,988	80,818	35.40	33.40
Guan	9,607	50,064	24.70	21.40
Mianyang (c)	2,650	30,000	46.70	n.a.

(a) n.a. = not available

(b) Figures refer to township- and village-run enterprises only. There are 20 township-run enterprises, the rest are village-run.

(c) Enterprise numbers include all township enterprises, but worker numbers refer only to those in township- and village-run enterprises.

Agricultural township enterprise employment figures are included in this table. By county they are as follows: Huairou n.a; Ling 28 enterprises, 354 workers; Jinniu 5 enterprises, 116 workers; Wenjiang 40 enterprises, 381 workers; Xindu 29 enterprises, 302 workers; Guan 54 enterprises, 485 workers; Mianyang n.a.

Sources: Interviews with representatives of the Township Enterprise Bureau in each county, September–December 1989. Figures for Jinniu and Wenjiang checked with those in Jiang Xuegui, *Chengdu Xiangzhengiye (1979–1988) [Chengdu's Township Enterprises (1979–1988)]*, Chengdu Chubanshe, Chengdu, 1989, pp. 69–92, 138–143, 626, 639.

their child. In one cloth shoe factory in this county the women's representative told me that, although they do not wish to, most women give up their factory job after their child is born. They find it too hard to look after a baby and keep working in the factory at the same time, so instead they do agricultural work. In a township-run carpet factory employing almost all women, the pattern was that young women worked in the factory until marriage, whereupon they took up carpet weaving as a form of outwork in their own home.

In these cases it appears that the withdrawal of older women from employment in township enterprises relates to the difficulties of combining such employment with child care and domestic work duties. Ellen Judd suggests, however, that such a pattern also relates to the patrilocal, exogamous marriage system. Judd found that in Qianrulin Village, Weifang Prefecture, Shandong, village-run factories are not willing to employ married women, who, as is the norm across rural China, come from other villages. In Zhangjiachedao Village, also in Weifang Prefecture, Judd found that in theory a woman who had married out could continue to work in her natal village but in practice rarely did so, and the shift work in the largest and preferred factory made such an arrangement extremely difficult.[19]

As with other areas of work, the patterns of women's employment in township enterprises that I have discussed here result partly from decisions made by women themselves and by families in managing their economies: decisions that are in turn influenced by assumptions about gendered dichotomies between 'inside' and 'outside' spheres, and 'light' and 'heavy' work. However, these patterns also result, in part, from the recruitment policies of township enterprises.

In private enterprises most workers either belong to the same family as the manager, or have obtained their job through personal connections or recommendation. In government-run enterprises, however, recruitment is more formalised. In all but two of the thirteen township enterprises run by township or village whose management I questioned on this issue, the main method for recruiting workers was by advertising and then requiring potential workers to sit an examination conducted either by the enterprise itself or by local government. This is somewhat different from the practice of commune- and brigade-run enterprises in the past, when the concern was mainly to provide employment for members of poor households or those with surplus labour, as well as for workers' children and those with personal connections with enterprise leaders. As others have noted, there has been a tendency in the 1980s to put more emphasis on skill or ability when recruiting into township enterprises, so as to improve profitability.[20]

Nevertheless, various other factors are also taken into consideration. For example, the children of present workers are sometimes still given preference, and often attempts are also made to equalise incomes in a community, either by assigning enterprise employment to members of poorer households, or by ensuring that at least one member of each household is employed in a township enterprise.

In addition, many enterprises have requirements for workers of a particular age or educational level. Commonly, the age of workers when first employed is between 18 and 25, though child labour is also recruited for the most un-skilled work, and older, more experienced people are sometimes employed in management, or in the most skilled work. A requirement for junior, and in some cases senior, secondary education amongst new workers is becoming increasingly common. Six enterprises that I visited stipulated this, though in one it had been introduced only the preceding year (see Appendix 2). In one sense, this condition works to the disadvantage of young women, since overall they attain lower levels of education than men. It may be, however, that a township enterprise requirement for junior secondary education will provide the incentive for families to keep their daughters at school for longer.

Enterprises also often stipulate the number of female and the number of male workers they require.[21] I found this to be the case in six out of thirteen enterprises I visited. One village-run clothing factory in Xindu County, Sichuan, for example, had a quota of 90 per cent female workers. In contrast, the managers of a township-run car parts factory said that in the last two years they had limited female employment to 30 per cent because most of the factory work was too heavy for women.

Five other enterprise leaders whom I interviewed did not stipulate particular requirements as regards the gender of their workers, but nevertheless expressed preferences. These reflected some of the widespread assumptions about women discussed elsewhere in this book. The two female managers of a township-run factory producing metal door and window frames said, for example, that they preferred hiring men because much of the work was too heavy for women. On the other hand, the head of a village-run cotton textile plant in Ling County voiced a preference for female workers, saying that textile making is female work since it requires patience and meticulousness.

Interestingly, the leaders of three enterprises employing mainly women said that this was not their preference. The (male) head of a township-run clothing factory in Huairou County, for example, said that he preferred to hire men. He claimed that men can do fine work as well as women and they are stronger. After marriage, and especially after childbirth, women do not work as effectively as men because they have too many other worries. He claimed that in a case where a choice had to be made between a potential male worker and a potential female worker with the same examination results he would take the man. Similarly, the head of a children's clothing factory said she preferred to hire men because women's burden of domestic work is too great. Most of her workers, however, were women, and in general, men were embarrassed at the thought of applying to work with so many women. Finally, the two female heads of a village-run chemical and electroplating enterprise said they preferred to hire men because they were more 'able' (*neng gan*), but, in practice, 70 per cent of the workers were women. These remarks suggest that particular assumptions about the type of work suitable for women do not always coincide with common stereotypes, and that even those industries commonly thought of as suitable for women often prefer to hire men.

Employment in urban areas

In the employment of rural people working in urban areas, there is, once more, a sharp gender division of labour. In Chengdu, for example, in 1989 some 95 per cent of the 63,000 members of the floating population hired to work in the construction industry were male, whereas about 84 per cent of the 12,000 members of the floating population hired as nannies were female. One large construction company hired 1,063 temporary rural workers in 1989, all of them male. In contrast, a leather clothing factory employed 90 temporary rural workers, 98 per cent of whom were young unmarried women. On Chengdu's Shaanxi Street, in the many private tailoring and shoe repair stalls that had been set up, 112 rural people were employed, of whom 70 per cent were women.[22]

These kinds of gender division of labour in Chinese industry are, of course, nothing new. Despite the Cultural Revolution claim that 'What men can do, women can do too', relatively few women worked in heavy industry, even in the 1970s. More women were employed in light industry, in particular in textiles, where they often comprised more than 50 per cent of the labour force. From the 1960s onwards, women also formed a significant proportion of the labour force in the newly established urban industries producing precision instruments, chemicals and drugs.[23]

It is important to note, though, that between the late 1950s and the 1970s the state did at least make some efforts to increase the number of women employed in traditionally male industries, and these efforts met with some success. Phyllis Andors claims, for example, that in the heavy industry sector, women formed a significantly larger proportion of the labour force in factories set up during or after the Great Leap Forward, than in older factories.[24]

After 1978 even the rhetoric changed, however, with the notion that 'What men can do, women can do too' being explicitly rejected as exaggerated.[25] In the 1980s and 1990s there has been considerable criticism, by the Women's Federation and others, of direct discrimination against urban women by state-run enterprises, for example in light industry, in which the work is considered 'suitable' for women.[26] However, there has been no criticism, but rather endorsement, of a segregation of industrial employment along gender lines.

The following two sections of this chapter examine the implications of gender divisions of labour (and, in the case of urban employment, of an urban/rural division of labour) for the experiences of rural women in both urban employment and in rural township enterprises. First I focus on women's experiences in urban industry and services. This is not a comprehensive analysis of rural women's work in urban areas. Instead it concentrates on the experience of rural women in three key areas of urban employment: domestic service; the small-scale private commerce and service sector; and light industries and textile factories.[27] Then in the final section there is a more detailed examination of women's experience of employment in township enterprises, this being by far the largest area of rural women's off-farm non-agricultural employment.

RURAL WOMEN'S EXPERIENCES OF URBAN EMPLOYMENT

Domestic service

Among the young rural women working away from home in non-agricultural occupations, a significant proportion are domestic workers or nannies (*baomu*) in urban households. The 1989–1990 study cited above found that in a sample survey of seven major cities, roughly nine per cent of the floating population worked in domestic service.[28] Another report estimated that at the end of 1988 there were approximately three million rural women working as nannies in towns and cities across China.[29]

The practice of hiring nannies, and the ways in which such employment is commonly perceived today, have antecedents in the employment of maids, or domestic servants, in pre-revolutionary China. Girls and women, most of them from very poor families, were bought by well-off families to undertake domestic work. Often they would be bought at the age of eight or nine and then married out at the age of eighteen or so. While in service, they commonly received no regular wages and their labour was entirely under the control of their owners.[30]

After the 1949 revolution the sale of women for domestic service largely ceased. However, in the 1950s and 1960s a small number of rural women continued to work in cities as maids or nannies for wealthier households. According to one report, these were mostly middle-aged women who left their husbands and children in search of work in order to overcome economic

171

difficulties resulting, for example, from natural disasters hitting their village or from the loss of a working member of the family. Many stayed in the city with the one employer for several years.[31]

During the Cultural Revolution the hiring of nannies was frowned upon as a form of bourgeois exploitation. Even with the revival of the practice in the 1980s considerable effort had to be put into explaining that the practice is not exploitative. It is, it was argued, a practical solution to the problems that so many urban couples face in coping with domestic work and child care. At the same time, it provides attractive employment for rural women for whom there is little other employment available, and it provides opportunities for them to gain new skills and contacts which will benefit both them and their village when they return home.[32]

What was generally not acknowledged by those arguing in this way, however, is that very few young urban women are willing to take on work as a nanny. A short story by Huo Da entitled 'Nanny', first published in 1983, clearly illustrates the low status of such work: when a young woman arrives seeking work as a nanny, her prospective employer assumes she is a peasant from outside Beijing, and is amazed when she learns that, in fact, the young woman is a Beijing resident waiting for employment (*daiye qingnian*). She thinks to herself: 'Does being a nanny count as a profession? . . . You must go into someone else's family, be meek and subservient and let others order you around; you have to do hard labour just in order to feed yourself; you're not much better than a beggar. To put it crudely, you're just a servant, a maid who can be ordered around, a little "maidservant" ("*lao mazi*")'.[33] Being a nanny, then, is scarcely considered a real job, for it has associations on the one hand, with domestic work which lacks status because it belongs to an 'inside' sphere, and on the other hand, with servitude.

Most women now seeking employment as nannies are young and unmarried rural women, the majority of whom work in the city for only a few years at most, returning to their village in their early twenties to get married. An investigation of 30,000 women working as nannies, undertaken in 1983 in Beijing, found that approximately 66 per cent were single and under the age of 25. On average these women had about four years of schooling. Most came from rural areas, either in the vicinity of Beijing or from other provinces. Amongst the approximately 20,000 live-in nannies, the largest single group, 8,700 or 44 per cent, came from Anhui Province. Eighty-three per cent of these came from the single county of Wuwei. The second largest group, 3,822, or 19 per cent, came from various counties in Hebei Province.[34]

In a second investigation of 1,257 nannies undertaken in Chengdu in 1989, it was found that 83.7 per cent were women. Some 90.4 per cent were peasants, and the majority came from suburban counties of Chengdu (33.3 per cent) or from other counties or municipalities in Sichuan province (62.8 per cent). Some 23.2 per cent were 18 or below. There were also some older nannies, however, with 14.6 per cent of them aged 50 or more. This study found that most women employed as nannies had either primary school education (40.1 per cent) or junior secondary school education (39.9 per cent).[35]

Women seeking work as nannies frequently come from the poorest, most backward rural areas. They are no longer necessarily motivated by desperate poverty, so much as by a lack of work resulting from a scarcity of land for agriculture and the paucity of any alternative employment.[36] For example, in Wuwei County, Anhui Province, a traditional supplier of nannies to Beijing, in 1985 agriculture could only absorb 50 per cent of the labour force. Township enterprises and sideline activities were only just developing, and 30 per cent of the labour force was without employment. Men, therefore, sought temporary work in urban factories or undertook long-distance transporting, and young women took jobs as nannies.[37]

In my conversations with eight rural women working, or seeking work, as nannies in Beijing and Hangzhou, one was a middle-aged illiterate woman who had been forced to seek work in the city because floods had destroyed her family's land and left them without a livelihood. The other seven were all in their teens or twenties. The primary reasons they gave for moving to the city to work as nannies were first, to escape farming or because there was 'too much labour and not enough land' at home, and second, to see the city and gain some independence.[38]

The majority of rural women (and men) coming to urban areas find jobs through personal connections or recommendations, or, once they get to the city, by waiting in informal labour markets on the street. However, since the early 1980s a number of women employed as nannies has also been recruited by domestic service companies. For example, the Beijing March 8th Domestic Service Company, established by the Beijing Municipal Women's Federation in 1983, recruits 4,000–5,000 nannies each year from across the country. The company's method of recruitment is to pay county Women's Federations a small fee to find women for them.[39]

The conditions under which nannies work are extremely varied. On the open market there are few guarantees of any sort, for either employer or employee. Women from areas with a tradition of sending young women to work as nannies, or from places which send large numbers of women, often belong to a network which provides them with support. In Beijing, the 'Anhui clique' (*Anhui bang*) has a reputation for providing very competent, but very wily, and sometimes criminal, nannies.[40] The older women teach the new, younger nannies all the 'tricks of the trade', and the nannies maintain contact in the city and help each other in times of need.

Domestic service companies do some screening of both potential nannies and employers, but beyond this they generally do not provide any protection or guarantees for the nannies they recruit. The Bejing March 8th Company is something of an exception; contracts written up with the company stipulate that employers must provide the nanny with meals and accommodation of the same standard as their own, and must pay a certain percentage of the nanny's medical expenses,[41] as well as a cash wage that has been agreed upon by the two parties. In theory, the nanny is required to report any maltreatment or infringement of her legal rights to the Domestic Service Company, which will then either take action itself or, in more serious cases, report the matter to the Public Security Bureau. In practice, however, the company has little control over what happens in individual households and cannot always prevent serious suffering. One young woman told me, for example, that in her first job as a nanny she had been badly physically abused by the grandfather of the child she was minding. She left and took a job with another family, who, however, worked her very hard and did not give her enough to eat. She wanted to leave but they prevented her from doing so. She herself was unwilling to leave or to contact the Domestic Service Company because she did not want her parents to find out about her troubles.[42]

Similarly, in 1993, the newly established magazine *Nongjianü Baishitong* (*Rural Women Knowing All*) published a disturbing report about a young woman who found work as a nanny through the March 8th Domestic Service Company, but who ended up in intensive care in a Beijing hospital after being beaten up several times by her employer. Subsequent stories and letters commenting on the original report, or offering accounts of the experiences of other nannies and employers, were not as horrific. They suggested, nevertheless, that nannies in China, as elsewhere, frequently suffer discrimination and abuse from their employers, and receive little in the way of legal, or other, protection.

Compared with the income they might gain from work in the fields, the wages that rural women earn in the city are high. In Hangzhou in 1995, for example, nannies generally earned a monthly wage of between 200 and 300 *yuan* (on top of food and accommodation), as compared to an average rural income of under 100 *yuan*.[43] As with employment in industry, the wages earned as a nanny have the added advantage of being 'cash in hand'. However, the initial pleasure that this affords many young women is generally greatly diminished when they find that prices are much higher in the city than at home, and they earn much less than urbanites. Most try to send a portion of their earnings home to their family, but find that the remainder they keep for themselves does not go very far at all.

The contribution to the family's income made by a young rural woman working in the city may give the woman more status in the family when she returns. Members of the Women's Federation certainly regard income contributed to the family as very important for improving women's status with regard to decision making and the use of resources. It may not necessarily have this effect, though. Research on young rural women working in Taiwanese factories suggests that despite the newness of the phenomenon, daughters' contributions to their families' incomes are simply accepted as the parents' due. This belief is reinforced by the fact that in Taiwan (as in rural China) young women marry out of their family and village. Any income they contribute before marriage is thus seen merely as part-repayment for the upbringing of a 'useless' daughter.[44]

In part because food and lodging is provided, employment as a nanny is one of the most important routes for young rural women seeking to leave their village and experience life in the city. Once there, however, they discover that nannies' wages are among the lowest for non-agricultural employment, their work hours are long and there are no fixed hours for work or rest, and clashes with employers are common.[45]

This, combined with the social stigma attached to such work, means that many young women who travel to cities originally to work as nannies, quickly leave their jobs in search of alternatives. Furthermore, whilst it remains an important source of employment for rural women in Beijing, in other cities, such as Hangzhou, the importance of domestic service as an entry point into the city appears to have declined through the 1990s, as other types of employment have expanded.

Employment in urban private enterprises in the commerce and service sector

Rather than working as nannies, some women seek employment in urban private enterprises (*getihu* and *siying qiye*) in the commerce and service sector, because the possibilities for earning higher incomes are somewhat greater, although very low wages are also common, and rural workers in private enterprises are often paid no more than one-third or one-quarter of the wage paid to local workers.[46]

For their part, private employers find that rural people are more willing to work in private enterprises than urban people, even with less pay. As Susan Young reports, in the 1980s urban young people were reluctant to take up private employment for fear of missing the benefits and security of work in the state sector. Even unemployed urban youths were sometimes reluctant to take work in a private enterprise because of the political insecurity surrounding the private sector, and because they feared that such work might jeopardise their chances of getting a job in a state or collective enterprise.[47] As a result, a large proportion of employees in urban private enterprises were rural residents. One investigation of 1.05 million *getihu* workers in Shenyang found, for example, that 0.52 million were rural surplus labour. The rest were job-waiting youth, people who had retired or resigned from state-run enterprises and 'socially idle personnel' (including ex-criminals and unemployed women).[48] Another report claimed that in Shanghai by the end of 1987, 56 per cent of about 150,000 workers surveyed were people from rural areas, where previously job-waiting youth and socially idle personnel had dominated employment in private enterprise.[49]

By the mid 1990s, concerns about political insecurity in the private sector had faded, and more and more urbanites were starting up their own private businesses. Other urban residents sought employment in private firms selling computers or offering consultancy services and the like. However, most employment in the private sector – as waiters and kitchen hands in restaurants, and as sales people in small clothing, repair and fruit and vegetable stalls – was shunned by urban people because of low wages, low status, and the lack of any prospects of career advancement, or even job security. Instead, most of such jobs were undertaken by rural people. In Hangzhou in 1995, for example, I found that the vast majority of restaurant waitresses were young rural women. Most worked more than eight hours a day without any days off except at New Year. They had no contracts or other form of job security, and turnover was high. Many said that their bosses looked down on them, and were rude and abusive.[50]

Media reports, also, suggest that both men and women, but especially young rural women, working in urban private enterprises frequently endure poor working conditions, exploitation and abuse. One report claimed that among the fifteen thousand or so workers hired by private enterprises in Beijing, the average workday is 9.4 hours. One quarter of them work more than ten hours. In the food and beverage trade, hired workers, most of whom are young rural women, work more than twelve hours a day. This report also claimed that some private employers also exploit inexperienced young peasant women, by paying only a portion of their wages each month or withholding wages for several months, so that they are forced to keep working against their will.[51]

Other media articles detail cases of sexual harassment and abuse by private employers. Reports of such abuse were a common element, for example, in accounts written by young rural women working in private restaurants and other businesses, published in a series on the experiences of the 'working sisters' ('*dagong mei*') – a term used to refer to young rural women working temporarily in the city – in *Nongjianü Baishitong* (*Rural Women Knowing All*), in 1994 and 1995.

Industry

Employment in urban factories

Some rural women turn to temporary work, not in the private commerce and service sector, but in industry, especially light industry and textiles, where they are once more desired as a cheap, flexible labour force, willing to undertake jobs that urbanites shun. Wages in such work tend to be little better than those that can be earned in domestic work and working conditions are, in many cases, considerably worse. Nevertheless, young women seek such jobs because they feel that their status as an industrial worker will be better than that of a nanny.[52]

Since the 1940s, and earlier in some cities, women have comprised a large proportion of the labour force in light industry and textiles.[53] In the early years of industrialisation most workers were drawn from the countryside, but between the 1950s and 1970s urban women made up almost the entire labour force, with strict limitations being placed on the employment of rural residents.

In the post-Mao era, however, patterns of employment shifted once more. There is a saying in Chinese cities today that 'Heavy industry is not heavy, light industry is not light' ('*zhonggongye bu zhong, qinggongye bu qing*'): it is widely felt that workers in light industries work harder and for longer hours for less pay and under worse conditions than in heavy industry or in the tertiary sector.[54] For this reason, since the early 1980s when young people were no longer allocated work and had a greater variety of employment to choose from, young urban women have been giving textile mills, in particular, a wide berth and have sought jobs in commerce and tourism instead.[55]

In order to alleviate labour shortages, employers in state-run textile industries have turned increasingly to hiring young rural women as contract or temporary workers.[56] In Wuhan, for example, by the mid-1980s approximately 10,000 rural women were working in the textile industry as contract workers. They comprised about one-third of workers on the production line in these industries.[57] At the same time, the private and foreign-funded light industrial and textile firms that sprang up in increasing numbers through the 1980s and 1990s also hired predominantly young, rural women.[58]

In both state and non-state industries, rural women workers suffer harsh working conditions and various forms of discrimination. As will become apparent in the following discussion, however, the scale of exploitation suffered by women in non-state industries is far above that found in the state sector.

State-run factories

In state-run factories, neither urban nor rural workers employed since the mid-1980s have been guaranteed life-long employment, as was previously the case for urban workers. Instead, they are employed on contracts of usually a few years' duration. The contracts stipulate conditions of employment, welfare benefits, company rules and so on. According to a State Council document of October 1991, peasants hired on a temporary basis by state-run industries are to receive more or less the same treatment as urban contract workers. In practice, however, the rural workers often receive fewer subsidies and welfare benefits than other contract workers, and sometimes receive none at all.[59]

Rural workers commonly also receive lower wages than their urban counterparts. In the Hangzhou No. 1 Cotton Factory in 1995, for example, the highest basic wage earned by a rural contract worker was 265 *yuan*, as compared to a maximum of 340 *yuan* for local workers.[60] The majority of both urban and rural production workers in the textile industry are on piece-rate wages. Rural workers are disadvantaged, however, in part because they are employed in tasks defined as being of lowest skill and they are remunerated at the lowest rate. They also tend to be put to work on the oldest, least reliable machines, so their productivity is low and, hence, they earn less.[61]

Working conditions in the textile mills, where rural women are concentrated, are widely acknowledged as being amongst the worst found in state-run industries. According to one report on textile mills in Suzhou, much of the machinery dates back to the 1950s and 1960s and production is highly labour-intensive. Workers are on their feet eight hours or more a day, constantly moving and under a good deal of mental stress. They work in dimly lit workshops with bad air circulation, extreme temperatures and high noise levels. The work is done in three rotating shifts and, unlike other industries which suffer from a labour surplus, work regulations and work quotas here are strictly enforced with very little flexibility. Workers must spend eight hours a day, often without meal breaks, to complete their quota.[62]

Furthermore, rural women workers often work under harsher conditions than urban women, even within the same factory. In Hangzhou textile factories, for example, while urban women work only one or two shifts, rural women are commonly expected to work three shifts. In addition, rural women are concentrated in the oldest workshops with the least reliable machinery and the worst working conditions. Urban women refuse to work in these workshops, but because they are young and ignorant, the rural women workers are more easily exploited.[63]

Private and foreign-funded factories

Whilst rural women working in state-run urban industry suffer various forms of discrimination and hardship, these are as nothing compared to the exploitation and abuse to which peasants working in private and foreign-funded firms are subjected. In many ways, as Dorothy Solinger says, 'these firms – perched on the edge of, or more often beyond, state oversight with their "slave-like conditions", unpaid overtime, abuse and disrespect – hearken back to the miseries of imperialist-run factories of the 1930s, whose "bullying and assaulting of workers" a foreign observer attributed to "pervasive racism"'.[64]

Thus, in Hangzhou in 1995, it appeared that rural workers in the non-state sector were most commonly employed without a contract and with no guarantees of even the most minimal forms of labour protection. In one privately run factory producing sellotape, the noise in the workshops was ear-splitting, and the workers told me that the chemical fumes caused skin problems in those who had been working there more than a few months. Like many others, this factory required a deposit of 300 *yuan* (that is, one month's wages) of each new employee – a measure aimed at preventing workers from leaving within one month. Despite this, turnover was so high that the factory was forced to advertise for new workers every month.[65]

Surveys and media reports, also, detail a range of abuse and exploitation that is in flagrant disregard of the state's regulations. For example, a random sample of 1,500 workers conducted by the Guangdong Provincial Federation of Trade Unions found that 39 per cent of employees were not given contracts upon entering the factory. Sixty-one per cent of them worked seven days a week, and 42 per cent worked ten hours a day or more. In two-thirds of the factories surveyed, incomes were lower than the local average.[66]

Rural workers also suffer humiliation by other employees and employers who look down on them as 'second class' workers and country bumpkins,[67] and physical abuse is common. According to one report, 18 per cent of workers in twenty factories in Guangdong claimed to have been regularly beaten or insulted.[68]

Rural women are far from passively accepting of the poor treatment they receive in textile mills and other factories, however. In the textile mills in Wuhan, for example, as a general rule one-third of rural workers stay only six months before returning home.[69]

Despite the fact that independent trade unions are illegal and the right to strike was removed from the constitution in 1982, there are also numerous instances of rural women workers going on strike. In one instance, more than two thousand workers in a Japanese-owned electronics factory in the Zhuhai Special Economic Zone, most of whom were women from north China, went on strike demanding wage increases and complaining of exploitation, lack of human rights and lack of trade union representation.[70] According to a *China Daily* report, between 1988 and 1993, 250,000 labour disputes and strikes occurred across the country, most of them in joint ventures. Most were sparked by ambiguous contracts, long working hours, low pay and poor safety conditions.[71]

It is clear from the above discussion that in hiring rural women urban employers in a range of trades exploit certain divisions: between male and female, and urban and rural workers, and between 'inside' and 'outside', 'light' and 'heavy' and 'unskilled' and 'skilled' work. Thus, as rural residents, such women can be expected to take on the 'unskilled', low paid tasks that urban women refuse. In service and light industries young rural women are preferred because they are believed to be physiologically and temperamentally more suited to such work than men, who for their part are seen as more suited to 'heavy' work, for example in construction. Women, especially young women, are also regarded as more docile and tractable than men. Furthermore, despite the strikes that have occurred in recent years, employers believe that as temporary workers whose strongest ties are still with their village, rural women are less likely to unite, for example, against poor working conditions. They can also be retrenched more easily in times of business contraction, or, in the case of textile and other light industries, once their eyesight and dexterity have deteriorated. In employers' eyes this advantage is reinforced by the expectation of the women themselves that after a few years they must return to their village to get married and take on domestic and agricultural duties.

From the point of view of rural women, employment in urban areas provides a much sought-after opportunity to get out of the village, and gives them higher incomes than they would have earned in agriculture. As I have argued, a gender division of labour between 'inside' and 'outside' means that fewer rural women than men enjoy such opportunities. Gender divisions of labour, in particular between 'heavy' and 'light' work, also mean that within urban employment, the experiences of rural women and men are rather different. This is not to say, however, that the experiences of the former are, in all respects, *worse* than the latter – in some ways they are, in some ways not.

Thus, on the one hand, it is likely that, as a group, young rural women working in urban areas suffer more exploitation and abuse than rural men, both because of their gender and because a greater proportion of the women are very young. In Chengdu in 1989, for example, a survey found that amongst the floating population, twenty per cent of the women were under the age of eighteen, as compared to thirteen per cent of the men.[72] Furthermore, for rural women exploitation includes not just lower wages and poor working conditions, but also sexual exploitation. As one report put it, 'long working hours in sweatshops, and filthy dormitories to sleep in at night are hazards for both men and women who drift towards the coast in search of work. But it is women who are most vulnerable in a world where strict Communist morality has crumbled and sex has become an exploitable commodity'.[73]

On the other hand, there appears to be no clear-cut difference between the wages earned by rural men in construction and heavy industry, and those earned by rural women in services and light industries – the variation in rural wages between urban enterprises within the same industry is as great as that between rural wages in different industries. And within any one industry, *both* rural women and men are concentrated at the very lowest end of the pay range. Furthermore, the conditions under which rural women work are not necessarily worse than those in which rural men work. The conditions endured by young rural women in textile mills, for example, are poor in comparison to those under which most urban people work, but so are those for rural men in the construction industry.

In this instance, an urban/rural divide, and the creation of an 'underclass' of rural workers in China's cities, is as significant in defining the experience and status of rural women workers, as is a gender division of labour. What then, has rural women's experience been in employment in rural township enterprises, where at least the risk of the stigma of being labelled a 'country bumpkin' is less?[74] This is the question to be addressed in the final section of the chapter.

RURAL WOMEN'S EXPERIENCE OF EMPLOYMENT IN TOWNSHIP ENTERPRISES

Participation in management

The young women who work as nannies or as temporary workers in urban areas have almost no chance to gain a position of any kind of authority or leadership status. For women working in township enterprises the chances are better, but still very slim.

In township- and village-run enterprises leaders are usually appointed by the township or village government or by other leaders.[75] A 1990 survey of four village-run enterprises in a village near Shanghai found that all but one of the sixteen people in charge of accounts or stores were female. However, the 22 skilled workers were all male, as were the six workshop heads, nine sales and marketing personnel and seven factory managers. This was despite the fact that 336 out of 395 of the ordinary workers were female.[76] Similarly, in my own fieldwork, Township Enterprise Bureaux commonly reported to me that women comprised approximately 25 per cent of workers appointed to full time positions in management or administration (including those of factory director and deputy director, workshop director, accountants and statisticians). Most of these women, however, occupied clerical positions, and a smaller number were workshop or section chiefs. In most counties no more than a few per cent of township enterprise factory directors or deputy directors were women.

In Jinniu District, Sichuan, for example, members of the Township Enterprise Bureau told me that of the twelve to fifteen per cent of workers involved full time in management or administration 25 per cent were women. However, of the 1,250 managers and deputy managers of township- and village-run enterprises only eight per cent were women. The representative of the bureau explained this poor representation of women in leadership positions in terms of three factors. First, women's lower levels of education; second, a traditional division of labour in which women work at home and men outside; and third, men's 'greater will power' (*yizhi*).

In Wenjiang County, Sichuan, where women comprise only about two per cent of managers in township-run enterprises, this was explained in the same terms as in Jinniu, with the additional comment that women are not appointed as factory directors because such a job requires a large amount of travelling to attend meetings and to seek out business.

Representatives of the Ling County Township Enterprise Bureau denied that education was a factor in determining the low proportion of women in enterprise leadership positions. Their explanations were otherwise the same as those given by the officials in Jinniu and Wenjiang, except that they also said that men do not like working under a woman, and men are better organisers than women.

Two final factors directly limiting the number of women gaining leadership positions in township enterprises are the small number of women in local government and Party organisations, and the patrilocal marriage system. Township enterprises depend heavily on a network of personal connections for obtaining raw materials and funds, and for securing business, and hence many of the most successful entrepreneurs in this sector are local government or Party cadres or former cadres.[77] Since, as discussed in Chapter 5, relatively very few women are appointed to positions in local governments or Party branches, women are also disadvantaged in relation to the management of township enterprises. Furthermore, in enterprises at village level and below, even those married women who might otherwise have the necessary skills and experience in leading an enterprise are disadvantaged by their break with their natal village and the perception of them as outsiders to the network of personal relations in the village they married into. Their chances of gaining positions of responsibility tend to depend on their husband or father-in-law occupying some kind of leadership role in the village. Ellen Judd, in her investigation of three villages in Shandong, found, for example, that the small number of women in minor positions of responsibility in village-run enterprises were not only all very able, but also well connected through kinship ties. They included a daughter-in-law of the village Party secretary, an uxorilocally married woman and wives of factory heads.[78]

Although I have no statistics, I suspect that in the larger privately run township enterprises the proportion of women in leadership positions is similar to that in township- and village-run enterprises. As discussed in Chapter 8, however, women appear to form a larger proportion of managers in small private enterprises and specialised households. This is in part because many of these are extensions of women's work in the courtyard economy, and in part, I suggest, because the small-scale and family-based nature of such enterprises means that management of them is a less obvious contravention of popular notions that women belong in the 'inside' sphere, whilst the 'outside' sphere of business is a man's realm.

Incomes

The incomes earned in township enterprises are generally lower than those earned in state-run enterprises. In my study of township- and village-run enterprises, average employee incomes (including bonuses) ranged from 100 *yuan* to 200 *yuan* per month (see Appendix 2). These findings are similar to those of the 1991 RDRI/CERU survey, according to which 22.6 per cent of township enterprise employees earned below 100 *yuan*, 65 per cent earned between 101 and 200 *yuan* and 12.4 per cent earned more than 200 *yuan*.[79] In contrast, a 1991 national survey of incomes amongst employees of state-run enterprises found that only 6.8 per cent earned below 100 *yuan*, 52.7 per cent earned between 101 and 200 *yuan* and 40.5 per cent earned more than 200 *yuan*.[80]

In the narrowest sense of the terms, the township enterprises I visited all practised the state policy of equal remuneration for equal work. The Women's Federation reports, however, that sometimes this is not the case.[81] The 1990 World Bank study mentioned above also found that when other variables (county, ownership and size of enterprise, enterprise profitability, worker occupation and age, and days worked) were held constant, women's incomes were fourteen per cent lower than men's.[82]

In practice, these differences in income are further exacerbated by differences in the ownership and industry of the enterprises in which women and men are employed, the profitability of the different enterprises, and the differences in male and female occupations within enterprises. Of these four factors, the latter two are the most significant.

Incomes vary a great deal between enterprises, but according to the 1990 World Bank study, and to the officials I interviewed, this relates primarily to enterprise profitability, which is not necessarily linked either to the ownership of the enterprise or to the type of production it is engaged in. The World Bank study found that an increase of ten percentage points in the ratio of profit to sales of an enterprise was associated with a five per cent increase in the level of pay.[83] It found that there was no significant difference in average profitability between private and other enterprises, and although incomes in private enterprises were somewhat less than in the others, this was mainly a regional effect.[84]

When I asked Township Enterprise Bureaux leaders about differences in levels of pay between light and heavy industries, they said that there was no obvious and consistent difference between the two. In my own limited survey of enterprises, I found only a very marginal difference in average worker incomes between light and heavy industries (see Appendix 2). These findings suggest, at least tentatively, that the gender division of labour, whereby female enterprise workers are found predominantly in light rather than in heavy industry, does not result in lower incomes.

Occupational differences within enterprises are, I would suggest, of far greater significance in determining wage differentials between male and female township enterprise workers. Not surprisingly, the fact that there are so few women in leadership positions means that very few women earn the highest incomes available: the 1990 World Bank study found that technical and management personnel earn between 10 and 30 per cent more than production workers.[85] In addition, while there is a good deal of variation between enterprise wage systems, most assign different wage rates according to the length of time the worker has been employed, or the skill and arduousness of the tasks they perform, or both. Women are disadvantaged in this system, both because they tend to work for shorter periods and because they are concentrated in areas of work defined as 'unskilled' and 'light'. Table 9.2 gives an illustration of the resulting pay differentials in two different enterprises in Huairou County, Beijing.

Somewhat surprisingly, however, the 1991 RDRI/CERU survey found the overall pattern of income distribution amongst female employees in 90 enterprises to be not very different from that amongst male employees. In fact, a slightly larger proportion of male employees (24.0 per cent) than of female employees (21.2 per cent) were found in the 'low' income range (below 100 *yuan*). The biggest differences between male and female incomes were observable in the 'middle' income range. Thus, 49.6 per cent of women had incomes in the 101–150 *yuan* range and 16.6 per cent had incomes in the 151–200 *yuan* range. In contrast, 40.1 per cent of men had incomes in the 101–150 *yuan* range and 23.7 per cent had incomes in the 151–200 *yuan* range.[86]

184

Table 9.2 *Graded wage rates in two township enterprises in Huairou County, Beijing*

(1) Township-run Agricultural Machine Factory

Work Classification	Income (Wage + Bonuses, *yuan*/month)	No. of Male Workers	No. of Female Workers
Heavy	275–300	130	0
Medium-heavy	170	0	20
Light	140–150	0	20
Apprentice	75	6	1

(2) Township-run Clothing Factory

Worker Classification	Income (Wage + Bonuses, *yuan*/month)	No. of Male Workers	No. of Female Workers
Worked more than 3 years	290	40	100
Up to 3 years	180	32	200
Apprentice	100	24	80

Source: Interviews with enterprise managers, September 1989

Working conditions and labour regulations

National regulations governing the protection of female workers in state-run enterprises are usually not implemented in township enterprises, and, in general, working conditions for women (and men) in township enterprises are much poorer than those in the state sector. Beyond this it is difficult to generalise. However, reports published since the mid-1980s, indicating that the Women's Federation has devoted some attention to improving conditions for women in township enterprises, suggest that there are, indeed, significant problems in relation to labour protection, but that at least attempts are being made to remedy these problems.

In May 1986 the Women's Federation, in conjunction with the Ministry of Labour, the Ministry of Health, and the All-China Federation of Trade Unions, promulgated a trial draft of provisional regulations on labour protection for female workers in township enterprises. At the same time, concerted efforts were begun across the country to investigate and improve labour protection and working conditions for female workers in township enterprises, and to have local governments formulate regulations on these matters. By late 1987, thirteen provinces and municipalities had drafted local regulations on labour protection for female workers.[87]

Despite continued calls for improvement in these matters, however, a national investigation of 144 township enterprises, conducted by the Women Workers' Section of the All-China Federation of Trade Unions in 1993, found that still only 40 per cent complied fully with the national Regulations Governing Labour Protection for Female Staff Members and Workers that had been introduced in 1988.[88]

In the following paragraphs I present a brief sketch of actual working conditions and labour protection measures for female workers in township enterprises at the end of the 1980s. This information is drawn, firstly, from my own sample of seventeen relatively large township- and village-run enterprises in rural Beijing, Shandong and Sichuan, and secondly, from a report, published in the internal journal of the Women's Federation, of an investigation of 180 township enterprises (including private enterprises as well as those run by villages and townships) in Shanxi province, undertaken by members of the Shanxi provincial Women's Federation.[89]

The Shanxi Women's Federation reported that working conditions, safety standards and labour protection regulations were generally better in township-run enterprises than in village-run enterprises, and the latter were better than those run privately. Working conditions tended also to be better in older, more established enterprises and those with larger profits, than in more recently established enterprises or those making smaller profits.

It found that in most township enterprises, factory buildings were simple and crude, equipment was backward, working conditions were poor, and there were no safety or protective measures, for example, in handling chemicals. In 90 per cent of township enterprises there were no regulations on labour protection for women during menstruation, pregnancy and lactation. In 36 per cent, although there were no fixed regulations, in fact labour protection measures were taken, but in 54 per cent no protection measures were taken for female workers. In village-run, joint-run and individual-run enterprises there was no protection for female workers.

The Federation reported that in many enterprises working hours were very long – in some as long as fifteen hours a day. They reported that welfare provisions were severely lacking. Among 22 enterprises only one had a clinic. None of them had female workers' washrooms, nursing rooms or change rooms, rest rooms for pregnant women, or child-care facilities.

In contrast to the findings of the Shanxi study, almost all the enterprise managers that I interviewed claimed that they gave maternity leave, the periods generally ranging from 50 to 110 days. Women commonly received a basic wage during this period, but no bonuses. A typical example was a village-run clothing factory in Xindu County, Sichuan, that had printed regulations to the effect that maternity leave was 90 days. During this time, workers on monthly wages would be paid their full wage. Workers on piece-rate wages would be paid 63 *yuan*. This compares to an average piece-rate wage of 70 *yuan* per month and an average income, including bonuses, of 150 *yuan* per month.

Most of the enterprises I visited gave nursing women time off for two periods of 30 minutes each, per day, but only one – a long-established agricultural machinery factory in Huairou County – had a nursing room. Only one enterprise, in Ling County, provided any child-care facilities. Representatives of other enterprises said that women with small children generally left them with relatives or in a village-run kindergarten.[90] The general lack of child-care facilities in township- and village-run enterprises is justified by officials in terms of the small number of women with babies working in such enterprises. However, at the same time this does, of course, reinforce the pattern whereby women withdraw from employment in township- and village-run enterprises after childbirth.

Some, but not all, township- and village-run enterprises that I visited had a Women's Congress or a Trade Union branch, or both, which included a women's representative, though in most of these cases the enterprise had only one women's representative and she was also a full-time worker. In Xindu County, the County Women's Federation advised that for every 30 women workers in a township enterprise there should be one women's representative. In actuality, in one village-run clothing factory that I visited there were three women's representatives for 306 workers, and in a township-run metal door and window frame factory employing 27 women there was one women's representative.

In the Shanxi survey it was found that 53.9 per cent of the township enterprises had established women's congresses, but not all of these had taken any measures toward women's labour protection. Usually the head of the women's congress was a female deputy factory director or another woman involved in management, and other members were full-time workers.

In off-farm non-agricultural employment, as in other areas of work, gendered dichotomies between 'inside' and 'outside', 'light' and 'heavy', and 'unskilled' and 'skilled' have contributed to major differences in the work experiences of women and men. Thus, because of their ties to the family, a larger proportion of female than of male industrial workers are employed in local township enterprises rather than in urban industry, and where women do work away from home it is usually for only a short period before they are married. Similarly, women are concentrated in light industry, commerce, catering and services, while men are employed predominantly in heavy industry, construction and transport work.

Rural women have suffered a number of problems in industrial employment in the post-Mao era. In urban areas, in particular, they have been exploited as both rural workers and as women who, it is assumed, will accept low paid, unpleasant work and harsh working conditions that urban residents shun, will be docile and uncomplaining, and will be good at work requiring dexterity and patience. In rural areas, some township enterprises discriminate against women in recruitment, and in others, women lose their jobs after marriage or the birth of a child. Work in township enterprises is often undertaken in poor conditions with few controls on safety or labour protection, women tend to be concentrated in 'unskilled', lower paid occupations, and there are few women in management. On the other hand, there is surprisingly little difference between the range of incomes earned by women in township enterprises and that earned by men. Furthermore, in recent years there has been a burgeoning growth in small, private enterprises, in which the chances for women to be involved in management and to have a degree of autonomy in their work are greater than in other sectors of non-agricultural employment.

Despite the problems, in comparison to alternative patterns, the process of industrialisation seen in rural China in the post-Mao era has had a number of advantages and benefits for women. The increasing shift toward light industry, commerce, catering and services has, for example, meant that a relatively large and growing proportion of women have been able to fulfil a desire to shift out of agriculture into industrial employment. China's particular focus on developing rural township enterprises has also provided more opportunities for women to be employed in industry. In addition, it has reduced the exploitation of rural women in industrial employment and to some extent has increased the potential for them to develop skills and a sense of autonomy and status, as well as to receive an income.

10

Conclusion

REFORMS undertaken in rural China since 1978, in particular, decollectivisation, diversification of the rural economy and strict family planning, have resulted in both change and continuity in the types of work undertaken by women and men, in gender divisions of labour and in the values associated with those divisions.

In some cases women have been able to take advantage of new work opportunities to enhance their position in society in terms of relations with others and access to, and control of, resources. On the whole, however, women have not benefited from the reforms to the same extent as men, and the reforms have not led to an improvement in rural women's position, either within the family or in the wider community. Rather, certain aspects of women's subordination have intensified and others have been altered or broken down, only to form new patterns of subordination.

In this book I have argued that central to this process has been a reinforcement and a redefinition of conceptual dichotomies between outside/inside, heavy/light and skilled/unskilled work. In each dichotomy the former term is associated with men, the latter with women. These dichotomies can be thought of as sets of values and assumptions relating to work and to gender identity. They shape the work opportunities and choices of women and men and the ways in which different types of work are perceived, and they contribute to the construction and maintenance of gender identities.

On the eve of reform, although women and men were, in reality, by no means confined to work in the 'inside' and 'outside' spheres respectively, expectations embodied in the traditional saying 'Men rule outside, women rule inside' (*'nan zhu wai, nü zhu nei'*) continued to exert an important influence on work patterns. They served to maintain and legitimate a gender division of labour in which domestic work and domestic sidelines were considered 'women's work'. Such work was seen as belonging to an 'inside' sphere in the sense that, firstly, it was physically located primarily within the home or courtyard. Secondly, it was seen as involving interaction largely only with family members, and it was undertaken for the benefit of the family, rather than for the collective.

Between the 1950s and the 1970s the state had made some attempts to reduce women's work in the 'inside' sphere. While these attempts met with little lasting success, a significant side-effect was the devaluation of 'inside' work as secondary to 'outside' production for the collective, and a corresponding view of women who were engaged primarily in such work as contributing less to society than others.

Although the CCP under Mao Zedong had increased women's involvement in 'outside' production undertaken for the collective and in political and economic leadership, in the late 1970s women's participation in these areas continued to be constrained both by beliefs that the 'outside' realm was a 'man's world' and by the demands of 'inside work' on their energy and time.

In addition, women's involvement in collective production was shaped by assumptions that women were less capable of 'heavy' and 'skilled' work than men. Such work was generally remunerated at higher rates than 'light' or 'unskilled' tasks. The categorisation of tasks as 'heavy' or 'light', 'skilled' or 'unskilled' varied, however, from one locality to another, and was, in many cases, linked with male peasant attempts to control labour-saving technology and to win higher remuneration rates for their work.

As a result of reforms that were initiated in rural China in 1978 there have been radical re-conceptualisations of the boundaries defining outside/inside, heavy/light and skilled/unskilled dichotomies. Nevertheless, I have argued here that since 1978 women have been constrained by the fact that such dichotomies still operate, and indeed have in some respects been reinforced. This has meant that despite major changes in work patterns, in the nature of different types of work and the ways in which work is organised, the rural reforms have resulted in neither a breakdown of gender divisions of labour, nor, on the whole, in a re-evaluation of women's and men's sides of the divisions. Instead, what is happening is that the content of women's work and men's work is changing, but the divisions remain, as does the secondary value placed on women's work, relative to men's.

Thus, shifts in strategies for economic development, and corresponding improvements in rural living conditions, have changed the nature of domestic work and the amount of time spent in such work by individual women. In particular, the improvement of basic amenities and the greater availability of consumer goods have reduced the time and effort required for domestic work. The implementation of strict family planning policies has also reduced domestic workloads in some families, although most continue to have at least two children.

No change has occurred, however, in the perception of domestic work as 'inside' women's work. On the other hand, the notion that women are, first and foremost, domestic workers has been reinforced by the state in the post-Mao era in its emphasis on women's roles as mothers and as the keepers of social stability and morality. The low regard in which domestic work is held, however, has been unaffected by reform. Thus, despite the value placed by the state on motherhood, and also despite the fact that decollectivisation and the diversification of the rural economy have blurred the boundaries between domestic work and income-generating work, a discourse in which the contribution of women's domestic work to the economy is trivialised, and in which domestic work is seen as petty drudgery rather than as 'real work', remains strong.

Domestic sidelines, now more commonly known as the 'courtyard economy', have also continued to be regarded as 'inside' work that is 'particularly suited to women'. Indeed, this view has been reinforced by the state, it being a central element in the encouragement of work in this sector as a source of employment for the mostly female labour deemed 'surplus' to the needs of agriculture, following the introduction of the production responsibility system. The characterisation of domestic sidelines as inside, women's work that is secondary to the main income-earning activities of the family has also enabled the state and individual capitalists to exploit women's labour in lines of production that are most commonly either poorly paid, or are highly profitable for only a short period.

As I have argued, however, over the last fifteen years work in the courtyard economy has also had a number of advantages for women. It has, for example, provided them with a greater degree of autonomy than industrial employment. In addition, some women have been able to use their work in this sector as a springboard into larger-scale, more profitable production, and to gain entry into the male, outside world of business leadership. It is, still, however, more common for management of a production venture to be taken over by the male head of the family once it has developed beyond a certain size.

The courtyard economy is now one of the most dynamic sectors of the rural economy, and, as is recognised by the All-China Women's Federation, it is possible that in the coming years women will develop their activities in this sector in such a way as to improve their economic and social status. I have argued, however, that the extent to which women will benefit from the courtyard economy or will be exploited depends very much on the kind of support and training with which they are provided.

Since 1978 some of the most radical shifts in rural gender divisions of labour and the ways in which work is perceived have occurred in relation to agriculture. In the early stages of reform, and still today in some less developed regions, a shortage of employment opportunities has led to the withdrawal of women from agriculture. This has been justified both by reference to the constraints on women imposed by their responsibility for 'inside' work, and through a re-assertion that women cannot do agricultural work because they are not physically strong enough and they lack the necessary technical skills.

In contrast, however, the expansion of opportunities for industrial employment that has characterised the reform process in more developed regions has led to a shift of men out of agriculture into more prestigious industrial jobs, while women have been left with the responsibility for agriculture, which is now regarded as the least desirable form of employment. This new gender division of labour has been achieved through, and legitimated by, a re-characterisation of agriculture as 'inside' work. Ironically, also, following the devaluation of agricultural work and its conceptual shift from the 'outside' to the 'inside' realm, the same references to women's physiological characteristics that were previously used as a justification for the restriction of women's employment in agricultural work are now being used to justify a concentration of women in such work.

The majority of rural women in the post-Mao era have continued to work either in the home or in the fields, but economic development has also involved major increases in the number of rural women, especially young, unmarried women, employed in off-farm non-agricultural work. The experiences of women in such work, as in other sectors, are shaped by gendered dichotomies and divisions of labour between outside/inside, heavy/light and skilled/unskilled work, and, in the case of employment in urban areas, by a rural/urban divide. Young rural women working in urban areas, for example as nannies, and as temporary workers in the private service sector and in light industries and textile mills, are exploited by employers both as young women who, it is assumed, will be naive, docile and uncomplaining, and as rural residents who will accept temporary, low-paid menial work that urban workers shun.

Fewer rural women than men work in urban areas, however, and they usually return to the countryside when they are in their early twenties in order to get married and to take over responsibility for the 'inside' sphere of domestic work, domestic sidelines and agriculture. Larger numbers of women work in local township enterprises, although even there they comprise only about 30 to 40 per cent of the labour force on average. They are concentrated in light industries and in unskilled occupations, with very few being involved in management. Average differences in income between male and female workers do not appear to be very marked however.

Whilst I have focused here on the impact of reform on women's work and gender divisions of labour, I have emphasised throughout that the changes that have occurred in divisions of labour and in the social implications of those divisions cannot be understood simply as a straightforward consequence of the

193

implementation of reform policies by the state. It must be recognised, first of all, that the changes in gender divisions of labour and in conceptual dichotomies that I have discussed in this study have both fed into, and themselves been constructed, maintained, and legitimated through other aspects of gender relations. For example, the continuation of the patrilocal marriage system, in which most women leave their natal family and village to join their husband's family upon marriage, leads to the perception of women as only temporary members of their natal family. As a consequence, girls are often given less education than boys, a problem that has become more serious in recent years as a result of rising education fees. In addition, upon marriage women are regarded as strangers to their new family and village, and to the kin and friendship networks that are so important in rural China for undertaking business and acquiring power, as well as for providing emotional and material support. Both their lower educational attainments and their marginalisation in local networks in turn disadvantage women in the 'outside' spheres of industrial employment, entrepreneurship and formal politics.

Gender segregation in education and the particular activities undertaken by the small numbers of women in positions of power, in particular the members of the Women's Federation, also shape, and are shaped by, perceptions of work and gender identity, and gender divisions of labour. Thus, a concentration of women in 'light' work, such as textiles and handicraft production, and in work associated with the 'inside' sphere, including domestic work and the court-yard economy, leads to an emphasis on training in these areas in vocational education for girls, and in the campaigns run by the Women's Federation on behalf of rural women. This in turn reinforces the view that women are most suited to 'light' and 'inside' work, whilst 'heavy' and 'outside' work is most appropriate for men.

Gendered dichotomies between heavy/light and outside/inside work have been further bolstered over the past fifteen years by state-sponsored shifts in social and political values. These shifts, transmitted through official pronouncements, through media articles, and through education, have included a reaction against women who are successful in the 'outside' sphere of politics and areas of 'male' work, such as heavy industry, as the epitome of Cultural Revolution-style radicalism and anarchy. The rejection of the Maoist slogan 'What men can do, women can do too', and the emphasis on physiological and psychological differences between the sexes, apparent in a vast array of media articles as well as in education, is also related to the current leadership's view that divisions of labour in general contribute to economic development and modernisation. Finally, a strong emphasis on the role of woman as mother and nurturer has been a central element in the post-Mao state's attempts to curb social disorder and to promote 'spiritual civilisation'.

Aside from examining the links between gender divisions of labour and other aspects of gender relations, we must also take account of the fact that changes in gender relations, along with other social, economic and political change, have been the outcome of a complex set of interactions between state and society, rather than the result merely of a top-down state imposition of policies on the people. Thus, for example, the shifts in social and political values discussed above would probably not have taken place were it not for the fact that the new values have received strong support from a wide section of the population, including women. To refer back to another example, the emergence of domestic sidelines and the 'courtyard economy' as one of the most important areas of employment for rural women cannot be understood solely in terms of a state manipulation of women as a cheap and flexible labour force, nor solely as a result of unequal power relations between women and men, although these factors are of great importance. It must also be recognised that women themselves choose to work in this sector because of certain advantages that it offers in comparison with other types of employment.

In this book I have developed an approach to the study of gender relations which integrates an examination of the material causes and consequences of gender divisions of labour with a study of the cultural values attached to those divisions, and which takes account of the complex interrelations between gender divisions of labour and other aspects of gender relations. I have used this approach to analyse the key dimensions of change in gender divisions of labour in rural China in a period in which major social, political and economic reforms have taken place. My analysis suggests that in rural China, divisions of labour and the meanings associated with those divisions are strongly influenced by the fact that a cultural dichotomy between 'men' and 'women' is linked with other dichotomies, by the particular forms those dichotomies take, and how they change. This is something that must be taken into account if the impact of reform on gender relations is to be understood, and if attempts to overcome women's subordination in rural China are to succeed.

It is to be hoped that in the future more detailed micro-studies will be undertaken in which regional differences in gender divisions of labour in rural China and the meanings attached to them are explored, and in which divisions within particular areas of work – for example in individual industries – are examined in more detail than was possible in mine. I would anticipate that such research would bear out the importance of the conceptual dichotomies discussed in this book, and may reveal that other dichotomies, for example between 'dangerous' and 'safe' industrial work, also shape gender relations in rural China.

I have made comparisons here between aspects of gender relations in rural China and in other developing societies. Furthering these comparisons may provide additional insights into the relationship between economic and social development and change in gender relations. I would argue, in addition, that while the particular conceptual dichotomies discussed in this book may not operate in societies other than rural China, the theoretical framework that I have developed may prove useful for the examination of the mechanics of change in gender relations in other societies.

Appendices

Appendix 1: Summary of information on sample families in rural Beijing, Shandong and Sichuan

(mu = 0.067 hectares; fen = 0.1 mu; li = 0.01 mu)

Location and Family No.	Family Membership	Amount of Cultivated Land and Crops Grown	Division of Labour in Agriculture*	Division of Labour in Other Remunerated Work	Division of Labour in Domestic Work
Huairou County, Beijing 1	Interviewee (54), husband, son, daughter-in-law, granddaughter (pre-school)	3 mu – corn and wheat	Son and daughter-in-law do field work. Interviewee runs specialised household, rearing pigs. She hires 30 person-days/ year to help.	Husband is retired worker. Son does occasional trading. Daughter-in-law works in factory.	Daughter-in-law makes breakfast. Interviewee does rest of the cooking, cleaning, makes clothes and looks after grandchild.
2	Interviewee (46), husband, 2 daughters, young male relative	3 mu – corn and wheat	Interviewee runs a specialised household, rearing pigs. Her daughters and male relative help. The four of them do field work.	Husband works in army factory in another township and comes home once a month.	Interviewee does all domestic work.
3	Interviewee (37), husband, 2 sons (at school), father- and mother-in-law	4 mu – vegetables	Father- and mother-in-law do most field work.	Interviewee runs a private enterprise making quilt covers and hires workers. Husband works in grocery shop.	Mother-in-law does most of the domestic work. She raises 13 chickens. Interviewee spends 3hrs/day on domestic work, mainly cooking. She also does the shopping.
4	Interviewee (36), husband, son and daughter (both at school)	58 mu – grain specialised household 2 mu – grain 3.2 fen – vegetables	Interviewee runs grain specialised household and works 7hrs/day in fields. Husband runs a specialised household rearing pigs, 2hrs/ day, and helps wife in fields. 4–5hrs/day. During busy season, the children and relatives help.		Interviewee does all domestic work.

5	Interviewee (44), husband, son and daughter (both at school)	3 mu – grain 4 mu – vegetables	Interviewee runs specialised household, growing fungi for Chinese medicine.	Husband is a carpenter.	Interviewee generally cooks, though husband sometimes helps. Interviewee does the washing and shopping. Whoever is around cleans.
6	Interviewee (27), husband, son (at school)	a few fen – vegetables and corn	Interviewee does field work. She and husband run specialised household rearing cows. Each work 4hrs/day. He does the heavier work.		Interviewee does all domestic work.
Ling County, Shandong 7	Interviewee (37), husband, son, daughter (both at school) father- and mother-in-law	3 mu – sesame and grain		Interviewee and husband run specialised household processing sesame seed paste. She does 6hrs/day.	Interviewee raises 2 pigs and several chickens. Mother-in-law does the rest of the domestic work.
8	Interviewee (48), husband, 3 children (at school and university)	All land (1 mu 2 fen) given to nephew		They run a private hotel.	Interviewee does all domestic work.
9	Interviewee (43), husband, daughter, son (at school)	3 mu plus 2 mu wild land that interviewee developed herself; grain for own consumption; cotton and vegetables to sell.	Interviewee, husband and daughter grow grain and cotton. Husband tends vegetables. Interviewee, husband and daughter all involved in raising bees.		Interviewee raises 4 pigs and she and daughter do the shopping. Daughter does the rest.

Location and Family No.	Family Membership	Amount of Cultivated Land and Crops Grown	Division of Labour in Agriculture*	Division of Labour in Other Remunerated Work	Division of Labour in Domestic Work
10	Interviewee (39), husband, 4 daughters (at school), father- and mother-in-law	5 *mu* – cotton 7 *fen* – vegetables for own consumption	Interviewee does field work 6hrs/day. (She does not grow much grain because it is too much work for one woman and they do not need it for livestock feed.)	Husband is electrician.	Mother-in-law does some washing. Otherwise inter- viewee does all domestic work.
11	Interviewee (37), husband, son and daughter (both at school) mother-in-law	4 *mu* – cotton 5 *fen* – vegetables	Interviewee does most of the field work, 5hrs/day. Husband shares work tending vegetables.	Husband works at cotton collection station 7–8 months/year.	Interviewee does all domestic work.
12	Interviewee (60), husband, son, daughter	3 *mu* 5 *fen* – cotton and grain 3 *fen* – vegetables for own consumption	Interviewee plants vegetables. Son plants cotton and grain.	Son and daughter are workers in township-run enterprises.	Interviewee does all domestic work. She raises a few ducks.
13	Interviewee (28), husband, (at school)	2 *mu* – grain for own consumption	Interviewee's uncle grows grain for them.	Interviewee runs a private enterprise sewing, and takes in students. Husband runs a private enterprise repairing bicycles.	Interviewee does the shopping and shares other domestic work with husband.
14	Interviewee (40), husband, daughter, 4 other children at school	no land		Interviewee and husband sell groceries. Oldest daughter works in county medicine factory.	Interviewee does all domestic work. She raises a few ducks.

	Household	Land	Field work	Other work	Domestic work
15	Interviewee (33), husband, 2 daughters (at school)	2 *mu* – cotton 2.5 *mu* – corn and wheat alternating 4 *fen* – vegetables for own consumption	Interviewee and husband each spend about 6hrs/day in fields. Husband tends vegetables.		Interviewee does all domestic work. She raises 20 chickens and 3 pigs.
16	Interviewee (51), husband, 2 children (at school)	2.7 *mu* – wheat and corn alternating 0.5 *mu* – vegetables and cotton alternating	Interviewee does the field work – 6hrs/day and raises 10 chickens and 2 pigs – 1hr/day.	Husband works 6hrs/day as cook in a bank.	Husband somtimes helps raise the 2 pigs and 10 chickens, and 2 daughters do their own washing. Otherwise, interviewee does all.
17	Interviewee (31), husband, 2 sons (at school)	5 *mu* – grain, cotton and vegetables	Interviewee and husband work in fields. She does 6hrs/day.	Husband drives tractor part-time.	Husband helps raise 2 pigs and 3 sheep. Otherwise, interviewee does all domestic work.
Xindu County, Sichuan 18	Interviewee (23), mother, father, brother, child (pre-school), husband's sister	1 *mu* 5 *fen* – rice, wheat and rape 4 *fen* – vegetables	Father does field work, 1hr/day. During busy season they all help.	Interviewee is village government secretary. Mother, father and brother work in local township enterprises. Mother also sews flour bags at home as outwork for county government. Interviewee pays husband's sister to look after child. Husband works away in army.	Whoever is free tends the 2 pigs and 4–5 chickens, and does the cooking. Her mother does the cleaning. Interviewee and her mother wash large items such as quilts, otherwise everyone does their own washing. Interviewee washes her child's clothes. She and her father do the shopping.

Location and Family No.	Family Membership	Amount of Cultivated Land and Crops Grown	Division of Labour in Agriculture*	Division of Labour in Other Remunerated Work	Division of Labour in Domestic Work
19	Interviewee (35), husband, child (at school)	2 mu 7 fen – rice, wheat and rape 3 fen 2 li – vegetables for own consumption	All three do field work, 1/2hr per day.	Interviewee is village accountant. Husband is carpenter.	Interviewee does most of the cooking, though husband also does some. She and husband go shopping together and both do washing. Interviewee, husband and child all do the cleaning.
20	Interviewee (47), husband, children and spouses, 2 grandchildren (pre-school) Total: 11 people	4 mu – rice, wheat rape and vegetables 4 fen – vegetables	Husband and children's spouses do field work, before and after work in factory each day, and on Sunday.	Husband is deputy head of village. All children and their spouses work in local glass factory.	Interviewee does all, including looking after her grandchildren. She raises 6 pigs and 10 chickens.
21	Interviewee (60), son, daughter-in-law (urban household reg) husband dead	1.3 mu – vegetables, rice, wheat and rape	Interviewee does field work and 2 married-out daughters help.	Son and daughter-in-law run specialised household making sofas.	Interviewee does all domestic work. She also takes her granddaughter to and from kindergarten.
22	Interviewee (54), husband, son, daughter-in-law, grandson	2.7 mu – rice, wheat and rape 3 fen – pig feed and vegetables	Son does most field work, 2hrs/day. On Sunday interviewee, husband and daughter-in-law also help.	Husband is party secretary in local glass factory. Son and daughter-in-law also work in glass factory.	Husband helps with cleaning the house and the 5 pigs and 100 chickens. Her son does the shopping on his way home from work. Interviewee does the rest.

	Household	Land	Field work	Employment	Domestic work
23	Interviewee (50), husband, 3 sons	3.25 mu – rice, wheat and vegetables. 3 fen – pig feed and vegetables	Youngest son (17) does field work, 7hrs/day.	Husband is deputy head of village government agricultural company. Oldest son is in army. Middle son works in a factory.	Interviewee does all domestic work. She raises 6 pigs, 10 chickens, 4–5 ducks and 1 goose.
24	Interviewee (41), husband, daughter, 2 sons (at school)	3 mu – rice, wheat and rape. 3 fen – vegetables	Interviewee's younger brother tends vegetables. The others do the rest of the field work.	Husband runs a restaurant and also works as a doctor. Interviewee runs a weighing station and helps in restaurant. Daughter works in a factory.	Interviewee does the shopping and most of the washing and cleaning. They do not cook at home.
Jinniu County, Sichuan 25	Interviewee (45), husband, 2 sons	1 mu	The land is given to neighbours to cultivate. The neighbours pay tax and fulfil government quotas and keep remaining profit.	Interviewee and husband run a hotel. One son is an electrician, one works for the railways.	Interviewee and husband do shopping for home and hotel. Cooking done by cooks hired for hotel. Interviewee does the rest.
26	Interviewee (36), husband, daughter (at school)	4 fen – grain for own consumption. 3.2 fen – vegetables for own consumption. 1 mu 5 fen – vegetables sold to the state	Interviewee and husband work in the fields, 2hrs at noon, after work until dark and all day Sunday. She is stronger and does most of the heavy work (he was a student for a long time). She carries water and fertiliser and spreads it. He digs, plants and pulls out weeds.	Interviewee works in small collective construction materials factory. Husband works in state factory.	Interviewee raises 5 chickens and does the shopping. She cooks breakfast and lunch. Child cooks evening meal. The whole family is involved in domestic work.
27	Interviewee (39), husband, son (at school)	2 mu 7 fen – rice and wheat for own consumption. 3 fen – vegetables for own consumption	Interviewee does most field work, 20hrs/week, before and after work in the factory. They also hire 5 person-days/year to help with field work.	Interviewee and husband work in a doufu factory (lianheti).	Interviewee does all domestic work. She raises 22 chickens.

Location and Family No.	Family Membership	Amount of Cultivated Land and Crops Grown	Division of Labour in Agriculture*	Division of Labour in Other Remunerated Work	Division of Labour in Domestic Work
28	Interviewee (37), husband, daughter (at school)	1 *mu* – grapes for market 3.5 *fen* – mushrooms for market 6 *fen* – grain for own consumption	Interviewee and husband do field work. She does the day-to-day work. They hire a young man to tend the mushrooms.	Husband is village government cadre.	Interviewee does the cooking. Husband sometimes helps. Interviewee does the washing. The whole family does the cleaning. Interviewee and husband do the shopping.
29	Interviewee (43), husband (urban household reg.), 2 sons (1 at school)	3 *fen* – vegetables Chicken farm built on remaining land – 1 *mu* 2 *fen*	Interviewee runs specialised household raising chickens. She and 2 hired workers do most of the work. 1 son helps.	Husband works in chemical factory in Chengdu.	Interviewee does all domestic work. She washes workers' clothes as well as her family's.
30	Interviewee (37), husband, daughter (at school)	2 *mu* 2 *fen* – rice, wheat and rape for own consumption 4 *fen* – vegetables for own consumption	Interviewee does the field work in the afternoons.	Husband works in township-run construction company. Interviewee runs a private sewing enterprise and gives outwork to 15 women.	Interviewee does the washing, cleaning and shopping. Mother-in-law does the cooking.
31	Interviewee (35), husband, son (at school)	2 *mu* 5 *fen* – rice, wheat and vegetables 3 *fen* – vegetables	Interviewee grows mushrooms and raises 10 chickens for own consumption. 4–5 person-days/ month hired. Husband helps with mushrooms when he comes home for lunch each day.	Husband works in factory.	Interviewee and husband both do domestic work.
32	Interviewee, husband (urban household reg.), 2 daughters, 1 son (handicapped or ill), mother	2 *mu* 5 *fen* – grain for own consumption 5 *fen* – vegetables for own consumption	Interviewee does most field work.	Interviewee runs a private enterprise machine-knitting jumpers. She hires 10 women. Husband works in state-run factory in Chengdu.	Interviewee's 70-year-old mother raises a few chickens. 2 pigs tended by whoever has time. Most of the rest of the domestic work is done by the interviewee's two daughters.

	Household	Land	Outside/field work	Domestic work
33	Interviewee (38), husband, son (at school)	1.76 *mu* – wheat, rice and rape for own consumption 2.5 *fen* – vegetables for own consumption and pig feed	During busy season husband is most important worker in fields, but otherwise she does all the work – about 1 day/ week.	Husband is accountant in village factory.	Interviewee does all domestic work. She raises 12 chickens and 3 pigs.
34	Interviewee (38), husband, 2 daughters (at school)	3 *mu* – rice, wheat, rape for sale and for own consumption 4 *fen* – vegetables for own consumption	Interviewee and husband both work in fields every day. There is no division of labour, but he works 1 hr/day more.	Husband does some temporary work in local factory during the agricultural slack season.	Interviewee and husband both do the shopping. Inter- viewee does the rest of the domestic work. She raises 1 chicken and 4 pigs.
Wenjiang County, Sichuan 35	Interviewee (38), husband, mother- and father-in-law, daughter, son (at school)	4 *mu* 5 *fen* – grain for own consumption and to meet state requirement 5 *fen* – pig feed	Interviewee does the day-to-day field work, watering and weeding 1 hr/day. During busy season all work more than 10 hrs/day in the fields. Husband does the planting. They ask others to help with the harvesting. Interviewee runs specialised household raising chickens. Husband does the buying and selling for this business. Daughter also works in the specialised household.	Husband works in township hospital 4 hrs/day.	Interviewee does the shopping. Interviewee does the cooking, cleaning and washing for herself, husband and parents- in-law. Daughter does the cooking, cleaning, and washing for herself and her brother. 4 pigs kept – unclear who tends them.
36	Interviewee (73), son, daughter-in- law, granddaughter, grandson (at school), husband dead	5 *mu* – rice, wheat and rape 5 *fen* – pig feed and vegetables for own consumption	Daughter-in-law does the field work. They are all involved in running a specialised household raising chickens.		Daughter-in-law does all domestic work. She raises 5 pigs.

Location and Family No.	Family Membership	Amount of Cultivated Land and Crops Grown	Division of Labour in Agriculture*	Division of Labour in Other Remunerated Work	Division of Labour in Domestic Work
37	Interviewee (55), husband, daughter, son (at school)	3 *mu* 5 *fen* – rice, wheat and rape 3 *fen* – vegetables for own consumption	They all do field work on Sunday.	Husband is retired teacher with pension. They run a tailoring school. Interviewee and daughter teach and sew, husband manages business deals and advertisement.	Interviewee does the shopping. Daughter does the rest. She raises 4 pigs and 5 chickens.
38	Interviewee (50), husband, daughter, son (at school)	3 *mu* 5 *fen* – all used for flowers and bonsai, except a few *fen* for vegetables for own consumption	Interviewee runs a specialised household growing flowers and bonsais. Husband, son and daughter help.	Husband is retired accountant.	All family members do domestic work.
39	Interviewee (38), husband, 2 daughters (1 at school), son	7 *mu* – wheat, pig feed and rice 2 *fen* – vegetables for pig feed and own consumption	During the slack season interviewee does the field work, 2 hrs/day, hoeing, watering, putting on fertiliser. During busy season she is helped by her children.	Husband works away in construction and only returns once a year at Spring Festival. Son and one daughter make car parts at home, for a township-run factory.	Interviewee does all domestic work. She raises 7 pigs and 12 chickens.
40	Interviewee (35), husband, mother-in-law, son (at school)	2 *mu* – wheat 1 *mu* – rice and wheat alternating 2 *fen* – pig feed	Interviewee manages field work during slack season and all are involved during busy season. Interviewee and mother-in-law raise 30 pigs and 10–20 chickens.	Husband is village Party Secretary.	Mother-in-law does the cooking sometimes. Interviewee does the rest.
41	Interviewee (60), son and daughter-in-law (urban household reg), grandson, husband dead	8 *fen* – rice, wheat and rape 1 *fen* – vegetables	Daughter-in-law does field work and raises 18 pigs, 13 chickens	Son works in county construction team.	Interviewee does the shopping and helps with the cooking. Daughter-in-law does the rest.

	Household	Land/crops	Field work	Domestic work
42	Interviewee (33), husband, son (at kindergarten)	a few *fen* – rice, wheat	Husband does field work (interviewee is crippled).	Husband is a contract truck driver.	Either the interviewee or her husband do the shopping. She does the rest. She raises a few chickens and 2 ducks.
43	Interviewee (40), husband, daughter, son (at school)	3 *mu* – wheat, rice and rape 4 *fen* – pig and chicken feed	During the busy season all do field work. They run a specialised household raising chickens. No division of labour, but she and daughter do longest hours.		The interviewee's father does the shopping for the two families. She and her daughter do the rest. Daughter raises pigs, 1 hr/day.
Guan County, Sichuan 44	Interviewee (66), husband, son, daughter-in-law, 2 grandchildren (at school)	4 *mu* 7 *fen* – rice and vegetables	Husband, son and daughter-in-law work 8 hrs/day in fields. Interviewee works 2 hrs/day in fields. They also raise goldfish and grow grapes.		Interviewee looks after her grandchildren. Daughter-in-law does all the domestic work. She raises 10 chickens and a few pigs.
45	Interviewee (33), husband, son (at school)	2 *mu* 1 *fen* – rice, wheat and vegetables	Interviewee works 5 hrs/day in fields, husband works 6 hrs/day in fields. He carries water and fertiliser, she pours it onto the fields.		Whoever has time does the shopping. Interviewee does the rest. She raises 6 chickens, 2 ducks and 2 pigs.
46	Interviewee (51), husband, 4 children, daughter-in-law, grandchild	3 *mu* 5 *fen* – rice and wheat 2.8 *fen* – rice and wheat	Interviewee works 6 hrs/day in field. Husband works 8 hrs/day in field. Women do weeding and harvesting. Men do ploughing using tractor. Men apply water and fertiliser.	Husband is a carpenter. 2 children work in factory.	Interviewee tends the pigs, does the washing and shopping for herself and her husband, and the cooking and cleaning for the whole family. Her husband helps with the cleaning.

Location and Family No.	Family Membership	Amount of Cultivated Land and Crops Grown	Division of Labour in Agriculture*	Division of Labour in Other Remunerated Work	Division of Labour in Domestic Work
47	Interviewee (48), husband, 3 sons, 3 daughters-in-law, 2 grandchildren	5 *mu* 9 *fen* – grain and vegetables	Interviewee and daughters-in-law do field work. Sons help a bit during busy season. Two daughters-in-law raise 170 pigs. One son and an elderly hired worker grow bonsai and flowers.	Two sons drive a tractor for other people. Husband runs a private enterprise crushing rocks.	Interviewee does the sweeping. One daughter-in-law does the cooking. All the women in the family do the washing. Interviewee does the shopping.
48	Interviewee (39), husband, mother- and father-in-law, 3 sons	3 *mu* – grain and vegetables	Interviewee does the field work, a few hours each day.	Husband and sons are contract loading workers.	Mother-in-law washes her own and her husband's clothes and helps tend the 3 ducks, 5–6 chickens, 6 geese, and 7 pigs. Interviewee does the rest.
49	Interviewee (48), husband, son, daughter-in-law, baby-grandchild, nanny	1 *mu* 2 *fen* – rice, wheat and rape	Interviewee does field work during slack season, 1 hr/day. During busy season the others help.	Interviewee is an accountant in a local enterprise 6 hrs/day. Husband, son and daughter-in-law work in a factory. Daughter-in-law works 6 hrs/day (she is nursing a baby). Husband and son work 8 hrs/day.	Interviewee does the shopping. She and daughter-in-law share the rest. The two take it in turns to look after interviewee's grandchild. They also hire a nanny for this.
50	Interviewee (27), husband, daughter (at school)	2.65 *mu* – rice, wheat and vegetables	Interviewee does field work – 2–3 hrs/day, 8 hrs in busy season. Husband helps with heavy work in busy season.	Husband drives a tractor for an income.	Interviewee does all, except that if it is raining and he cannot go out, husband helps her. Interviewee raises 2 pigs and 8 chickens.

	Household	Land	Agricultural work	Employment	Domestic work
51	Interviewee (36), husband (urban household reg), daughter (at school)	1 *mu* 2 *fen* – rice, wheat and rape 1 *fen* – vegetables for own consumption	Interviewee does the field work. During slack season this amounts to 1/2 hr/day for vegetables, 1 month/year for grain. During busy season she works 10 hrs/day for 15 days and 3 hrs/day for 15 days. Husband helps during busy season. Last year interviewee grew sugar cane, but it was too much trouble.	Interviewee works in factory 8 hrs/day and during slack season makes plastic grain bags at home. Husband works in township hospital 8 hrs/day.	Interviewee does the shopping and washing and raises 2 pigs. Her husband helps with other domestic work 1 hr/day.
Mianyang County, Sichuan 52	Interviewee (48), husband, 2 sons (1 at school)	3.88 *mu* – grain and vegetables	Two hired workers do the field work and raise 37 pigs.	Interviewee runs a private enterprise in food processing. She is helped by one son and her husband who is a retired worker. They also hire 16 workers for this business.	Interviewee and husband do the shopping. She does some washing and sweeping. Two hired workers do the rest.
53	Interviewee (38), husband (urban household reg), 2 children (at school)	3 *mu*	Workers hired for the cake business help with field work when the electricity stops.	Interviewee runs a private enterprise making cakes, and hires 12 workers. Husband works in Public Security Bureau.	Interviewee is helped by a hired worker.
54	Interviewee (34), husband (urban household reg), daughter (at school)	7.2 *fen* – vegetables	Interviewee does field work, 2hrs/day.	Husband is a factory worker. Interviewee dredges sand from river.	Interviewee does all domestic work.
55	Interviewee (52), husband, daughter, son	1.17 *mu* – vegetables		Husband is a tax collector. He is retired on a pension, but continues some employment. Daughter works in factory. Son is a temporary worker.	Interviewee does most of the domestic work. Daughter and husband help.

Location and Family No.	Family Membership	Amount of Cultivated Land and Crops Grown	Division of Labour in Agriculture*	Division of Labour in Other Remunerated Work	Division of Labour in Domestic Work
56	Interviewee (37), husband (urban household reg), 2 children	5 *fen* – vegetables	Interviewee does most of the field work, 2 hrs/week.	Interviewee runs a grocery shop and a recreation room. Husband works in a fertiliser shop.	Interviewee and husband share domestic work.
57	Interviewee (47), husband, mother, daughter	1 *mu* 4 *fen* – vegetables	Interviewee does most of the field work, 1 hr/day. Husband and daughter do 1/2 hr/day each.	Interviewee and daughter run a tailoring school with 90 students. Husband works in a state factory.	Interviewee's mother does the cooking and raises 2 pigs. The rest of the family help with domestic work.
58	Interviewee (38), husband, mother, mother- and father-in-law, son (at school)	2.12 *mu* – vegetables	Interviewee does 6–7 hrs/day field work, husband does 1 hr/day.	Mother- and father-in-law are retired cadres on pensions.	Interviewee does most of the domestic work. She raises 2 pigs.
59	Interviewee (26), husband, son (at school)	1 *mu* 8 *fen* – vegetables	Interviewee does the field work, 8 hrs/day.	Husband works in a village-run factory and lives elsewhere.	Interviewee does all domestic work. She used to raise pigs, but stopped because she does not have time.
60	Interviewee (28), husband, mother- and father-in-law, daughter (pre-school)	1 *mu* 5 *fen* – vegetables	Interviewee and husband do 1/2 hr/day field work each.	Interviewee works in village-run fur factory. Husband is an accountant in a township-run enterprise.	All adult family members involved in domestic work. Parents-in-law raise 11 chickens. Husband does 2 hrs/day.

* Times given refer to agricultural slack season, unless otherwise stated.

Source: Interviews with rural women, August–December 1989

Appendix 2: Employment in sample township enterprises in rural Beijing, Shandong and Sichuan

Location	Enterprise	Ownership	Products	Start of Operation	Number of Workers	Percentage of Female Workers	Age of Workers	Workers' Education	Average Wage (*yuan*/month)
Huairou County, Beijing	1	Township	Agricultural machinery	1958	180	27.8	Average: 30 Oldest: 52 Youngest: 18	a. & b. 0 c. 115 d. 9F 49M e. 1F 6M	150 (including bonuses)
	2	Township	Clothing	1980	610	78.7	Average: 21 Oldest: 50 Youngest: 18	a. & b. 0 c. 80% d. 15% e. 5%	160 (including bonuses)
Ling County, Shandong	3	Village	Cotton ginning		220	52			138
	4	Village	Cotton textiles	1979	167	61.7			100
	5	Village	Cotton spinning		200	90			120
	6	Township (processes for county factory)	Carpets	1982	150 in factory 350 at home or in village workshops	96–98	in factory: Youngest: 16 Oldest: 21		
	7	County	Carpets		420	80	Average: 27 Oldest: 50 Youngest: 16	c. minimum requirement	

Location	Enterprise	Ownership	Products	Start of Operation	Number of Workers	Percentage Female Workers	Age of Workers	Workers' Education	Average Wage (yuan/month)
Ling County, Shandong (contd.)	8	Township	Cloth shoes	1981	125	67.2	Oldest: <20 Youngest: 15	c. majority	100 (incl. bonuses)
	9	Township (contract with provincial company)	Artificial silk	1987	82	73	Oldest: 20 Youngest: 16	c. average	100
Xindu County, Sichuan	10	Village	Clothing	1983	340	90	Average: 25 Oldest: 40 Youngest: 18	c. minimum requirement	150
	11	Township	Metal door and window frames	1984	120	25	Average: 24 Oldest: 62 (2 skilled workers) Unskilled: Oldest: 36 Youngest: 18	c. minimum requirement d. majority	
Jinniu District, Sichuan	12	Township	Fibreglass cooling towers	1979	316	33.9	Average: 30 Oldest: 56 Youngest: 18	a. & b. 0 c. 37.5% d. 60% e. 2.5%	145 (incl. bonuses)
	13.	Village	Chemical products, electro-plating	1978	90	70	Average: 30 Oldest: 46 Youngest: 18	c. average d. requirement for workers hired after 1988	150

								Education	Wages
Wenjiang County, Sichuan	14	Township	Car parts	1978	226	46.9	Average (F): 22 Oldest (F): 34 Youngest (F): 17 Average (M): 25.5 Oldest (M): 52 Youngest (M): 18	a. & b. 0 c. 146 (minimum requirement) d. 30 F, 50 M	123.33 (incl. bonuses)
	15	Township (subsidiary of state-run factory in Chengdu)	Nylon thread	1987	80	80	Average: 21 Youngest: 17 Oldest (F): 36 (Head) Oldest (M): 42 (in management)	c. average	160 (incl. bonuses)
Guan County, Sichuan	16	Township	Chemicals	1979	127	26	Average: 38 Youngest: 17	a. 0 b. 101 c. & d. 26 d. 5 F	116.66
	17	Cooperative (sub-production team unit)	Children's clothing	1987	126	97.6	Average: 25 Oldest: 45 (skilled worker) Youngest: 17 (apprentice)	a. & b. 0 c. minimum requirement e. 2	156.7 (incl. bonuses)

a. illiterate
b. primary school graduate
c. junior secondary school graduate
d. senior secondary school graduate
e. secondary or tertiary vocational school graduate

Source: Interviews with managers of township enterprises, September–December 1989

Notes

INTRODUCTION

1　For examples, see the articles in Andrew Watson, ed., *Economic Reform and Social Change in China*, Routledge, London and New York, 1992, pp. 171–199.

2　See, in particular, Elisabeth Croll, *Chinese Women Since Mao*, Zed Books, London and M. E. Sharpe, Armonk, New York, 1983; Delia Davin, 'The implications of contract agriculture for the employment and status of Chinese peasant women', in Stephen Feuchtwang, Athar Hussain and Thierry Pairault, eds, *Transforming China's Economy in the Eighties, Vol. 1, The Rural Sector, Welfare and Employment*, Westview Press, Boulder and Zed Books, London, 1988, pp. 137–144; Emily Honig and Gail Hershatter, *Personal Voices, Chinese Women in the 1980s*, Stanford University Press, Stanford, California, 1988; Christina Gilmartin, Gail Hershatter, Lisa Rofel and Tyrene White, eds, *Engendering China. Women, Culture, and the State*, Harvard University Press, Cambridge, Massachusetts and London, 1994; Ellen Judd, *Gender and Power in Rural North China*, Stanford University Press, Stanford, California, 1994.

3　The differentiation of these levels of meaning is inspired in part by Sylvia Junko Yanagisako's discussion of a similar outside/inside dichotomy underlying perceptions of gender amongst first and second generation Japanese Americans (Sylvia Junko Yanagisako, 'Mixed metaphors: native and anthropological models of gender and kinship domains', in Jane Fishburne Collier and Sylvia Junko Yanagisako, eds, *Gender and Kinship, Essays Toward a Unified Analysis*, Stanford University Press, Stanford, California, 1987.

4　Institute of Population Studies, Chinese Academy of Social Sciences, ed., *Sampling Survey Data of Women's Status in Contemporary China*, International Academic Publishers, Beijing, 1994.

1　THEORISING GENDER

1　Engels' analysis of the origins of women's subordination is discussed in more detail in Chapter 2.

2　For more thorough critiques see Karen Sacks, 'Engels revisited: women, the organization of production, and private property', in Michelle Rosaldo and Louise Lamphere, eds, *Woman, Culture, and Society*, Stanford University Press, Stanford, California, 1974; Rosalind Delmar, 'Looking again at Engels's "Origins of the family, private property and the state" ', in Juliet Mitchell and Ann Oakley, eds, *The Rights and Wrongs of Women*, Penguin, Harmondsworth, 1976, pp. 271–287; and Michelle Barrett, *Women's Oppression Today. Problems in Marxist Feminist Analysis*, 5th edn, Verso, London, 1986.

3 Friedrich Engels, *The Origin of the Family, Private Property and the State*, Progress Publishers, Moscow, 1977 (1884), pp. 5–6.

4 Alison Jaggar, *Feminist Politics and Human Nature*, Rowman and Allanheld, New Jersey, and Harvester Press, Sussex, 1983, p. 217.

5 *Ibid.*, p. 134.

6 *Ibid.*, p. 76.

7 Engels, *The Origin of the Family*, p. 155.

8 See, for example, Karl Marx, *Capital*, 1967, p. 351, cited in Jaggar, *Feminist Politics*, p. 68.

9 Engels, *The Origin of the Family*, p. 158.

10 Karl Marx and Friedrich Engels, *Selected Works*, 1968, p. 334, cited in Jaggar, *Feminist Politics*, p. 68.

11 Clare Burton, *Subordination. Feminism and Social Theory*, George Allen and Unwin, Sydney, 1985, p. 32.

12 Kay Ann Johnson, *Women, the Family and Peasant Revolution in China*, University of Chicago Press, Chicago and London, 1983, p. 88. Mao Zedong and his followers became known for their 'voluntarist' brand of Marxism, that is, for the emphasis they placed on the role of the 'superstructure' in historical change. As Johnson notes, however, 'the dominant Chinese theoretical view of women and the family, in sharp contrast to many other issues, has remained firmly rooted in the mechanistic, materialistic, economistic mainstream of the inherited orthodoxy (Johnson, *Women, the Family and Peasant Revolution*, p. 221).

13 Michelle Barrett, *Women's Oppression Today*, p. 9.

14 For example, Sheila Rowbotham, *Women, Resistance and Revolution*, Allen Lane, London, 1972; Claudie Broyelle, *Women's Liberation in China*, translated by M. Cohen and G. Herman, Humanities Press, Atlantic Highlands, New Jersey, 1977.

15 Two other important works on women in China written in this period are *Women, the Family and Peasant Revolution in China*, by Kay Ann Johnson, and *Patriarchy and Socialist Revolution in China*, by Judith Stacey. These differ from the others in that they focus on the family as the key site of women's subordination rather than on gender divisions of labour. Thus, Johnson argues that 'women's secondary roles and relatively low participation rates in major areas of the economy deprived them of important means of influence and narrowed the sphere in which they could act. But it did not in itself cause the basic subordination of women, which derived from fundamental principles of kinship organisation and family formation, both of which in turn organised society' (p. 25). Johnson and Stacey, like the other scholars mentioned above, develop important insights into gender relations in China. I would argue that like them, however, in attempting to focus on the most fundamental cause of women's subordination, they have underestimated the importance of the links between different aspects of gender relations, whether they be gender divisions of labour or family relations.

16 Compare Barrett, *Women's Oppression Today*, p. 84: 'The concept of ideology is an intractable one for Marxist feminism, not least because it remains inadequately theorised in both Marxist and feminist theory.'

17 Iris Young, 'Beyond the unhappy marriage: a critique of the dual systems theory', in Lydia Sargent, ed., *Women and Revolution*, South End Press, Boston, 1980, pp. 50–52.

18 *Ibid.*, p. 51.
19 *Ibid.*, p. 54.
20 *Ibid.*, p. 54.
21 Michelle Rosaldo, 'Woman, culture, and society: a theoretical overview', in Rosaldo and Lamphere, *Woman, Culture, and Society*, p. 17.
22 *Ibid.*, p. 18.
23 *Ibid.*, p. 31.
24 Sherry Ortner, 'Is female to male as nature is to culture?', in Rosaldo and Lamphere, *Woman, Culture, and Society*, pp. 83–84.
25 *Ibid.*, p. 72.
26 Henrietta Moore, *Feminism and Anthropology*, 3rd edn, Polity Press, Cambridge, 1991, pp. 15–16.
27 Marilyn Strathern, 'No nature, no culture: the Hagen case', in Carol MacCormack and Marilyn Strathern, eds, *Nature, Culture and Gender*, Cambridge University Press, Cambridge, 1980, p. 177.
28 *Ibid.*, p. 179.
29 Michelle Rosaldo, 'The use and abuse of anthropology: reflections on feminism and cross-cultural understanding', *Signs: Journal of Women in Culture and Society*, vol. 5, no. 3, 1980, p. 401. As Rosaldo notes, however, the opposition between a public male sphere and a private female sphere did not begin in the Victorian era, but can be traced to ancient Greek philosophy (Rosaldo, 'The use and abuse of anthropology', p. 401).
30 Rosaldo, 'The use and abuse of anthropology', p. 402; Genevieve Lloyd, *The Man of Reason. 'Male' and 'Female' in Western Philosophy*, Methuen, London, 1984.
31 Carol MacCormack, 'Nature, culture and gender: a critique', in MacCormack and Strathern, *Nature, Culture and Gender*, p. 10.
32 Rosaldo, 1974, 'Woman, culture, and society: a theoretical overview', pp. 22–24.
33 Olivia Harris, 'The power of signs: gender, culture and the wild in the Bolivian Andes', in MacCormack and Strathern, *Nature, Culture and Gender*, p. 24.
34 Ortner, 'Is female to male', pp. 71, 76.
35 MacCormack, 'Nature, culture and gender: a critique', p. 2.
36 Joan Scott, 'Deconstructing equality-versus-difference: or, the uses of post-structuralist theory for feminism', *Feminist Studies*, vol. 14, no. 1, 1988, p. 35.
37 See, for example, the articles in Jane Fishburne Collier and Sylvia Junko Yanagisako, eds, *Gender and Kinship. Essays Toward a Unified Analysis*, Stanford University Press, Stanford, California, 1987.

2 PATTERNS FROM THE PAST

1 For more detailed analyses of gender relations and state policies on gender relations between the 1900s and the 1970s, see Delia Davin, *Woman-Work. Women and the Party in Revolutionary China*, Clarendon Press, Oxford, 1976; and Elisabeth Croll, *Feminism and Socialism in China*, Routledge and Kegan Paul, London, Henley and Boston, 1978. Croll's work includes an examination of Guomindang policies on gender relations, an issue not discussed here.
2 John Lossing Buck, *Land Utilization in China*, Council on Economic and Cultural Affairs Inc., New York, 1956 (1937), p. 289.

3   There were exceptions, however. See Kay Ann Johnson, *Women, the Family and Peasant Revolution in China*, University of Chicago Press, Chicago and London, 1983, pp. 12–13.

4   Marion Levy, *The Family Revolution in Modern China* (2nd edn), Octagon Books, New York, 1963, p. 80.

5   Buck, *Land Utilization in China*, pp. 290, 293.

6   Margery Wolf, *Revolution Postponed. Women in Contemporary China*, Methuen, London, 1985, p. 81; Emily Ahern, 'The power and pollution of Chinese women', in Margery Wolf and Roxane Witke, eds, *Women in Chinese Society*, Stanford University Press, Stanford, California, 1975, pp. 193–214.

7   Buck further divided the wheat and rice regions into eight areas. The boundaries of these areas and regions were determined largely by physical factors, such as climate and soil type, which affected land use (Buck, *Land Utilization in China*, pp. 23–24). For details of variations in women's participation rates in agriculture between areas see Buck, p. 293.

8   Davin, *Woman-Work*, p. 118.

9   Buck, *Land Utilization in China*, p. 292.

10   Davin, *Woman-Work*, p. 118.

11   *Ibid.*, p. 121.

12   Francis Hsu, *Under the Ancestors' Shadow. Chinese Culture and Personality*, Routledge and Kegan Paul, London, 1949, p. 67.

13   Fei Hsiao-Tung and Chang Chih-I, *Earthbound China. A Study of Rural Economy in Yunnan*, University of Chicago Press, Chicago, 1945, p. 31.

14   *Ibid.*, p. 145.

15   For a detailed discussion of the development of commercialisation and family production in handicrafts and other subsidiary activities see Philip Huang, *The Peasant Economy and Social Change in North China*, Stanford University Press, Stanford, California, 1985; and Philip Huang, *The Peasant Family and Rural Development in the Yangzi Delta, 1350–1988*, Stanford University Press, Stanford, California, 1990.

16   Sidney Gamble, *Ting Hsien. A North China Rural Community*, Stanford University Press, Stanford, 1954, pp. 288–301.

17   Fei Hsiao-Tung and Chang Chih-I, *Earthbound China*, pp. 239–244.

18   Buck, *Land Utilization in China*, p. 298.

19   Hsu, *Under the Ancestors' Shadow*, pp. 67–74.

20   Lucien Bianco, *Origins of the Chinese Revolution, 1915–1949*, Stanford University Press, California, and Oxford University Press, London, 1971 (1967), p. 104.

21   *Ibid.*, p. 91.

22   Frederic Wakeman, *The Fall of Imperial China*, Free Press, New York, 1975; Bianco, *Origins of the Chinese Revolution*.

23   See Ida Pruitt, *A Daughter of Han. The Autobiography of a Chinese Working Woman*, Stanford University Press, Stanford, California, 1945.

24   Carl Riskin, *China's Political Economy. The Quest for Development Since 1949*, Oxford University Press, Oxford, 1987, p. 15.

25   Emily Honig, *Sisters and Strangers. Women in the Shanghai Cotton Mills, 1919–1949*, Stanford University Press, Stanford, California, 1986; Gail Hershatter, *The Workers of Tianjin, 1900–1949*, Stanford University Press, Stanford, California, 1986.

217

26 Marjorie Topley, 'Marriage resistance in rural Kwangtung', in Wolf and Witke, *Women in Chinese Society*, pp. 67–88.

27 Johnson, *Women, the Family and Peasant Revolution*, p. 40.

28 Davin, *Woman-Work*, p. 28; Johnson, *Women, the Family and Peasant Revolution*, p. 55.

29 Such legislation was opposed not only by male peasants. Women, who as mothers and mothers-in-law had, after years of subjugation, finally attained some measure of authority through control of daughters and daughters-in-law, also felt threatened by reforms that would give young women greater autonomy. Young wives had the most to gain from legislation such as the Marriage Law, but they were also the most vulnerable. It was women from this group who were most active in the CCP's women's organisations, but at the same time, there were many who dared not fight the opposition of husband and mother-in-law.

30 Johnson, *Women, the Family and Peasant Revolution*.

31 *Ibid.*, p. 220.

32 See, for example, William Hinton, *Fanshen*, Monthly Review Press, New York, 1966, p. 397.

33 Davin, *Woman-Work*, pp. 65–66.

34 Johnson, *Women, the Family and Peasant Revolution*, p. 102.

35 Margery Wolf, 'Chinese women: old skills in a new context', in Michelle Rosaldo and Louise Lamphere, eds, *Woman, Culture and Society*, Stanford University Press, Stanford, California, 1974, p. 171.

36 This was the precursor to *ZGFN*.

37 Phyllis Andors, *The Unfinished Liberation of Chinese Women. 1949–1980*, Indiana University Press, Bloomington, and Wheatsheaf Books, Sussex, 1983, p. 37.

38 I must stress, though, that the connection I am making here is between changes in economic strategy and changes in policy on women. This does not necessarily imply the same correlation between economic strategy and the real rate of employment amongst urban women. As I argue elsewhere, there is evidence to suggest that since 1978, for example, despite urban unemployment problems and pressures on women to withdraw from the paid labour force, the overall employment rate of women has not declined. Instead, it has declined in some sectors of the economy, but increased in others (Tamara Jacka, 'Back to the wok: women and employment in Chinese industry in the 1980s', *Australian Journal of Chinese Affairs*, no. 24, 1990, pp. 1–24).

39 Marina Thorborg, 'Chinese employment policy in 1949–1978 with special emphasis on women in rural production', in *Chinese Economy Post-Mao. A Compendium of Papers Submitted to the Joint Economic Committee Congress of the United States, vol. 1 Policy and Performance*, US Government Printing Office, Washington, 1978, pp. 538–539.

40 *Ibid.*, p. 582.

41 *Ibid.*, p. 592.

42 William Parish and Martin Whyte, *Village and Family in Contemporary China*, University of Chicago Press, Chicago and London, 1978, pp. 203, 238.

43 Thorborg, 'Chinese employment policy', pp. 600–601.

44 *ZGFN*, March 1962, editorial.

45 *RMRB*, 20 November 1964.

46 Erika Platte, 'The private sector in China's agriculture: an appraisal of recent changes', *Australian Journal of Chinese Affairs*, no. 10, 1983, p. 82.

47 Friedrich Engels, *The Origin of the Family, Private Property and the State*, Progress Publishers, Moscow, 1977 (1884), p. 158.

48 Alison Jaggar, *Feminist Politics and Human Nature*, Rowman and Allanheld, New Jersey, and Harvester Press, Sussex, 1983, p. 72.

49 Andors, *The Unfinished Liberation of Chinese Women*, p. 55; Thorborg, 'Chinese employment policy', pp. 566–567.

50 Thorborg, 'Chinese employment policy', p. 542.

51 Isabel Crook and David Crook, *The First Years of Yangyi Commune*, 2nd edn, Routledge and Kegan Paul, London, Boston and Henley, 1979, p. 128; Thorborg, 'Chinese employment policy', p. 551.

52 Thorborg, 'Chinese employment policy', p. 584.

53 Croll, *Feminism and Socialism in China*, p. 290.

54 Johnson, *Women, the Family and Peasant Revolution*, p. 167.

55 Riskin, *China's Political Economy*, p. 187.

56 Andors, *The Unfinished Liberation of Chinese Women*, p. 146.

57 The next national congress was not held until 1978, however.

58 This type of work is identified in Chinese as *funü gongzuo*. Henceforth in this book I will use Delia Davin's term 'woman-work' when referring to such work. Although clumsy, this term is, as Davin suggests, preferable to the common but misleading translation of *funü gongzuo* as 'women's work' (Davin, *Woman-Work*, p. 17).

59 Ruth Sidel and Victor Sidel, *The Health of China. Current Conflicts in Medical and Human Services for One Billion People*, Zed Press, London, 1982, p. 80.

60 Johnson, *Women, the Family and Peasant Revolution*, p. 202.

61 Parish and Whyte, *Village and Family in Contemporary China*, p. 204.

62 Emily Honig, 'Socialist revolution and women's liberation in China – a review article', *Journal of Asian Studies*, vol. 49, no. 2, 1985, p. 335.

3 POST-MAO REFORMS

1 Deborah Davis and Ezra Vogel, 'Introduction: the social and political consequences of reform', in Deborah Davis and Ezra Vogel, eds, *Chinese Society on the Eve of Tiananmen. The Impact of Reform*, Council on East Asian Studies, Harvard University, Cambridge, Massachusetts and London, 1990, pp. 3–4.

2 Much of the groundwork for these shifts had, in fact, already been laid between 1976 and 1978, and was based on arguments made by Deng Xiaoping in 1974 and 1975 (Andrew Watson, 'The management of the industrial economy: the return of the economists', in Jack Gray and Gordon White, *China's New Development Strategy*, Academic Press, London and New York, 1982, pp. 87–103).

3 Modernisation of agriculture, industry, science and technology, and defence.

4 For example, as suggested below, the state's attempts to promote 'spiritual civilisation' have been a response to what is seen as a decline in morals and social order, these being regarded, in part, as undesired side-effects of the 'open door policy' and the development of a market economy.

5 Marilyn Young, 'Chicken Little in China: some reflections on women', in Arif Dirlik and Maurice Meisner, eds, *Marxism and the Chinese Experience*, M. E. Sharpe, Armonk, New York and London, 1989, pp. 262–263.

6   *Ibid.,* pp. 261–263.
7   Emily Honig and Gail Hershatter, *Personal Voices. Chinese Women in the 1980s,* Stanford University Press, Stanford, California, 1988, pp. 14–40.
8   Young, 'Chicken Little in China', pp. 258–259.
9   Quoted in Jean Robinson, 'Of women and washing machines: employment, housework, and the reproduction of motherhood in socialist China', *China Quarterly,* no. 101, 1985, p. 51. For further discussion of the reaffirmation of the image of woman as mother, and of the consequences for gender relations in rural areas, see Chapters 4–6.
10 Tamara Jacka, 'Back to the wok: women and employment in Chinese industry in the 1980s', *Australian Journal of Chinese Affairs,* no. 24, 1990, pp. 1–24.
11 This meeting was later to be pinpointed as the beginning of the reform period, even though a number of the policy changes put forward had already been heralded at meetings earlier in the year (Dorothy Solinger, 'The Fifth National People's Congress and the process of policy making: reform, readjustment and the opposition', *Asian Survey,* vol. 22, no. 12, 1982, pp. 1248–1249).
12 Andrew Watson, 'Agriculture looks for "shoes that fit": The production responsibility system and its implications', *World Development,* vol. 11, no. 8, 1983, p. 712; Carl Riskin, *China's Political Economy. The Quest for Development Since 1949,* Oxford University Press, Oxford, 1987, pp. 286–287.
13 Watson, 'Agriculture looks for "shoes that fit" ', p. 717.
14 For details see Nongcun Diaocha Lingdao Xiaozu Bangongshi [Office of the Lead Group on Rural Investigation], *Nongcun zai biange zhong qianjin – lai zi jiceng de diaocha baogao [The Progress of Rural Areas in Reform – Report on a Grass-Roots Investigation],* Nongye Chubanshe, PRC, 1987, p. 20.
15 Watson, 'Agriculture looks for "shoes that fit" ', p. 717.
16 Andrew Watson, 'The family farm, land use and accumulation in agriculture', *Australian Journal of Chinese Affairs,* no. 17, January 1987, p. 24.
17 David Zweig, 'Peasants, ideology, and new incentive systems: Jiangsu Province, 1978–1981', in William Parish, ed., *Chinese Rural Development. The Great Transformation,* M. E. Sharpe, Armonk, New York and London, 1985, pp. 141–163.
18 Watson, 'The family farm', p. 22.
19 Watson, 'Agriculture looks for "shoes that fit" ', p. 719.
20 Watson, 'The family farm', p. 4.
21 Andrew Watson, 'New structures in the organization of Chinese agriculture: A variable model', *Pacific Affairs,* vol. 57, no. 4, 1984–85, pp. 624–627; Tyrene White, 'Political reform and rural government', in Deborah Davis and Ezra Vogel, eds, *Chinese Society on the Eve of Tiananmen,* pp. 38–39.
22 Sulamith Potter and Jack Potter, *China's Peasants. The Anthropology of a Revolution,* 2nd edn, Cambridge University Press, Cambridge, 1991, p. 281.
23 Scott Rozelle, 'Decision-making in China's rural economy: the linkages between village leaders and farm housholds', *China Quarterly,* no. 137, 1994, pp. 123–124.
24 Sample surveys suggest that in more than half the villages of eastern China, decisions relating to crop planting are made under a system of 'unified management' (*tongyi jingying*), in which village leaders assign particular areas to be planted with particular crops. They are able to command peasant compliance with their plans in part through their ability to provide, or deny, access to farm equipment. Scott Rozelle found,

however, that in the poorer inland province of Hubei it is more common for rural households to make their own decisions over crop planting (Rozelle, 'Decision-making in China's rural economy', pp. 110–111).

25 Victor Nee and Su Sijin, 'Institutional change and economic growth in China: the view from the villages', *Journal of Asian Studies*, vol. 49, no. 1, 1990, pp. 18–21; Andrew Watson, ed., 'The management of the rural economy: the institutional parameters', in Watson, *Economic Reform and Social Change in China*, pp. 182–188.

26 Nee and Su, 'Institutional change and economic growth', pp. 18–21. More recently, local governments have been increasing various levies and fees on peasant families. Indeed, in the 1990s in parts of rural China, such a heavy burden of charges has been imposed on peasant families that they have reacted with riots and violence. There has been little sign, however, of any significant improvement in the provision of collective welfare and other services; much of the money is used instead either to line village and township cadres' own pockets, or to meet the demands of government departments at higher levels (*Inside China Mainland,* vol. 15, March 1993, pp. 28–40).

27 CCP, 'Communique of the Third Plenary Session of the 11th Central Committee of the Communist Party of China', *Peking Review*, no. 52, 29 December 1978, p. 13.

28 Robert Ash, 'The agricultural sector in China: performance and policy dilemmas during the 1990s', *China Quarterly*, no. 131, 1992, p. 555.

29 Andrew Watson, 'Market reform and agricultural growth: the dynamics of change in the Chinese countryside in 1992', in Joseph Cheng and Maurice Brosseau, eds, *China Review 1993*, Chinese University of Hong Kong, 1993, pp. 1–20.

30 CCP, 'Communique', p. 12.

31 'Decision on some problems in accelerating the development of agriculture', quoted in William Byrd and Lin Qingsong, eds, *China's Rural Industry. Structure, Development and Reform*, published for the World Bank, Oxford University Press, Oxford, 1990, p. 10.

32 Riskin, *China's Political Economy*, p. 289. For a more detailed discussion of specialised households and private enterprises, see Chapter 8.

33 A survey of 272 villages across the country found, for example, that in 1987 the average gross income earned from one person-day's labour in grain production was 6.49 *yuan*. The income earned in forestry was 1.18 times this amount, and the incomes earned in industry, transport, and in commerce, catering and services, were respectively 2.54, 3.16 and 1.37 times the amount earned in grain production (Nongcun Diaocha Bangongshi [Office of Rural Investigation], *'Nongcun gaige yu fazhan zhong de ruogan xin qingkuang'* ['Certain new situations arising in economic reform and development'], *Nongye Jingji Wenti [Issues in Agricultural Economics]*, no. 3, 1989, p. 55).

34 Harry Wu, 'The industrialisation of China's rural labour force since the economic reform', Working Paper no. 92/6, Chinese Economy Research Unit, University of Adelaide, 1992, pp. 4–5, pp. 28–29.

35 For an indication of the geographical distribution of township enterprise employment, see Chapter 9.

36 Guojia Tongjiju [State Statistical Bureau], *Zhongguo Tongji Nianjian, 1992 [Statistical Yearbook of China, 1992]*, Zhongguo Tongji Chubanshe, Beijing, 1992, pp. 307, 310; Guojia Tongjiju [State Statistical Bureau], *Zhongguo Tongji Nianjian,*

1994 [Statistical Yearbook of China, 1994], Zhongguo Tongji Chubanshe, Beijing, 1994, p. 276.

37   Guojia Tongjiju, *Zhongguo Tongji Nianjian*, 1992, p. 276.

38   Azizur Khan, Keith Griffin, Carl Riskin and Zhao Renwei, 'Household income and its distribution in China', *China Quarterly*, no. 132, 1992, p. 1056. This latter study was based on a survey of 10,258 rural households in 28 provinces. For a comparison of the methodology and findings of this and the World Bank studies, see Khan et al., 'Household income', pp. 1055–1058.

39   Hiroyuki Kato, 'Regional development in the reform period', in Ross Garnaut and Liu Guoguang, *Economic Reform and Internationalisation: China and the Pacific Region*, Allen & Unwin, Australia, 1992, p. 118.

40   Khan et al., 'Household income', p. 1040.

41   Institute of Population Studies, Chinese Academy of Social Sciences, ed., *Sampling Survey Data of Women's Status in Contemporary China*, International Academic Publishers, Beijing, 1994, p. 232. It should be stressed that this was a survey of *married couples living together*. Had single people (or those living separately from their spouses) been included, it is likely that the concentration of women in the lowest income brackets would have been even more striking.

42   Khan et al., 'Household income', pp. 1041–1042, p. 1044.

43   For details of incentives and disincentives, and of exceptions to the one-child policy, see Elisabeth Croll, 'Introduction: fertility norms and family size in China', in Elisabeth Croll, Delia Davin and Penny Kane, eds, *China's One-Child Family Policy*, Macmillan, London, 1985, pp. 1–36; Delia Davin, 'The single-child policy in the countryside', in Croll, Davin and Kane, *China's One-Child Family Policy*, pp. 37–82; and Delia Davin, "Never mind if it's a girl, you can have another try", in Jorge Delman, Clemens Stubbe Ostergaard and Flemming Christiansen, eds, *Remaking Peasant China. Problems of Rural Development and Institutions at the start of the 1990s*, Aarhus University Press, Denmark, 1990, pp. 81–91.

44   Athar Hussain and Liu Hong, 'Compendium of Literature on the Chinese Social Security System', *China Programme, Research Working Papers*, no. 3, STICERD, London School of Economics, 1989, pp. 56–82.

45   *SWB* 19 April 1995 FEW/0380 WG/12.

46   *ZGFN*, September 1981, p. 46; *RMRB*, 9 April 1983.

47   For reports on female infanticide see *ZGNMB* 16 January 1983; *Guangming Ribao* 14 October 1988. In the 1980s and 1990s statistics have revealed unusually high proportions of males amongst babies in rural China. In the 1980s many scholars believed that this imbalance in sex ratios was a result of female infanticide. More recently, however, scholars have shown that the major causes are sex specific abortions and the underreporting of female births (Terence Hull, 'Rising sex ratios in China: evidence from the 1990 population census', *Briefing Paper no. 31*, Australian Development Studies Network, Australian National University, Canberra, 1993).

48   Davin, 'Never mind', pp. 81–91.

49   Elisabeth Croll, *Chinese Women Since Mao*, Zed Books, London and M. E. Sharpe, Armonk, New York, 1983, pp. 121–123; Davin, 'Never mind', pp. 87–88.

50   Davin, 'Never mind', p. 86.

51   Vivienne Shue, 'Emerging state-society relations in rural China', in Delman, Ostergaard and Christiansen, *Remaking Peasant China*, 1990, p. 60.

4 FAMILIES

1 Margery Wolf, *Revolution Postponed. Women in Contemporary China*, Methuen, London, 1985, p. 183.

2 For more detailed discussions of the Chinese family see Maurice Freedman, ed., *Family and Kinship in Chinese Society*, Stanford University Press, Stanford, California, 1970; Margery Wolf, *Women and the Family in Rural Taiwan*, Stanford University Press, Stanford, California, 1972; William Parish and Martin Whyte, *Village and Family in Contemporary China*, University of Chicago Press, Chicago and London, 1978, Chapter 3; and Elisabeth Croll, *The Politics of Marriage in Contemporary China*, Cambridge University Press, Cambridge, 1981.

3 This rough definition of the term '*jia*', corresponds to that of Myron Cohen (Myron Cohen, 'Developmental process in the Chinese domestic group', in Freedman, *Family and Kinship in Chinese Society*) and other western scholars. Some scholars, however, use the term '*hu*' (household) to refer to this type of unit (e.g., Sulamith Potter and Jack Potter, *China's Peasants. The Anthropology of a Revolution*, 2nd edn, Cambridge University Press, Cambridge, 1991, pp. 215–216). In terms of composition, as Ellen Judd points out, the household and the family in China are usually identical. However, in Chinese discourse the term '*jia*' is more ambiguous and flexible than '*hu*'. The former is used more often in reference to domestic relations and kinship, and my feeling is that it is the term preferred by ordinary people. The latter term is more common in politico-administrative and economic discourse, and refers to a unit of control and regulation by the state, and, particularly since economic reforms were introduced, to a unit of production and reproduction (Ellen Judd, *Gender and Power in Rural North China*, Stanford University Press, Stanford, California, 1994, pp. 117, 167–174). Unless otherwise indicated, in this book the terms 'family' and 'household' are interchangeable, although their usage is coloured by nuances similar to the above.

4 'Nuclear' families are those containing one married couple or remnant thereof, with or without unmarried children. 'Stem' families contain two generations with one married couple, or remnant thereof, in each, with or without unmarried children. 'Grand' families contain two or more generations with two or more married couples, or remnants thereof, in each, with or without unmarried children (Wolf, *Revolution Postponed. Women in Contemporary China*, p. 183).

5 Parish and Whyte, *Village and Family in Contemporary China*, pp. 132–133.

6 Guo Zhigang, '*Bijiao jiating moshi bianhua dingliang yanjiu zhibiao de tantao*' ['An inquiry into research standards for comparing changes in family type'], *Renkou yu Jingji [Population and the Economy]*, no. 2, 1988, pp. 52–58.

7 Wang Shuhui, '*Funü shengming zhouqi yu jiating jiegou*' ['Women's life cycle and the structure of the family'], *Hunyin yu Jiating [Marriage and the Family]*, October 1987, pp. 14–16.

8 Guojia Tongjiju [State Statistical Bureau], *Zhongguo Tongji Nianjian, 1992 [Statistical Yearbook of China, 1992]*, Zhongguo Tongji Chubanshe, Beijing, 1992, p. 98.

9 *SWB*, 15 February 1989 FE/0385 B2/7; *RMRB*, 17 September 1988.

10 Wang Shuhui, '*Funü shengming zhouqi yu jiating jiegou*', p. 15.

11 *Ibid.*

12 The national divorce rate was 0.7 per thousand in 1980, and 1.5 per thousand in 1993 (Guojia Tongjiju [State Statistical Bureau], *Zhongguo Tongji Nianjian, 1994, [Statistical Yearbook of China, 1994]*, Zhongguo Tongji Chubanshe, Beijing, 1994, p. 655).

13 For example, Parish and Whyte, *Village and Family in Contemporary China.*

14 See, for example, Teodor Shanin, ed., *Peasants and Peasant Societies*, Penguin, Harmondsworth, 1971.

15 See, for example, Philip Huang, *The Peasant Family and Rural Development in the Yangzi Delta, 1350–1988*, Stanford University Press, Stanford, California, 1990. Huang draws explicitly on a model of the family farm developed by A.V. Chayanov that has been extremely influential in peasant studies. In this model, peasant families seek to deploy their labour power in such a way as to achieve a balance between the satisfaction of family needs and the drudgery of work (A.V. Chayanov, 1925, *Organizatsiya krest'yanskogo khozyaistva*, translated by D. Thorner, R. Smith and B. Kerblay as *The Theory of Peasant Economy*, Irwin, Illinois, 1966, pp. 5–7).

16 Ellen Judd, '*Niangjia:* Chinese women and their natal families', *Journal of Asian Studies*, vol. 48, no. 3, 1989, p. 533.

17 Wolf, *Women and the Family in Rural Taiwan*, pp. 160–163.

18 Amartya Sen, 'Gender and Cooperative Conflicts' in Irene Tinker, ed., *Persistent Inequalities. Women and World Development*, Oxford University Press, New York and Oxford, 1990, p. 126.

19 *Ibid.*

20 *Ibid.*

21 cf. Hanna Papanek, 'To each less than she needs, from each more than she can do' in Tinker, *Persistent Inequalities. Women and World Development*, p. 164.

22 Hugh Baker, *Chinese Family and Kinship*, Macmillan, London and Basingstoke, 1979, p. 43.

23 Delia Davin, *Woman-Work. Women and the Party in Revolutionary China*, Clarendon Press, Oxford, 1976, p. 125.

24 Emily Honig and Gail Hershatter, *Personal Voices. Chinese Women in the 1980s*, Stanford University Press, Stanford, California, 1988, pp. 168–173.

25 Parish and Whyte, *Village and Family in Contemporary China*, p. 213; Wolf, *Revolution Postponed. Women in Contemporary China*, pp. 231–237.

26 *ZGFN*, July 1991, p. 24.

27 Croll, *The Politics of Marriage in Contemporary China*, p. 41.

28 Parish and Whyte, *Village and Family in Contemporary China*, p. 180.

29 For discussions of the reasons behind high and increasing bride-price payments, see Parish and Whyte, *Village and Family in Contemporary China*, pp. 186–188; and Zhang Sehua and Liu Zhongyi, '*Zai Fujian Qingliuxian gao'e caili chengwei nongmin fudan*' ['In Qingliu County, Fujian, high bride-prices have become a burden for peasants'], *ZGFN*, December, 1986, pp. 14–22.

30 *ZGFNB*, 4 July 1986.

31 *Time*, 11 November 1991.

32 *NMRB*, 31 October 1986.

33 Song Meiya, '*Yi zhuang zhangfu qiangjian qizi an*' ['A case of a man raping his wife'], *ZGFN*, January 1991, pp. 14–15.

34 Honig and Hershatter, *Personal Voices. Chinese Women in the 1980s*, p. 174.

35 *ZGFN*, June 1984, p. 20.

36 *ZGFN*, July 1984, p. 17.

37 *Ibid.*

38 *Peking Review*, 30 March 1973, quoted in Elisabeth Croll, *Feminism and Socialism in China*, Routledge and Kegan Paul, London, Henley and Boston, 1978, pp. 311–316.

39 FBIS, 10 March 1980, quoted in Jean Robinson, 'Of women and washing machines: employment, housework, and the reproduction of motherhood in socialist China', *China Quarterly*, no. 101, 1985, p. 52.

40 *ZGFN*, July 1986, p. 11.

41 Wei Ziqian, '*Kaifa haizi danao de shenmi qianli*' ['Developing the mysterious potential of a child's brain'], *Nongjianü Baishitong [Rural Women Knowing All]*, no. 5, 1995, p. 39.

42 Wolf, *Revolution Postponed. Women in Contemporary China*, p. 223.

43 Martin Yang, *A Chinese Village. Taitou, Shantung Province*, Columbia University Press, New York, 1945.

44 Davin, *Woman-Work. Women and the Party in Revolutionary China*, p. 76.

45 Parish and Whyte, *Village and Family in Contemporary China*, pp. 209–215.

46 For example, Croll, *The Politics of Marriage in Contemporary China*, p. 159.

47 The table presented here provides only a summary of the study's findings. Further details, including information on decision making on other issues, and on decision making according to the age of the wife, are given in Institute of Population Studies, Chinese Academy of Social Sciences, ed., *Sampling Survey Data of Women's Status in Contemporary China*, International Academic Publishers, Beijing, 1994, pp. 312–316.

48 Elisabeth Croll, 'Some implications of the rural economic reforms for the Chinese peasant household', in Ashwani Saith, ed., *The Re-emergence of the Chinese Peasantry. Aspects of Rural Decollectivisation*, Croom Helm, London, 1987, p. 126.

49 Examples of exceptions to this pattern are mentioned above. See also *NMRB*, 7 March 1987. However, I would argue that these exceptions, singled out for comment as they are, merely confirm the general rule.

50 *Women in the Villages, Men in the Towns*, UNESCO, Geneva, 1984.

51 Delia Davin, 'China: the new inheritance law and the peasant household', *Journal of Communist Studies*, vol. 3, no. 4, 1987, p. 58.

52 Jonathan Ocko, 'Women, property, and law in the People's Republic of China', in Rubie Watson and Patricia Ebrey, eds, *Marriage and Inequality in Chinese Society*, University of California Press, Berkeley, 1991, pp. 324–325.

53 *NMRB*, 26 June 1985.

54 *RMRB*, 21 April 1988.

55 Davin, 'China: the new inheritance law', p. 62.

56 *Ibid.*, p. 60.

5 EDUCATION AND POLITICS

1 Guojia Tongjiju Renkou Tongjisi [Population Statistics Department, State Bureau of Statistics], *Zhongguo Renkou Tongji Nianjian, 1991 [Chinese Population Statistical Yearbook, 1991]*, Zhongguo Tongji Chubanshe, Beijing, 1992, pp. 63–65.

2 *Ibid.*, p. 57.

3 Suzanne Pepper, *China's Education Reform in the 1980s. Policies, Issues, and Historical Perspectives*, Institute of East Asian Studies, University of California, Berkeley, 1990, pp. 70–71.

4 *Ibid.*, p. 91.

5 *Ibid.*, p. 97.

6 Pepper, *China's Education Reform in the 1980s*, p. 99.

7 Zhang Ning, 'A conflict of interests: current problems in educational reform', in Andrew Watson, ed., *Economic Reform and Social Change in China*, Routledge, London and New York, 1992, p. 154.

8 Jiao Fengjun, '*Nongcun jiaoyu de fazhan, kunjing yu chulu*' ['Developments, difficulties and solutions in rural education'], *Lilun Jianshe [The Construction of Theory]*, no. 2, 1994, p. 62.

9 Li Kejing, 'Strategic approaches to eliminating illiteracy in China', *Social Sciences in China*, no. 2, 1992, p. 30.

10 *SWB*, 1 November 1990 FE/0910 B2/5.

11 *ZGNMB*, 22 May 1983; Fujian Education Commission, 'An investigation of the status of primary education among rural school-age girls', *Chinese Education. A Journal of Translations*, vol. 22, no. 2, 1989, p. 63.

12 The female proportion of primary enrolments declined from 45.5 per cent in 1976 to 43.7 per cent in 1983. However, it then increased to 45.6 per cent in 1988 and 46.8 per cent in 1993 (Zhonghua Quanguo Funü Lianhehui Funü Yanjiusuo and Shaanxisheng Funü Lianhehui Yanjiushi [Research Institute of the All-China Women's Federation and Research Office of Shaanxi Provincial Women's Federation], *Zhongguo Funü Tongji Ziliao, 1949–1989 [Statistics on Chinese Women, 1949–1989]*, Zhongguo Tongji Chubanshe, Beijing, 1991, p. 125; Guojia Tongjiju [State Statistical Bureau], *Zhongguo Tongji Nianjian, 1994, [Statistical Yearbook of China, 1994]*, Zhongguo Tongji Chubanshe, Beijing, 1994, p. 571). The female proportion of regular secondary school enrolments dropped from 40.4 per cent in 1976 to 39.4 per cent in 1983, but then rose to 41.3 per cent in 1988 and 43.7 per cent in 1993 (Zhonghua Quanguo Funü Lianhehui, *Zhongguo Funü Tongji Ziliao*, pp. 136–137; Guojia Tongjiju, *Zhongguo Tongji Nianjian*, 1994, p. 571).

13 For details on these schools, see Heidi Ross, 'The "crisis" in Chinese secondary schooling', in Irving Epstein, ed., *Chinese Education. Problems, Policies and Prospects*, Garland Publishing, New York and London, 1991, pp. 77–79.

14 Pepper, *China's Education Reform in the 1980s*, p. 108.

15 *Zhongguo Jiaoyu Nianjian, 1949–1981 [Chinese Education Yearbook, 1949–1981]*, Zhongguo Da Baikequanshu Chubanshe, Beijing, 1984, p. 1023; Guojia Tongjiju [State Statistical Bureau], *Zhongguo Tongji Nianjian, 1986 [Statistical Yearbook of China, 1986]*, Zhongguo Tongji Chubanshe, Beijing, 1986, p. 756; Guojia Tongjiju, *Zhongguo Tongji Nianjian*, 1994, p. 586.

16 Börge Bakken, 'Backwards reform in Chinese education', *Australian Journal of Chinese Affairs*, no. 19/20, 1988, p. 153.

17 Fujian Education Commission 'An investigation of the status of primary education among rural school-age girls', pp. 54–56.

18 *Ibid.*, pp. 56–57.

19 Wang Shuhui, 'Educational level of female teenagers and young adults declines', *Chinese Education. A Journal of Translations*, vol. 22, no. 2, 1989, p. 21.

20 *Zhongguo Jiaoyu Nianjian, 1949–1981*, p. 1005; Guojia Tongjiju, *Zhongguo Tongji Nianjian, 1986*, p. 750; Guojia Tongjiju, *Zhongguo Tongji Nianjian, 1994*, p. 581.

21 There are some exceptions to this pattern, however. In Wenjiang County, Sichuan, for example, Education Bureau officials told me that the drop-out rate from junior secondary school is higher amongst boys than amongst girls. The reason they gave was that boys can rely on their physical strength to earn money, whereas girls can only rely on their education (Interview, October 1989).

22 *China Daily*, 12 October 1985.

23 Interviews with County Education Bureau officials, September–December 1989.

24 Emily Honig and Gail Hershatter, *Personal Voices. Chinese Women in the 1980s*, Stanford University Press, Stanford, California, 1988, pp. 14–23.

25 *Ibid.*, pp. 14–16.

26 *Gei Shaonü de Xin [Letters to Young Girls]*, Shanghai, Shanghai Renmin Chubanshe, 1984, quoted in Honig and Hershatter, *Personal Voices. Chinese Women in the 1980s*, pp. 15–16.

27 Guojia Tongjiju, *Zhongguo Tongji Nianjian, 1994*, p. 571.

28 Pepper, *China's Education Reform in the 1980s*, p. 97.

29 Zhonghua Quanguo Funü Lianhehui, *Zhongguo Funü Tongji Ziliao*, p. 150.

30 Beverley Hooper, 'Gender and education', in Epstein, ed., *Chinese Education. Problems, Policies, and Prospects*, pp. 357–359; Tamara Jacka, 'Back to the wok: women and employment in Chinese industry in the 1980s', *Australian Journal of Chinese Affairs*, no. 24, 1990, pp. 1–24.

31 *Renmin Jiaoyu [People's Education]*, October 1985, p. 12.

32 Interview, October 1989.

33 Nan Ning, '*Xingbie qishi: jiaoyu de tanxi*' ['Sexual discrimination: the sigh of education'], *ZGFN*, February, 1989, pp. 4–5.

34 Zhongguo Qingnian Bao *[China Youth Daily]*, 13 March 1982, p. 4, quoted in Honig and Hershatter, *Personal Voices. Chinese Women in the 1980s*, p. 18.

35 Yang Chengxun, '*Jingji tizhi gaige yu funü jiefang*' ['Economic reform and women's liberation'], *Funü Shenghuo [Women's Life]*, no. 1, 1986, p. 4.

36 Honig and Hershatter, *Personal Voices. Chinese Women in the 1980s*, p. 30.

37 The following discussion is limited to forms of political activity sanctioned by the state. It does not include peasant rebellions or other violence, forms of non-cooperation such as strikes, subterfuge, bribery, or corruption, all of which are, nevertheless, important avenues for the articulation of rural interests. See John Burns, 'Chinese Peasant Interest Articulation', in David Goodman, ed., *Groups and Politics in the People's Republic of China*, M. E. Sharpe, Armonk, New York, 1984, pp. 126–151.

38 Sulamith Potter and Jack Potter, *China's Peasants. The Anthropology of a Revolution*, 2nd edn, Cambridge University Press, Cambridge, 1991, p. 336.

39 Ellen Judd, *Gender and Power in Rural North China*, Stanford University Press, Stanford, 1994, p. 125.

40 Zhonghua Quanguo Funü Lianhehui, *Zhongguo Funü Tongji Ziliao*, p. 572; *SWB*, 19 October 1992 FE/1515 C1/3-5.

41 *ZGFN*, October 1984, p. 48; *NMRB*, 11 March 1986; *NMRB*, 28 July 1986.

42 Zhang Jinyun and Hu Zhaoqing, '*Nongcun nü dangyuan shao, lao wenti ying yinqi*

zhongshi' ['The problem of old age and scarcity of women Party members must be given attention'], *FNGZ*, July 1988, pp. 14–15.

43 *RMRB*, 2 March 1988.

44 Ellen Judd, *Gender and Power in Rural North China*, p. 229.

45 A 'leading cadre' is usually someone with the status of director, deputy director or secretary, or their equivalents, in any particular body.

46 ACWF, '*Quanguo Fulian Shujichu xiang wujie changwei de gongzuo huibao*' ['Work report given by the secretariat of the All-China Women's Federation to the standing committee of the Fifth National Women's Congress'], *FNGZ*, April 1984, pp. 4–8.

47 Zhonggong Zhongyang Zuzhi Bu and Zhonghua Quanguo Funü Lianhehui [Central Organisation Department of the CCP and The All-China Women's Federation], '*Zai gaige kaifang zhong jiaqiang peiyang xuanba nü ganbu de yijian*' ['Views on strengthening the training and election of women cadres during reform'], *FNGZ*, May 1988, pp. 9–10.

48 *SWB*, 22 August 1990, FE/0849 B2/3.

49 Zhang Jinyun and Hu Zhaoqing, '*Nongcun nü dangyuan shao, lao wenti ying yinqi zhongshi*', pp. 14–15.

50 *ZGFNB*, 11 January 1988.

51 Burns, 'Chinese Peasant Interest Articulation', pp. 131, 142.

52 Amongst the counties I visited in 1989, Ling County in Shandong maintained a target of 24 per cent women delegates to the People's Congress. Guan County, Sichuan, had a target of 20 to 22 per cent women delegates to the People's Congress, and had also maintained a quota system since before the reforms whereby every group of leading cadres from village level up was required to include at least one woman. Xindu and Jinniu counties in Sichuan had dropped quotas, but in the latter a quota of one woman in each group of leading cadres had been reintroduced in 1989 as a reaction to declines in women's political representation (Interviews with members of County Women's Federations, September–December 1989).

53 For a summary of the different views on the topic see Cui Yuxiang, '*Guanyu funü canzheng wenti yanjiu zongshu*' ['A summary of research on women's participation in politics'], in Zhongguo Renmin Daxue Shubao Ziliao Zhongxin, Fuyin Baokan Ziliao, *Funü Zuzhi yu Huodong* [Press clippings on *Women's Organisations and Activities*, Centre for Books and Newspaper Materials, Chinese People's University], no. 6, 1993, pp. 42–45.

54 Ma Yinan, '*Guanyu wanshan funü quanyi baozhangfa de ruogan sikao*' ['Some thoughts on how to perfect the Women's Rights Protection Law'], *Zhongguo Faxue [Chinese Legal Studies]*, no. 5, 1995, p. 102.

55 Marilyn Young, 'Chicken Little in China: some reflections on women', in Arif Dirlik and Maurice Meisner, eds, *Marxism and the Chinese Experience*, M. E. Sharpe, Armonk, New York and London, 1989, pp. 262–263.

56 Ross Terrill, *The White-Boned Demon. A Biography of Madame Mao-Zedong*, William Morrow, New York 1984, pp. 16, 391.

57 *Ibid.*, p. 391.

58 Important exceptions in the 1980s and 1990s have been the newly emerging women's research groups and women's studies departments in universities across China (for details see Liu Jinxiu, '*Minjian funü xueshu tuanti yilan*' ['A guide to non-

governmental academic women's groups'] in Beijingshi Funülianhehui and Beijing Funü Wenti Lilun Yanjiuhui [The Beijing Women's Federation and The Beijing Women's Issues Theory Research Group] eds, *Zhongguo Funü Lilun Yanjiu Shi Nian [Ten Years of Theoretical Research on Chinese Women's Issues]*, Zhongguo Funü Chubanshe, Beijing, 1992, pp. 580–584).

In addition, in the 1980s many trade unions established women's groups and a number of professional women's organisations were set up. All such organisations belong officially, however, to the state-controlled All-China Women's Federation (Article 6, Clause 25, Constitution of the All-China Women's Federation, *RMRB*, 13 September 1983).

59 *ZGFN*, November 1980, pp. 2–3, quoted in Honig and Hershatter, *Personal Voices. Chinese Women in the 1980s*, p. 318.

60 In the late 1980s, suggestions that mass organisations such as the Women's Federation be given independence were supported by the then General Secretary of the CCP, Zhao Ziyang. In the Women's Federation the possibility that autonomy might soon become a reality generated a good deal of excitement, though there was also trepidation that this would result in a loss of funding and of authority that the Federation could ill afford (Interviews with Women's Federation cadres, Beijing and Chengdu, August–December 1989). With the demise of Zhao Ziyang and the brutal suppression of pro-democracy protests in 1989, however, Party control over mass organisations tightened once more.

61 See, for example, *RMRB*, 18 April 1983, for a directive from the Secretariat of the CCP Central Committee setting out the main tasks of the Women's Federation.

62 *RMRB*, 13 September 1983.

63 Zhou Limin, '*Kaichuang xin jumian yao you "ban bian tian"*' ['In initiating a new phase we need "half the sky"'], *ZGFN*, November 1982, p. 42.

64 *RMRB*, 13 September 1983.

65 Interviews with members of County Women's Federations, Beijing, Shandong and Sichuan, September–December 1989.

66 Tan Yingzi, '*Jiceng fulian mianlin de xin wenti*' ['New problems faced by grass-roots women's federations'], *FNGZ*, January 1989, p. 24; Zhang Jinyun and Hu Zhaoqing, '*Nongcun nü dangyuan shao, lao wenti ying yinqi zhongshi*', pp. 15, 17.

67 Shandongsheng Fulian [Shandong Provincial Women's Federation], '*Weirao gaige jiaqiang jiceng funü zuzhi jianshe*' ['Strengthen the establishment of grass-roots women's organisations in line with reform'], *FNGZ*, October 1986, p. 13.

68 Tan Yingzi, 1989, '*Jiceng fulian mianlin de xin wenti*', p. 24.

69 Interviews with members of county Women's Federations, September–December 1989. In many places, however, Women's Congresses now raise their own funds through entrepreneurial activities. In one county in Hubei, for example, village Women's Congresses have reportedly overcome a shortage of funding by cultivating land or fish ponds assigned to them by the village government, or by running private enterprises (*ZGFN*, September 1988, p. 30). The question that springs to mind here is: How much time is left for woman-work when such activities are undertaken?

70 *NMRB*, 17 March 1986.

71 For details see Jacka, 'Back to the wok'.

72 *ZGNMB*, 29 May 1984; *NMRB*, 13 November 1987.

73 Kang Keqing, '*Fenfa ziqiang kaichuang funü yundong xin jumian*' ['Let us rouse all

our strength to initiate a new phase in the women's movement'], *Xinhua Yuebao [New China Monthly]*, no. 9, 1983, p. 63.

74 ACWF, '*Xin shiqi nongcun funü gongzuo de xin renwu*' ['New tasks for rural woman-work in the new era'], *FNGZ*, August 1986, pp. 2–5.

75 *Ibid.*, p. 3.

76 Huang Qizao, '*Zai di si qi pinkun diqu xianji fulian zhuren peixun ban shang de zongjie jianghua*' ['Concluding speech at the fourth training class for heads of county level Women's Federations of poor areas'], *FNGZ*, November 1989, p. 2.

77 A woman is counted each time she participates in a session, regardless of how many other sessions she has participated in.

78 *NMRB*, 9 March 1987.

79 See, for example, *RMRB*, 27 January 1985.

80 ACWF, '*Guanyu zai quanguo gezu nongcun funü zhong shenru kaizhan xue wenhua, xue jishu, bi chengji, bi gongxian jingsai huodong de lianhe tongzhi*' ['Joint circular on the thorough development of activities to study culture and technology and compete in achievements and contribution amongst rural women of all nationalities across the country'], *FNGZ*, April 1989, pp. 11–12.

81 Ma Lizhen, '*Ba "shuang xue shuang bi" huodong tuixiang xin jieduan*' ['Advance the "double study, double compete" activities to a new stage'], *ZGFN*, March 1992, p. 4.

82 *RMRB*, 11 October 1994, p. 1. For further discussion of the 'double study, double compete' campaign see Shirin Rai and Zhang Junzuo, '"Competing and learning": women and the state in contemporary rural mainland China', *Issues and Studies*, vol. 30, no. 3, 1994, pp. 51–66.

83 Potter and Potter, *China's Peasants. The Anthropology of a Revolution*, p. 200; William Parish and Martin Whyte, *Village and Family in Contemporary China*, University of Chicago Press, Chicago and London, pp. 171–172; Anita Chan, Richard Madsen and Jonathan Unger, *Chen Village under Mao and Deng*, University of California Press, Berkeley, 1992 (1984), pp. 186–212.

84 Potter and Potter, *China's Peasants. The Anthropology of a Revolution*, pp. 186–212. See also, Chan et al., *Chen Village under Mao and Deng*, pp. 186–212.

6 DOMESTIC WORK

1 This is also a common feature of western discussions of domestic work, as Christine Delphy has pointed out (Christine Delphy, *Close to Home. A Materialist Analysis of Women's Oppression*, Hutchinson, London, 1984, pp. 78–92).

2 However, it is also seen as a domestic sideline, and when larger numbers of domestic livestock are kept and bring in substantial cash income, the activity is redefined as a family business or 'specialised household'. (See Chapter 8.)

3 *Xinhua*, 29 February 1960, quoted in Phyllis Andors, *The Unfinished Liberation of Chinese Women. 1949–1980*, Indiana University Press, Bloomington, and Wheatsheaf Books, Sussex, 1983, p. 51.

4 *ZGFN*, April 1978, p. 16.

5 This was the case even in instances where the woman clearly also did a large proportion of the work in the fields.

6 Margery Wolf, *Revolution Postponed. Women in Contemporary China*, Methuen, London, 1985, p. 138.

7   Christine Bose, 'Technology and changes in the division of labour in the American home', in Elizabeth Whitelegg, ed., *The Changing Experience of Women*, Martin Robertson, Oxford, 1982, pp. 226–238.

8   Zhang Juan and Ma Wenrong, '*Daqiuzhuang "funü hui jia" de sisuo*', ['Thoughts on "women returning home" in Daqiu Village'], *ZGFN*, January 1988, pp. 8–10.

9   For example, *RMRB*, 9 July 1988; *RMRB*, 17 September 1988.

10 Zhang Juan and Ma Wenrong, '*Daqiuzhuang "funü hui jia" de sisuo*', p. 9.

11 *Ibid.*

12 *RMRB*, 9 July 1988.

13 For a more detailed discussion of this topic, see Tamara Jacka, 'Back to the wok: women and employment in Chinese industry in the 1980s', *Australian Journal of Chinese Affairs*, no. 24, 1990, pp. 1–24.

14 Zhang Juan and Ma Wenrong, '*Daqiuzhuang "funü hui jia" de sisuo*', p. 10.

15 By domestic work she is referring to meal preparation, cleaning and washing (Interview, October 1989).

16 Wang Shuhui, '*Sichuan nongcun funü de zhiye jiegou*' ['The structure of women's work in rural Sichuan'], *Hunyin yu Jiating [Marriage and the Family]*, November 1987, p. 20.

17 *Ibid.*

18 Jill Matthews, *Good and Mad Women. The Historical Construction of Femininity in Twentieth-Century Australia*, 2nd edn, Allen & Unwin, Australia, 1992, pp. 56–57.

19 *Ibid.*, p. 58.

20 *Ibid.*, p. 59.

21 This is the reason for the inclusion of the private plot in Table 6.1 and its exclusion in Table 6.2.

22 It is perhaps useful to note that the *Sample Survey of Women's Status in Contemporary China*, conducted in 1991 by the Institute of Population Studies, Chinese Academy of Social Sciences, gathered detailed information on the time spent by men and women on various daily activities, including domestic work tasks, in urban areas, but not in rural areas (Institute of Population Studies, Chinese Academy of Social Sciences, *Sampling Survey Data of Women's Status in Contemporary China*, International Academic Publishers, Beijing, 1994).

23 It should be noted that whereas the figures in Table 6.1 refer to the time spent in particular tasks by the family as a whole, those in Table 6.2 refer to the time spent in each task by the individual women interviewed. Information on the gender division of labour in domestic work in these women's families is given in Appendix 1.

24 Elisabeth Croll, *The Family Rice Bowl: Food and the Domestic Economy in China*, United Nations Research Institute for Social Development, Geneva, 1982, pp. 298, 300.

25 *Ibid.*, p. 299.

26 Elisabeth Croll, *Women in Rural Development in China*, International Labour Office, Geneva, 1985 (1979), p. 114.

27 World Bank, *The Health Sector in China*, Report no. 4664-CHA, 1984.

28 *SWB*, 5 December 1990 FE/WO157 A/2.

29 Anita Chan, Richard Madsen and Jonathan Unger, *Chen Village under Mao and Deng*, University of California Press, Berkeley, 1992 (1984), p. 215.

30 Guojia Tongjiju [State Statistical Bureau], *Zhongguo Tongji Nianjian, 1990 [Statistical Yearbook of China, 1990]*, Zhongguo Tongji Chubanshe, Beijing, 1990, p. 322; Guojia Tongjiju [State Statistical Bureau], *Zhongguo Tongji Nianjian, 1994 [Statistical Yearbook of China, 1994]*, Zhongguo Tongji Chubanshe, Beijing, 1994, p. 285.

31 *NMRB*, 11 January 1989.

32 Croll, *The Family Rice Bowl: Food and the Domestic Economy in China*, pp. 298, 300.

33 *Ibid.*, p. 177.

34 *Ibid.*, p. 299.

35 *Ibid.*

36 Guojia Tongjiju, *Zhongguo Tongji Nianjian, 1990*, p. 316; Guojia Tongjiju, *Zhongguo Tongji Nianjian, 1994*, p. 280.

37 Guojia Tongjiju, *Zhongguo Tongji Nianjian, 1990*, p. 322; Guojia Tongjiju, *Zhongguo Tongji Nianjian, 1994*, p. 285.

38 Guojia Tongjiju, *Zhongguo Tongji Nianjian, 1990*, p. 322; Guojia Tongjiju, *Zhongguo Tongji Nianjian, 1994*, p. 285.

39 Jan Myrdal, *Report from a Chinese Village*, Penguin Books, Harmondsworth and Melbourne, 1967, pp. 295–306.

40 Delia Davin, *Woman-Work. Women and the Party in Revolutionary China*, Clarendon Press, Oxford, 1976, p. 130.

41 Institute of Population Studies, *Sampling Survey Data*, p. 274.

42 Börge Bakken, 'Backwards reform in Chinese education', *Australian Journal of Chinese Affairs*, no. 19/20, 1988, p. 135.

43 *ZGFN*, July 1981, p. 29.

44 *Ibid.*

45 Penny Kane, *The Second Billion. Population and Family Planning in China*, Penguin Books, Melbourne, 1987, pp. 192–193.

46 Jean Oi, 'The fate of the collective after the commune', in Deborah Davis and Ezra Vogel, eds, *Chinese Society on the Eve of Tiananmen. The Impact of Reform*, Harvard Contemporary China Series:7, 1990, pp. 17, 26.

47 *NMRB*, 9 March 1987.

48 *NMRB*, 29 May 1987.

49 *China Daily*, 24 May 1991.

50 Marina Thorborg, 'Chinese employment policy in 1949–1978 with special emphasis on women in rural production', in *Chinese Economy Post-Mao. A Compendium of Papers Submitted to the Joint Economic Committee Congress of the United States, vol. 1, Policy and Performance*, US Government Printing Office, Washington, 1978, p. 601.

7 AGRICULTURE

1 Elisabeth Croll, *The Family Rice Bowl: Food and the Domestic Economy in China*, United Nations Research Institute for Social Development, Geneva, 1982, p. 313.

2 Marina Thorborg, 'Chinese employment policy in 1949–1978 with special emphasis on women in rural production', in *Chinese Economy Post-Mao. A Compendium of Papers Submitted to the Joint Economic Committee Congress of the United States, vol. 1, Policy and Performance*, US Government Printing Office, Washington, 1978, pp. 584, 586.

3 *Ibid.*, p. 596.

4 Isabel Crook and David Crook, *The First Years of Yangyi Commune*, 2nd edn, Routledge and Kegan Paul, London, Boston and Henley, 1979, p. 128. See also Thorborg, 'Chinese employment policy in 1949–1978', p. 551.

5 Margery Wolf, *Revolution Postponed. Women in Contemporary China*, Methuen, London, 1985, p. 84.

6 *Ibid.*, p. 85.

7 *Ibid.*, pp. 83–84.

8 Fei Juanhong '*Wo guo nongcun gaige yu liang xing laodong fengong*' ['China's rural reforms and the division of labour between the sexes'], *Shehui Kexue Yanjiu [Social Science Research]*, no. 2, 1994, p. 81.

9 Appendix 1 also contains some information on the gender division of labour in agriculture in the families that I interviewed in 1989.

10 Jeffrey Taylor, 'Rural employment trends and the legacy of surplus labour, 1978–86', *China Quarterly*, no. 116, 1988, p. 743.

11 Li Qingzeng (unpub.), '*Lun nongcun shengyu laodongli de zhuanyi zhanlue*' ['A discussion of strategies for the diversion of rural surplus labour'], Rural Development Institute, Chinese Academy of Social Sciences, 1986.

12 Taylor, 'Rural employment trends', p. 748.

13 Li Qingzeng, '*Lun nongcun shengyu laodongli de zhuanyi zhanlue*', pp. 6–7.

14 Zhongguo Nongcun Chanye Jiegou Yanjiu Keti Zu, 'Report on the study of the structure of rural production in China, 1982–2000', p. 7, quoted in Taylor 'Rural employment trends', p. 737.

15 *FNGZ*, September 1984, p. 24.

16 *FNGZ*, July 1986, p. 12.

17 See, for example, Wu Kaiti, '*Yao chongfen fahui funü de zuoyong*' ['We must bring women's abilities into full play'], *ZGFN*, May 1979, pp. 38–42.

18 These issues are discussed in relation to Third World countries and the USSR in Susan Bridger, *Women in the Soviet Countryside. Women's Roles in Rural Development in the Soviet Union*, Cambridge University Press, Cambridge, 1987, p. 2, pp. 220–222.

19 William Hinton, 'Transformation in the countryside. Part Two: unresolved issues and the responsibility system', *US–China Review*, vol. 8, no. 4, 1984, p. 13.

20 Guojia Tongjiju Renkou Tongjisi [Population Statistics Department, State Bureau of Statistics], *Zhongguo Renkou Tongji Nianjian, 1991 [Chinese Population Statistical Yearbook, 1991]*, Zhongguo Tongji Chubanshe, Beijing, 1992, p. 73; Zhonghua Quanguo Funü Lianhehui Funü Yanjiusuo and Shaanxisheng Funü Lianhehui Yanjiushi [Research Institute of the All-China Women's Federation and Research Office of Shaanxi Provincial Women's Federation], *Zhongguo Funü Tongji Ziliao, 1949-1989 [Statistics on Chinese Women, 1949–1989]*, Zhongguo Tongji Chubanshe, Beijing, 1991, p. 253.

21 Meng Xianfan, ' "*Nan gong nü geng*" *yu Zhongguo nongcun nüxing de fazhan*' [' "Men work in industry while women plough" and rural women's development'], *Shehui Kexue Zhanxian [Social Sciences Frontline]*, no. 1, 1995, p. 248.

22 Guojia Tongjiju Renkou Tongjisi, *Zhongguo Renkou Tongji Nianjian, 1991*, p. 73; Zhonghua Quanguo Funü Lianhehui, *Zhongguo Funü Tongji Ziliao*, p. 253.

23 Philip Huang, *The Peasant Economy and Social Change in North China*, Stanford

University Press, Stanford, California, 1985, p. 213. See also Yuen-fong Woon, 'From Mao to Deng: Life satisfaction among rural women in an emigrant community in South China', *Australian Journal of Chinese Affairs*, no. 25, 1991, p. 156.

24 *ZGNMB*, 29 April 1984.

25 *ZGNMB*, 2 May 1988, quoted in Huang Xiyi, 'Changes in the economic status of rural women in the transformation of modern Chinese society', *Social Sciences in China*, no. 1, 1992, p. 89.

26 Ellen Judd, 'Alternative development strategies for women in rural China', *Development and Change*, vol. 21, no. 1, 1990, pp. 28–30.

27 *Ibid.*, p. 30.

28 This does not include approximately 1,500 contract and temporary workers employed outside the county. The majority of these workers are men in the construction industry. They generally do not return home in the busy season because they are too far away.

29 Figures checked with Jiang Xuegui, ed., *Chengdu Xiangzhenqiye (1979–1988) [Chengdu's Township Enterprises (1979–1988)]*, Chengdu Chubanshe, Chengdu, 1989.

30 In this table, the category 'other' includes 3 families in which the interviewee's husband was dead, 3 in which information on the division of labour was incomplete, and 6 in which the division of labour could not be accounted for in the other categories. Further information on the families included in this table is to be found in Appendix 1.

31 Li Xiaoyun, Lin Zhibin, Liu Yonggong and Li Ou (unpub.), 'The contribution of women to agricultural and household activities in rural areas. A case study in Ningjin County', Centre for Integrated Agricultural Development, Beijing Agricultural University, Beijing, 1992.

32 Ester Boserup, *Woman's Role in Economic Development*, St. Martin's Press, New York, 1970, p. 16.

33 *Ibid.*, p. 81.

34 Barbara Jancar, *Women under Communism*, John Hopkins University Press, Baltimore and London, 1978, p. 20.

35 Thorborg, 'Chinese employment policy', p. 580. In areas of south and southeast China the feminisation of agriculture has a longer history. Kathy Le Mons Walker, for example, claims that in Nantong County in the Yangzi Delta, commercialisation and industrialisation of the rural economy in the early part of the twentieth century involved women taking over family farming, while men moved into off-farm wage labour (Kathy Le Mons Walker, 'Economic growth, peasant marginalization, and the sexual division of labour in early twentieth-century China', *Modern China*, vol. 19, no. 3, 1993, pp. 370–376). Yuen-fong Woon says that in Chikan Zhen, in the Pearl River Delta, a feminisation of agriculture between the mid-nineteenth century and 1949 was connected to the migration overseas of thousands of people, most of them young men (Yuen-fong Woon, 'From Mao to Deng: Life satisfaction among rural women in an emigrant community in South China', *Australian Journal of Chinese Affairs*, no. 25, 1991, pp. 154–155).

36 Sulamith Potter and Jack Potter, *China's Peasants. The Anthropology of a Revolution*, 2nd edn, Cambridge University Press, Cambridge, 1991, pp. 299–300.

37 This was the case, for example, in family no. 41, Wenjiang (Appendix 1). For a more detailed discussion of this practice, and of variations of it, see Flemming Christiansen,

'Social division and peasant mobility in mainland China: the implications of the hu-k'ou system', *Issues and Studies*, vol. 26, no. 4, 1990, pp. 32–33.

38 Christiansen, 'Social division and peasant mobility', p. 36.

39 Potter and Potter, *China's Peasants. The Anthropology of a Revolution*, p. 306. The system of job inheritance in urban industry was formally abolished in 1983, but may still be practised illegally (Christiansen, 'Social division and peasant mobility in mainland China', p. 31).

40 Potter and Potter, *China's Peasants. The Anthropology of a Revolution*, pp. 306–311.

41 William Lavely, 'Marriage and mobility under rural collectivism', in Rubie Watson and Patricia Ebrey, eds, *Marriage and Inequality in Chinese Society*, University of California Press, Berkeley, 1991, p. 288. It is much rarer for a man to marry a woman with a higher status than his own, in part because of a traditional resistance to such marriages (Ji Ping, Zhang Kaiti and Liu Dawei, 'Marriage motivated population movement in the outskirts of Beijing', *Social Sciences in China*, vol. 7, no. 1, 1986, p. 293), and in part because, under the patrilocal marriage system, a woman's status and standard of living are greatly influenced by the status of the family she marries into, but a man's status is little affected by that of his wife's family (Lavely, 'Marriage and mobility under rural collectivism', p. 288).

42 These are generally men who were originally classified as peasants but who then obtained urban household registration. It is much rarer for a man born with urban household registration to marry a peasant.

43 Wolf, *Revolution Postponed. Women in Contemporary China*, p. 107.

44 Nongcun Diaocha Bangongshi [Office of Rural Investigation], '*Nongcun gaige yu fazhan zhong de ruogan xin qingkuang*' ['Certain new situations arising in economic reform and development'], *Nongye Jingji Wenti [Issues in Agricultural Economics]*, no. 3, 1989, pp. 42–57.

45 Wang Jinjin, '*Dangjin, Zhongguo, qiaoran xingqi de funü jiefang lang chao*' ['The tide of women's liberation that is softly rising in China today'], *ZGFN*, March 1991, pp. 8–11.

46 *Ibid.*, p. 8.

47 *Hunyin yu Jiating [Marriage and the Family]*, May 1986, p. 13.

48 Shi Chenglin, '*Lun xiandai nongcun funü zai laoli zhuanyi zhong de diwei he zuoyong*' ['A discussion of the status and function of rural women in the present movement of labour'], *Fujian Luntan: Jingji, Shehui Ban [Fujian Tribune: Economy and Society Edition]*, no. 9, 1987, pp. 54–56.

49 Wang Shuhui, '*Sichuan nongcun funü de zhiye jiegou*' ['The structure of women's work in rural Sichuan'], *Hunyin yu Jiating [Marriage and the Family]*, November, 1987, pp. 20–29.

50 It is probable that earlier instances of the feminisation of agriculture in parts of rural China were accompanied by similar shifts in perception. This is suggested in Kathy Walker's discussion of the feminisation of agriculture in Nantong County in the early twentieth century (see Note 35 above). Walker argues that women 'were not merely left behind as men moved into off-farm work but were deliberately "defined back" to the home/farm where their added roles in agriculture became, in effect, a new variant of older seclusion norms' (Walker, 'Economic growth, peasant marginalization, and the sexual division of labour in early twentieth-century China', p. 374).

51 *ZGFN*, May 1982, p. 30. See also *Hunyin yu Jiating*, May 1986, p. 13.

52 Appendix 1, family no.10.

53 See, for example, the quotation cited below referring to the situation in Chen Village. Helen Siu reports also that 'evidence from Nanxi and Minlong rural communes shows that agricultural income increased severalfold after the reforms and at times might have surpassed wages in the factories. But young peasants are leaving the villages at an alarming rate' (Helen Siu, 'The politics of migration in a market town', in Deborah Davis and Ezra Vogel, eds, *Chinese Society on the Eve of Tiananmen. The Impact of Reform*, Harvard University Press, Cambridge, Massachusetts and London, 1990, p. 76.

54 *NMRB*, 13 May 1986, cited in Ole Odgaard, 'Collective control of income distribution: a case study of private enterprises in Sichuan province', in Jorgen Delman, Clemens Stubbe Ostergaard, and Flemming Christiansen, *Remaking Peasant China. Problems of Rural Development and Institutions at the start of the 1990s*, Aarhus University Press, Denmark, 1990, p. 107. See also, Note 31, Chapter 3.

55 Wang Jinjin, '*Dangjin, Zhongguo, qiaoran xingqi de funü jiefang lang chao*', pp. 8–11.

56 Meng Xianfan, ' *"Nan gong nü geng" yu Zhongguo nongcun nüxing de fazhan*', pp. 249–250.

57 *ZGNMB*, 29 April 1984.

58 *Women in the Villages, Men in the Towns*, UNESCO, Geneva, 1984, pp. 299–300.

59 Meng Xianfan, '*Gaige zhong nongcun nüxing de jingji jihui – dui liang ge cunzhuang de diaocha*' ['The economic opportunities for rural women during reform – a survey of two villages'], *Funü Yanjiu Luncong [Collection of Women's Studies]*, no. 3, 1994, pp. 27–31.

60 For a further example, see Huang, *The Peasant Economy and Social Change in North China*, p. 213. I noted a similar pattern in some of the families I interviewed in 1989 (see Appendix 1, families 24, 26, 37, 57 and 60).

61 Anita Chan, Richard Madsen, and Jonathan Unger, *Chen Village under Mao and Deng*, University of California Press, Berkeley, 1992 (1984), p. 297.

62 *Ibid.*, pp. 267–308. For further discussion of the use of immigrant labour in agriculture in the Pearl River delta region see Tao Xiaoyong, '*Zhujiang sanjiaozhou diqu de dai geng jingying ji qi jingji, shehui yingxiang*' ['The subcontracting of land in the Pearl River delta region and its economic and social implications'], *Nongye Jingji Wenti [Issues in Agricultural Economics]*, October, 1986, pp. 16–18.

8 ENTREPRENEURS ON THE FARM

1 These activities were also undertaken to some extent by collective units.

2 Philip Huang, *The Peasant Family and Rural Development in the Yangzi Delta, 1350–1988*, Stanford University Press, Stanford, California, 1990, p. 203.

3 Elisabeth Croll, *Chinese Women Since Mao*, Zed Books, London and M. E. Sharpe, Armonk, New York, 1983, p. 36.

4 Elisabeth Croll, 'The promotion of domestic sideline production in rural China 1978–79', in Jack Gray and Gordon White, eds, *China's New Development Strategy*, Academic Press, UK, 1978, p. 237.

5 Huang, *The Peasant Family and Rural Development in the Yangzi Delta, 1350–1988*, p. 218.

6 Zhang Ruihua, '*Nongcun tingyuan jingji chutan*' [A preliminary investigation of the rural courtyard economy'], in Zhongguo Renmin Daxue Shubao Ziliao Zhongxin, Fuyin Baokan Ziliao, *Funü Zuzhi yu Huodong* [Press clippings on *Women's Organisations and Activities*, Centre for Books and Newspaper Materials, Chinese People's University], no. 8, 1987, p. 65.

7 *ZGFNB*, 18 August 1986.

8 *NMRB*, 17 May 1988.

9 Xu Yan, '*Liyong tingyuan gao te yang xinxi shichang shi guanjian*' ['Market information is the key to profiting from specialised production in the courtyard', *Nongjianü Baishitong [Rural Women Knowing All]*, January 1995, pp. 60–61.

10 Huang, *The Peasant Family and Rural Development in the Yangzi Delta, 1350–1988*, pp. 217–218.

11 Sulamith Potter and Jack Potter, *China's Peasants. The Anthropology of a Revolution*, 2nd edn, Cambridge University Press, Cambridge, 1991, p. 331.

12 Victor Nee and Su Sijin, 'Institutional change and economic growth in China: the view from the villages', *Journal of Asian Studies*, vol. 49, no. 1, 1990, p. 9.

13 Interviews conducted in Ling County, September 1989.

14 Interview with members of Xindu County Women's Federation, October 1989.

15 Maria Mies, *The Lace Makers of Narsapur. Indian Housewives Produce for the World Market*, Zed Press, London, 1982, p. 172.

16 *Ibid.*, p. 176.

17 See, for example, *ZGFN*, March 1979, p. 5.

18 *ZGFNB*, 20 June 1986.

19 Potter and Potter, *China's Peasants*, p. 321.

20 *ZGNMB*, 22 May 1983.

21 Shanxisheng Huairenxian Fulian [The Women's Federation of Huairen County, Shanxi Province] '*Tingyuan ziyou zhi fu lu*' ['The courtyard itself is a way to get rich'], *FNGZ*, September, 1984, p. 24; *NMRB*, 8 March 1985; *NMRB*, 17 July 1986. The lack of any clear definition of the category 'domestic sidelines' or 'courtyard economy', and the considerable overlap between activities undertaken in this sector and in other sectors means, however, that any statistics on the subject should be taken only as a rough guide.

22 Delia Davin, 'The implications of contract agriculture for the employment and status of Chinese peasant women', in Stephan Feuchtwang, Athar Hussain, and Thierry Pairault, eds, *Transforming China's Economy in the Eighties. Vol. 1, The Rural Sector, Welfare and Employment*, Westview Press, Boulder, and Zed Books, London, 1988, p. 140.

23 Xu Yan, '*Liyong tingyuan gao te yang xinxi shichang shi guanjian*', pp. 60–61.

24 Davin, 'The implications of contract agriculture for the employment and status of Chinese peasant women', p. 138.

25 One study notes that in rural markets in the county towns of Heilongjiang there has recently been an increase, in both absolute terms and as a proportion of the total, in the numbers of women selling produce. In a survey of 2,803 people marketing produce it was found that 66 per cent were women (*Zhongguo Nongcun Jingji [Chinese Rural Economy]*, June 1988, p. 63). This is similar to the pre-1949 situation discussed in Chapter 2.

26 Ellen Judd, *Gender and Power in Rural North China*, Stanford University Press, Stanford, 1994, pp. 125–126.

27 Not mentioned here are 'joint household enterprises' (*lianheti*), which are non-agricultural enterprises run jointly by two or more families. In 1991 there were approximately 849,000 such enterprises registered across China (*Zhongguo Xiangzhenqiye Nianjian, 1992, [Chinese Township Enterprise Yearbook, 1992]*, Nongye Chubanshe, Beijing, 1993, p. 137).

28 *Ibid.* Both these statistics and subsequent ones referring to *siying qiye* and specialised households should be taken only as rough indications of the real situation. Because of the political insecurity of the private sector for much of the 1980s, *getihu* have sometimes avoided registration, or have falsely registered as collectives or as specialised households. Consequently, the statistics are likely to underrepresent the number of *getihu*. At the same time, however, these statistics are likely to have been boosted by the inclusion of non-agricultural specialised households. Statistics that I collected from county Township Enterprise Bureaux in Sichuan in 1989 included non-agricultural specialised households as private enterprises. It is not clear, however, whether this is also the case for the national statistics cited here.

29 The majority of these, however, had been falsely registered as *getihu*, as joint household or joint-share enterprises, or as collectives (Susan Young, 'Wealth but not security: attitudes towards private business in China in the 1980s', *Australian Journal of Chinese Affairs*, no. 25, 1991, pp. 117–119).

30 Zhou Qiren and Du Ying, 'Specialized households: a preliminary study', *Social Sciences in China*, vol. 5, no. 3, September 1984, p. 65.

31 *SWB*, 5 October 1988 FE/W0046/A/1. This figure is also likely to be inflated, however. In 1985 the State Bureau of Statistics stipulated that specialised households must conform to the following criteria: (1) at least 60 per cent of the household's labour time must be devoted to specialised production or marketing; (2) at least 60 per cent of the household's income must be derived from the specialised line of production; (3) at least 80 per cent of specialised products or services must be for sale (except for grain-producing households, for which the commodity rate is set at a minimum of 60 per cent); (4) the income the household derives from selling its specialised product or service must be at least double the average income from sales earned by local non-specialised households (*Jingjixue Wenzhai [Selections on Economics]*, January 1986, p. 59). Considerable regional variations in the standards set for specialised households nevertheless persist.

 Another factor contributing to statistical inaccuracies is the false registration of some ventures as specialised households. This occurs largely because, although in practice they function in the same way as *getihu*, specialised households are commonly seen as specialisations of the collective economy. As such, through the 1980s they were more politically secure than *getihu*. They were also more often given preferential treatment by local governments, for example, with respect to credit and the supply of raw materials.

32 See Appendix 1, families no. 4; 5; 38; 6; 1 and 2; 29, 35, 36 and 43.

33 See Appendix 1, families no. 7, 52 and 53; 8 and 25; 37 and 57; 56; 32; 30.

34 *RMRB*, 31 October 1986. In comparison, another large-scale study undertaken in 1988 found that women constituted only 21 per cent of owners of private enterprises

(Azizur Rahman Khan, Keith Griffin, Carl Riskin and Zhao Renwei, 'Household income and its distribution in China', *China Quarterly*, no. 132, 1992, pp. 1042).

35 In absolute terms, however, most women running specialised households in this county were engaged in processing.

36 In the early 1980s, a distinction was commonly made in the Chinese literature between two categories of specialised households, according to the ways in which they had evolved. 'Contract' specialised households (*chengbao zhuanyehu*) were those that contracted specific production tasks from their production team. In most cases, the work contracted was in agriculture. 'Self managed' specialised households (*ziying zhuanyehu*) were those that had started out as households that contracted land and at the same time undertook domestic sidelines. Then, finding the 'sidelines' to be most profitable they concentrated on turning them into their major line of production (Zhou Qiren and Du Ying, 'Specialized households: a preliminary study', pp. 50–52). According to a number of reports, in the early to mid-1980s the latter type of specialised household clearly outnumbered the former (Richard Conroy, 'Laissez-faire socialism? Prosperous peasants and China's current rural development strategy', *Australian Journal of Chinese Affairs*, no. 12, 1984, p. 21; Song Linfei, 'The present state and future prospects of specialized households in rural China', *Social Sciences in China*, vol. 5, no. 4, 1984, p. 118). They engaged primarily in animal husbandry and handicraft production. More recently, however, specialised households have also engaged in other activities, including cash crop production, transport, and various services.

37 Interview with head of Huairou County Women's Federation, 6 September 1989.

38 Jilinsheng Fulian Xuanjiaobu [Propaganda and Education Department of the Jilin Provincial Women's Federation], '*Tigao funü kexue wenhua suzhi shi bashi niandai funü yundong xin tedian zhi yi*' ['Improving women's scientific and cultural quality is a new characteristic of the women's movement of the '80s'], *FNGZ*, September, 1984, pp. 14–15; *NMRB*, 12 June 1986; Xu Yan, '*Liyong tingyuan gao te yang xinxi shichang shi guanjian*', pp. 60–61.

39 Interview, October 1989.

40 Interviews with Ran Moying, Research Office of the Sichuan Provincial Women's Federation, and Li Dongshan, Institute of Sociology, Sichuan Academy of Social Sciences, October 1989.

41 Zhao Xishun, ed., *Gaige yu Nongcun Jiating [Reform and the Rural Family]*, Sichuansheng Shehui Kexueyuan Chubanshe, Sichuan, 1988, pp. 67–68.

42 *Ibid.*, p. 73.

43 Jilinsheng Fulian Xuanjiaobu, '*Tigao funü kexue wenhua suzhi shi bashi niandai funü yundong xin tedian zhi yi*', p. 14.

44 Of the remainder, 42 per cent were run by educated youth or demobilised soldiers, 9 per cent were run by 'skilled peasants', 5 per cent were run by 'talented people' (i.e., people formerly accused of being 'capitalist-roaders') and 1 per cent were run by people 'engaged in illegal activities' (*Beijing Review,* no. 9, 1984, p. 18, quoted in Conroy, 'Laissez-faire socialism?', p. 23).

45 Shanxisheng Huairenxian Fulian [The Women's Federation of Huairen County, Shanxi Province] '*Tingyuan ziyou zhi fu lu*' ['The courtyard itself is a way to get rich'], *FNGZ*, September, 1984, pp. 24–25.

46 Ester Boserup, *Woman's Role in Economic Development*, St. Martin's Press, New York, 1970, p. 221.
47 Ellen Judd, 'Alternative development strategies for women in rural China', *Development and Change*, vol. 21, no. 1, 1990, p. 37.
48 Shanxisheng Hairenxian Fulian, '*Tingyuan ziyou zhi fu lu*', pp. 25–26.
49 An important example is the Federation's campaign against calls for women to 'return to the kitchen' to relieve employment pressures in state-run industries. See Tamara Jacka, 'Back to the wok: women and employment in Chinese industry in the 1980s', *Australian Journal of Chinese Affairs*, no. 24, 1990, pp. 1–24.

9 INDUSTRY

1 Christopher Findlay and Andrew Watson, 'Surrounding the cities from the countryside', in Ross Garnaut and Liu Guoguang, eds, *Economic Reform and Internationalisation: China and the Pacific Region*, Allen & Unwin in association with Pacific Trade and Development Conference Secretariat, Australian National University, 1992, pp. 64–65.
2 See Guojia Tongjiju [State Statistical Bureau], *Zhongguo Tongji Nianjian, 1994 [Statistical Yearbook of China, 1994]*, Zhongguo Tongji Chubanshe, Beijing, 1994, pp. 361–362.
3 Chen Chunlai, Andrew Watson and Christopher Findlay, 'One state – two economies: current issues in China's rural industrialisation', Chinese Economy Research Unit Working Paper no. 91/16, University of Adelaide, 1990, p. 2.

It should be noted that joint ventures and foreign companies are not included in the discussion of township enterprises, even though some of them are located in villages and townships. They are, instead, discussed in the section on rural women's employment in urban areas.
4 Guojia Tongjiju, *Zhongguo Tongji Nianjian, 1994*, p. 362.
5 In 1984 private enterprises were included in the statistics for the first time. This meant that private enterprises that had developed in previous years were counted for the first time in 1984. Consequently, the growth rate in township enterprise employment for the period 1983–1985 is exaggerated in the statistics and is therefore not included here.
6 *Zhongguo Xiangzhenqiye Nianjian, 1992 [Chinese Township Enterprise Yearbook, 1992]*, Nongye Chunbanshe, Beijing, 1993, pp. 134–135; Guojia Tongjiju, *Zhongguo Tongji Nianjian*, 1994, p. 362.
7 Wang Tuoyu, 'Regional Imbalances', in William Byrd and Lin Qingsong, *China's Rural Industry. Structure, Development, and Reform*, Published for the World Bank, Oxford University Press, Oxford, 1990, p. 260.
8 *Ibid.*, pp. 260–261.
9 Dorothy Solinger, 'The Chinese Work Unit and Transient Labor in the Transition from Socialism', *Modern China*, vol. 21, no. 2, 1995, p. 178, note 1.
10 Li Mengbai and Hu Xin, eds, *Liudong Renkou Dui Da Chengshi Fazhan de Yingxiang ji Duice [The Influence of the Floating Population on Large Cities and Policy Responses]*, Jingji Ribao Chubanshe, Beijing, 1991, pp. 126, 216–218, 264.
11 *Ibid.*, pp. 7–13.
12 Men working away from home, whilst also mostly young and unmarried, include

some who are married and have families. They too are termed 'temporary' workers, but they are more likely than women to spend long periods away, moving from one temporary position to another, and only very occasionally returning home.

13 *NMRB*, 27 November 1986; *RMRB*, 31 October 1986; Quanguo Fulian Quanyibu Shengchanfulichu [Production Welfare Office, Legal Rights Department of the All-China Women's Federation] 1988, '*Xiangzhenqiye nügong laodong baohu ying yun er xing*' ['Labour protection for female workers in township enterprises must be carried out'], *FNGZ*, March 1988, pp. 6–7; *RMRB* 11 October 1994.

14 *RMRB*, 31 October 1986.

15 Harry Wu, 'The rural industrial enterprise workforce', in Christopher Findlay, Andrew Watson, and Harry Wu, eds, *Rural Enterprises in China*, Macmillan, Houndmills and London, and St Martin's Press, New York, 1994, p. 120.

16 Duan Daohuai, Jin Zhenji, Zhang Zhunying and Shi Suoda, 'Building a new countryside: Chinese women in rural enterprises', in Noeleen Heyzer, ed., *Daughters in Industry. Work Skills and Consciousness of Women Workers in Asia*, Asian and Pacific Development Centre, Kuala Lumpur, 1988, p. 84.

17 Wu, 'The rural industrial enterprise workforce', Table 6.4, p. 128. The survey found that the female labour force in township enterprises was on average younger than both the male labour force in township enterprises and the total working-age population. Some 55.2 per cent of male employees in township enterprises were aged between 17 and 29, and 25.4 per cent were aged between 30 and 39. In the national labour force, 43.4 per cent were aged between 17 and 29, whilst 25.7 were aged between 30 and 39 (Wu, 'The rural industrial enterprise workforce', pp. 7–8 and Table 6.4). It should be noted that none of these figures takes into account child labour, which, however, has been substantial in the 1980s and 1990s. Surveys from Hebei Province suggest, for example, that child labour makes up 10 per cent of the labour force in some counties (*Liaowang* [Overseas edition], no. 24, 1988, cited in Ole Odgaard, *Private Enterprises in Rural China*, Avebury, England, 1992, p. 170).

18 Duan Daohuai et al., 'Building a new countryside', p. 84.

19 Ellen Judd, 'Alternative development strategies for women in rural China', *Development and Change*, vol. 21, no. 1, 1990, p. 32.

20 Keith Griffin, *Institutional Reform and Economic Development in the Chinese Countryside*, Macmillan Press, London and Basingstoke, 1984, p. 219.

21 This practice is not limited to township enterprises. In 1995 I noted that advertisements for work in various enterprises in Hangzhou contained similar stipulations.

22 Guo Furen, ed., *Chengdu Liudong Renkou [Chengdu's Floating Population]*, Chengdu Chubanshe, Chengdu, 1990, pp. 14, 250, 254, 258.

23 Phyllis Andors relates this to the fact that many of the experiments in small-scale 'street industry', designed in part to draw 'housewives' into production, were in these areas, and that 'women's participation in the pilot projects ensured their absorption into the larger projects that evolved' (Phyllis Andors, *The Unfinished Liberation of Chinese Women 1949–1980*, Indiana University Press, Bloomington, and Wheatsheaf Books, Sussex, 1983, p. 87).

24 *Ibid.*

25 *ZGFN*, July 1979, p. 9; *RMRB*, 24 June 1988.

26 Tamara Jacka, 'Back to the wok: women and employment in Chinese industry in the 1980s', *Australian Journal of Chinese Affairs*, no. 24, 1990, pp. 1–24.

241

27 Prostitution, which is dominated by young rural women, is not discussed in this book. According to one estimate, in 1993 between 600,000 and 800,000 people were employed in the prostitution industry, mostly in the Special Economic Zones and large cities in the coastal provinces, but also in interior cities (Central People's Broadcasting Station 1993, p. 71). For research on prostitution in China see Dan Guangnai, *Zhongguo Changji – Guoqu he Xianzai [Prostitution in China – Past and Present]*, Falü Chubanshe, Beijing, 1995.

28 Li Mengbai and Hu Xin, eds, *Liudong Renkou*, p. 10.

29 *NMRB*, 11 January 1989.

30 Rubie Watson, 'Wives, concubines, and maids: servitude and kinship in the Hong Kong region, 1900–1940', in Rubie Watson and Patricia Ebrey, eds, *Marriage and Inequality in Chinese Society*, University of California Press, Berkeley, 1991, pp. 231–255; Maria Jaschok, *Concubines and Bondservants: the Social History of a Chinese Custom*, Zed Press, London, 1988.

31 Chen Baoming and Sun Zijun, 'The social function of housekeepers', *Chinese Sociology and Anthropology. A Journal of Translations*, vol. 17, no. 2, 1984–85, p. 97.

32 Guo Furen, *Chengdu Liudong Renkou*, pp. 274–275.

33 Huo Da, '*Baomu*' ['Nanny'] in Yan Chunde, ed., *Xin Shiqi Nüzuojia Bai Ren Zuopin Xuan [A Collection of Works By One Hundred Recent Women Writers]*, Haixia Wenyi Chubanshe, Fuzhou, 1985, p. 719.

34 Beijing Demographic and Urban Development Research Group, 'Family hired help in the Beijing area', *Chinese Sociology and Anthropology. A Journal of Translations*, vol. 20, no. 2, 1987–88, pp. 36–37.

35 Guo Furen, *Chengdu Liudong Renkou*, p. 270.

36 *Ibid.*, p. 274.

37 *Jingji Ribao [Economics Daily]*, 4 August 1985.

38 Interviews conducted in Beijing, August–September 1989, and in Hangzhou, October 1995.

39 Interview with representative of March 8th Domestic Service Company, Beijing, August 1989.

40 For this reason, the Beijing March 8th Domestic Service Company now refuses to hire nannies from Anhui, but they nevertheless still find employment in Beijing.

41 30 per cent in the contract I saw.

42 Interview conducted in Beijing, August 1989.

43 Interviews conducted in Hangzhou, October and November 1995.

44 Lydia Kung, *Factory Women in Taiwan*, UMI Research Press, Ann Arbor, Michigan, 1983, p. xv.

45 Guo Furen, *Chengdu Liudong Renkou*, p. 272.

46 Guowuyuan Yanjiushi [State Council Research Office], ed., *Geti Jingji Diaocha yu Yanjiu [Research and Investigation into the Private Economy]*, (Internal Document), Jingjikexue Chubanshe, Beijing, 1986.

47 Susan Young, 'Wealth but not security: attitudes towards private business in China in the 1980s', *Australian Journal of Chinese Affairs*, no. 25, 1991, pp. 123–124.

48 He Jianzhang and Zhu Qianfang (unpub.), 1987, p. 1, '*Geti jingji de fazhan qushi ji duice – Shenyangshi diaocha baogao*' ['Development trends and policies on the

private economy - an investigation report from Shenyang'], also translated in *Chinese Economic Studies*, vol. 21, no. 2, winter 1987–88.

49 Lu Zhonghe, '*Shanghai geti jingji fazhan de chengjiu, wenti ji guanli yijian*' ['Comments on the successes, problems and management of the development of Shanghai's private economy'], *Shanghai Jingji [Shanghai Economy]*, no. 2, 1988, p. 55.

50 Interviews conducted in Hangzhou, August–November 1995.

51 *Zhongguo Laodong Renshi Bao [Chinese Labour Newspaper]*, 16 March 1988. For further examples, see *Qiangjiang Wanbao [Qiangjiang Evening Paper]*, 24 December 1992.

52 Interview with representative of March 8th Domestic Service Company, Beijing, August 1989.

53 For accounts of the employment of women in textile factories in Shanghai and Tianjin in the first half of the 20th century see Emily Honig, *Sisters and Strangers. Women in the Shanghai Cotton Mills, 1919–1949*, Stanford University Press, Stanford, California, 1986; and Gail Hershatter, *The Workers of Tianjin, 1900–1949*, Stanford University Press, Stanford, California, 1986.

54 Duan Chengde, Sichuan Provincial Women's Federation, personal communication, October 1989.

55 Wu Jikang, 'Why young women are shying away from jobs in textile mills', *Chinese Sociology and Anthropology. A Journal of Translations*, vol. 20, no. 2, 1987–88, p. 21. See also Lisa Rofel, 'Hegemony and productivity: workers in post-Mao China', in Arif Dirlik and Maurice Meisner, eds, *Marxism and the Chinese Experience*, M. E. Sharpe, Armonk, New York and London, 1989, p. 246.

56 The media reports on the situation in textile mills all claim that it is shortages of urban workers that is driving employers to recruit rural women. Yet it may be that in some cases employers are retrenching urban women while recruiting rural women in preference because they are cheaper (personal communication, Ma Guonan, 1992).

57 Bao Ronglan, '*Xin shenghuo de tiansuankula – nongcun nühetonggong shenghuo jilu*' ['The sweetness and bitterness of a new life – a record of the lives of rural female contract workers'], *ZGFN*, January 1989, p. 6.

58 At the beginning of the 1980s, foreign funded firms, including Chinese/foreign joint ventures and wholly foreign firms, were concentrated in the Special Economic Zones of Shenzhen, Zhuhai, Shantou and Xiamen, where they enjoyed tax concessions and lax labour regulations. Through the 1980s and 1990s, however, they spread in increasing numbers to other cities, towns and townships in the south and southeast provinces, and gradually moved further and further inland.

59 Solinger, 'The Chinese work unit and transient labor', pp. 161–165.

60 Interview, Hangzhou, October 1995.

61 Sally Sargeson, personal communication, August 1993.

62 Wu Jikang, 'Why young women are shying away from jobs in textile mills', pp. 22–24.

63 Personal communication, August 1993.

64 Solinger, 'The Chinese work unit and transient labor', p. 165.

65 Interviews with rural workers, conducted in Hangzhou, August–November 1995.

66 Xinhua, 23 February 1994, cited in Solinger, 'The Chinese work unit and transient labor', p. 166.

67 For examples, see Bao Ronglan, '*Xin shenghuo de tiansuankula – nongcun nühetonggong shenghuo jilu*'.

68 Agence France Presse, 20 February 1994, cited in Solinger, 'The Chinese work unit and transient labor', p. 166.

69 *Ibid.*, p. 6.

70 Pat and Roger Howard, 'The campaign to eliminate job security in China', *Journal of Contemporary Asia*, vol. 25, no. 3, 1995, p. 351.

71 Cited in Solinger, 'The Chinese work unit and transient labor', p. 175.

72 Guo Furen, *Chengdu Liudong Renkou*, Appendix.

73 *South China Morning Post*, 18 March 1993.

74 For some township enterprise workers a similar kind of stigma is, nevertheless, still a problem. In the 1980s and 1990s most township enterprise employees worked in the same village or county in which they were resident, and my comments in the following section relate to these workers. It should be noted, however, that with increases in labour mobility, the employment in township enterprises of migrants from other counties and provinces is increasing. These migrants are hired as temporary workers and suffer forms of discrimination similar to those suffered by temporary workers in urban employment. For examples, see Helen Siu, 'The politics of migration in a market town', in Deborah Davis and Ezra Vogel, eds, *Chinese Society on the Eve of Tiananmen. The Impact of Reform*, Harvard University Press, Cambridge, Massachusetts and London, 1990, p. 77; and Anita Chan, Richard Madsen and Jonathan Unger, *Chen Village under Mao and Deng*, University of California Press, Berkeley, 1992 (1984), p. 304.

75 Alan Gelb, 'TVP workers' incomes, incentives, and attitudes', in Byrd and Lin, *China's Rural Industry. Structure, Development, and Reform*, p. 286.

76 Fei Juanhong, '*Wo guo nongcun gaige yu liang xing laodong fengong*' ['China's rural reforms and the division of labour between the sexes'], *Shehui Kexue Yanjiu [Social Science Research]*, no. 2, 1994, p. 80.

77 In addition, local governments often appoint cadres from their midst to management positions in township enterprises in order to maintain influence or control over the enterprise (Wu, 'The rural industrial enterprise workforce', p. 141; Guowuyuan Yanjiushi Nongcun Jingjizu, Zhongguo Shehui Kexueyuan Nongcun Fazhan Yanjiusuo [The Rural Economy Group of the State Council Research Office and The Rural Development Research Institute of the Chinese Academy of Social Sciences], eds, *Bie Wu Xuanze – Xiangzhen Qiye yu Guomin Jingji de Xietiao Fazhan [There is a Choice – The Co-ordinated Development of Township Enterprises and the National Economy]*, Gaige Chabanshe, Beijing, 1990, p. 148). According to the 1991 RDRI/CERU survey, 24.4 per cent of the 90 enterprise managers also held village cadre positions, 20 per cent held township cadre positions and 1.1 per cent held county cadre positions. Furthermore, 47.8 per cent of the managers were former township and village cadres, 10 per cent were former cadres above township level, or had worked in state-owned enterprises, and 17.8 per cent had worked in local supply and marketing cooperatives or credit cooperatives, or in other rural enterprises (Wu, 'The rural industrial enterprise workforce', p. 141).

78 Judd, 'Alternative development strategies for women in rural China', p. 33.

79 Wu, 'The rural industrial enterprise workforce', Table 6.9, p. 143.

80 Guojia Tongjiju [State Statistical Bureau], 1992, p. 137, cited in Wu, 'The rural industrial enterprise workforce', pp. 142–143.

81 Shanxisheng Fulian Diaoyanshi Quanyibu [The Legal Rights Section of the Research Office of the Shanxi Provincial Women's Federation], *'Xiangzhenqiye nügong laobao xianzhuang de diaocha'*, ['An investigation into labour protection for female workers in township enterprises'], *FNGZ*, September 1988, pp. 25–27.

82 Gelb, 'TVP workers' incomes, incentives, and attitudes', pp. 292–294.

83 *Ibid.*, p. 292.

84 *Ibid.*, pp. 291–292. Other surveys suggest, however, that while average profitability and incomes in private enterprises are similar to, or lower than, those in township or village-run enterprises, the range of profitability and incomes is much greater. One national survey estimates, for example, that 700,000 private enterprises earn more than 10,000 *yuan* per year. However, there are also private enterprises that earn incomes substantially below 3,000 *yuan* per year (*Jingji Cankao*, 8 April 1990, cited in Ole Odgaard, *Private Enterprises in Rural China*, Avebury, England, 1992, p. 161.)

85 Gelb, 'TVP workers' incomes, incentives, and attitudes', p. 297.

86 Wu, 'The rural industrial enterprise workforce', Table 6.9, p. 143.

87 Quanguo Fulian Quanyibu Shengchanfulichu [Production Welfare Office, Legal Rights Department of the All-China Women's Federation], *'Xiangzhenqiye nügong laodong baohu ying yun er xing'* ['Labour protection for female workers in township enterprises must be carried out'], *FNGZ*, March 1988, pp. 6–7.

88 Tan Shen, *'Dangdai zhongguo funü zhuangkuang de fenxi yu yuze'* ['Analysis and forecasts on the situation of women in contemporary China'], *Shehuixue Yanjiu [Sociological Research]*, no. 3, 1994, p. 74.

89 Shanxisheng Fulian Diaoyanshi Quanyibu [The Legal Rights Section of the Research Office of the Shanxi Provincial Women's Federation], *'Xiangzhenqiye nügong laobao xianzhuang de diaocha'*, ['An investigation into labour protection for female workers in township enterprises'], *FNGZ*, September 1988, pp. 25–27. The report claims that at the end of 1987 women working in township enterprises in Shanxi numbered 780,000, or 34.7 per cent of the total workforce in these enterprises. In textiles, clothing, printing, food and beverages, services and processing industries, they made up 80 to 90 per cent of workers.

90 While few township enterprises themselves provide child care, in some places they have nevertheless improved public child-care facilities more indirectly through taxes and other funds to local governments. In other places, however, local governments prefer to use such revenue for more immediately 'profitable' ventures. See Chapter 6.

Bibliography

ENGLISH LANGUAGE SOURCES

Ahern, Emily, 'The power and pollution of Chinese women', in Wolf, Margery and Witke, Roxane, eds, *Women in Chinese Society*, Stanford University Press, Stanford, California, 1975, pp. 193–214.

Andors, Phyllis, *The Unfinished Liberation of Chinese Women. 1949–1980*, Indiana University Press, Bloomington and Wheatsheaf Books, Sussex, 1983.

Ash, Robert, 'The agricultural sector in China: performance and policy dilemmas during the 1990s', *China Quarterly*, no. 131, 1992, pp. 545–576.

Baker, Hugh, *Chinese Family and Kinship*, Macmillan, London and Basingstoke, 1979.

Bakken, Börge, 'Backwards reform in Chinese education', *Australian Journal of Chinese Affairs*, no. 19/20, 1988, pp. 127–163.

Barrett, Michelle, *Women's Oppression Today. Problems in Marxist Feminist Analysis* (5th edn), Verso, London, 1986.

Beijing Demographic and Urban Development Research Group, 'Family hired help in the Beijing area', *Chinese Sociology and Anthropology. A Journal of Translations*, vol. 20, no. 2, 1987–88, pp. 34–47.

Bianco, Lucien, *Origins of the Chinese Revolution, 1915–1949*, Stanford University Press, California, and Oxford University Press, London, 1971 (1967).

Bose, Christine, 'Technology and changes in the division of labour in the American home', in Whitelegg, Elizabeth, ed., *The Changing Experience of Women*, Martin Robertson, Oxford, 1982, pp. 226–238.

Boserup, Ester, *Woman's Role in Economic Development*, St. Martin's Press, New York, 1970.

Bridger, Susan, *Women in the Soviet Countryside. Women's Roles in Rural Development in the Soviet Union*, Cambridge University Press, Cambridge, 1987.

Broyelle, Claudie, *Women's Liberation in China*, translated by Cohen, M. and Herman, G., Humanities Press, Atlantic Highlands, New Jersey, 1977.

Buck, John, *Land Utilization in China*, Council on Economic and Cultural Affairs, New York, 1956 (1937).

Burns, John, 'Chinese Peasant Interest Articulation', in Goodman, David, ed., *Groups and Politics in the People's Republic of China*, M. E. Sharpe, Armonk, New York, 1984, pp. 126–151.

Burton, Clare, *Subordination. Feminism and Social Theory*, Allen & Unwin, Sydney, 1985.

Byrd, William, and Lin Qinsong, eds, *China's Rural Industry. Structure, Development and Reform*, published for the World Bank, Oxford University Press, Oxford, 1990.

CCP, 'Communique of the Third Plenary Session of the 11th Central Committee of the Communist Party of China', *Peking Review*, no. 52, 29 December 1978, pp. 6–16.

Central People's Broadcasting Station, 'CPBS looks at the prostitution phenomenon', broadcast, May 2, Beijing, printed in *Inside China Mainland*, vol. 15, July 1993, pp. 71–74.

Chan, Anita, Madsen, Richard and Unger, Jonathan, *Chen Village under Mao and Deng*, University of California Press, Berkeley, 1992 (1984).

Chayanov, A.V., *Organizatsiya krest'yanskogo khozyaistva*, 1925, translated by Thorner, D., Smith, R. and Kerblay, B. 1966, as *The Theory of Peasant Economy*, Irwin, Illinois, 1966.

Chen Baoming and Sun Zijun, 'The social function of housekeepers', *Chinese Sociology and Anthropology. A Journal of Translations*, vol. 17, no. 2, 1984–85, pp. 96–106.

Chen Chunlai, Watson, Andrew and Findlay, Christopher, 'One state – two economies: current issues in China's rural industrialisation', Chinese Economy Research Unit Working Paper no. 91/16, University of Adelaide, 1990.

China Daily
12 October 1985.
24 May 1991.

Christiansen, Flemming, 'Social division and peasant mobility in mainland China: the implications of the *hu-k'ou* system', *Issues and Studies*, vol. 26, no. 4, 1990, pp. 23–42.

Cohen, Myron, 'Developmental process in the Chinese domestic group', in Freedman, Maurice, ed., *Family and Kinship in Chinese Society*, Stanford University Press, Stanford, California, 1970, pp. 21–36.

Collier, Jane Fishburne and Yanagisako, Sylvia Junko, eds, *Gender and Kinship. Essays Toward a Unified Analysis*, Stanford University Press, Stanford, California, 1987.

Conroy, Richard, 'Laissez-faire socialism? Prosperous peasants and China's current rural development strategy', *Australian Journal of Chinese Affairs*, no. 12, 1984, pp. 1–34.

Croll, Elisabeth, *Feminism and Socialism in China*, Routledge and Kegan Paul, London, Henley and Boston, 1978.

Croll, Elisabeth, *The Politics of Marriage in Contemporary China*, Cambridge University Press, Cambridge, 1981.

Croll, Elisabeth, *The Family Rice Bowl: Food and the Domestic Economy in China*, United Nations Research Institute for Social Development, Geneva, 1982.

Croll, Elisabeth, 'The promotion of domestic sideline production in rural China 1978–79', in Gray, Jack and White, Gordon, eds, *China's New Development Strategy*, Academic Press, London, 1982, pp. 235–254.

Croll, Elisabeth, *Chinese Women Since Mao*, Zed Books, London and M. E. Sharpe, Armonk, New York, 1983.

Croll, Elisabeth, 'Introduction: fertility norms and family size in China', in Croll, Elisabeth, Davin, Delia, and Kane, Penny, eds, *China's One-Child Family Policy*, Macmillan, London, 1985, pp. 1–36.

Croll, Elisabeth, *Women in Rural Development in China*, International Labour Office, Geneva, 1985 (1979).

Croll, Elisabeth, 'Some implications of the rural economic reforms for the Chinese peasant household', in Saith, Ashwani, ed., *The Re-emergence of the Chinese*

Peasantry. Aspects of Rural Decollectivisation, Croom Helm, London, 1987, pp. 105–136.

Crook, Isabel and Crook, David, *The First Years of Yangyi Commune*, 2nd edn, Routledge and Kegan Paul, London, Boston and Henley, 1979.

Davin, Delia, *Woman-Work. Women and the Party in Revolutionary China*, Clarendon Press, Oxford, 1976.

Davin, Delia, 'The single-child policy in the countryside', in Croll, Elisabeth, Davin, Delia, and Kane, Penny, eds, *China's One-Child Family Policy*, Macmillan, London, 1985, pp. 37–82.

Davin, Delia, 'China: The new inheritance law and the peasant household', *Journal of Communist Studies*, vol. 3, no. 4, 1987, pp. 52–63.

Davin, Delia, 'The implications of contract agriculture for the employment and status of Chinese peasant women', in Feuchtwang, Stephan, Hussain, Athar, and Pairault, Thierry, eds, *Transforming China's Economy in the Eighties. Vol. 1, The Rural Sector, Welfare and Employment*, Westview Press, Boulder, and Zed Books, London, 1988, pp. 137–144.

Davin, Delia, ' "Never mind if it's a girl, you can have another try" ', in Delman, Jorgen, Ostergaard, Clemens Stubbe, and Christiansen, Flemming, *Remaking Peasant China. Problems of Rural Development and Institutions at the start of the 1990s*, Aarhus University Press, Denmark, 1990, pp. 81–91.

Davis, Deborah and Vogel, Ezra, 'Introduction: the social and political consequences of reform', in Davis, Deborah, and Vogel, Ezra, eds, *Chinese Society on the Eve of Tiananmen. The Impact of Reform*, Council on East Asian Studies, Harvard University, Cambridge, Massachusetts and London, 1990, pp. 1–12.

De Koninck, Rodolphe, 'La réhabilitation de l'agriculture familiale en République Populaire de Chine: quelques intérrogations' ['The rehabilitation of family-based agriculture in the People's Republic of China: some questions'], *TRAVAIL, Capital et Société [LABOUR, Capital and Society]*, vol. 18, no. 1, 1985, pp. 44–67.

Delmar, Rosalind, 'Looking again at Engels's "Origins of the family, private property and the state" ', in Mitchell, Juliet, and Oakley, Ann, eds, *The Rights and Wrongs of Women*, Penguin, Harmondsworth, 1976, pp. 271–287.

Delphy, Christine, *Close to Home. A Materialist Analysis of Women's Oppression*, Hutchinson, London, 1984.

Duan Daohuai, Jin Zhenji, Zhang Zhunying and Shi Suoda, 'Building a new countryside: Chinese women in rural enterprises', in Heyzer, Noeleen, ed., *Daughters in Industry. Work Skills and Consciousness of Women Workers in Asia*, Asian and Pacific Development Centre, Kuala Lumpur, 1988, pp. 69–104.

Engels, Friedrich, *The Origin of the Family, Private Property and the State*, Progress Publishers, Moscow, 1977 (1884).

Fei Hsiao-Tung and Chang Chih-I, *Earthbound China. A Study of Rural Economy in Yunnan*, University of Chicago Press, Chicago, 1945.

Findlay, Christopher and Watson, Andrew, 'Surrounding the cities from the countryside', in Garnaut, Ross and Liu Guoguang, eds, *Economic Reform and Internationalisation: China and the Pacific Region*, Allen & Unwin in association with the Pacific Trade and Development Conference Secretariat, Australian National University, 1992, pp. 49–78.

Freedman, Maurice, ed., *Family and Kinship in Chinese Society*, Stanford University Press, Stanford, California, 1970.

Fujian Education Commission, 'An investigation of the status of primary education among rural school-age girls', *Chinese Education. A Journal of Translations*, vol. 22, no. 2, 1989, pp. 53–64.

Gamble, Sidney, *Ting Hsien. A North China Rural Community*, Stanford University Press, Stanford, 1954.

Gelb, Alan, 'TVP workers' incomes, incentives, and attitudes', in Byrd, William and Lin Qingsong, ed., *China's Rural Industry. Structure, Development, and Reform*, Published for the World Bank, Oxford University Press, Oxford, 1990, pp. 280–298.

Gilmartin, Christina, Hershatter, Gail, Rofel, Lisa and White, Tyrene, eds, *Engendering China. Women, Culture and the State*, Harvard University Press, Cambridge, Massachusetts, London, 1994.

Gray, Jack and White, Gordon, *China's New Development Strategy*, Academic Press, London and New York, 1978.

Griffin, Keith, ed., *Institutional Reform and Economic Development in the Chinese Countryside*, Macmillan Press, London and Basingstoke, 1984.

Harris, Olivia, 'The power of signs: gender, culture and the wild in the Bolivian Andes', in MacCormack, Carol and Strathern, Marilyn, eds, *Nature, Culture and Gender*, Cambridge University Press, Cambridge, 1980, pp. 70–94.

Hershatter, Gail, *The Workers of Tianjin, 1900–1949*, Stanford University Press, Stanford, California, 1986.

Hinton, William, *Fanshen*, Monthly Review Press, New York, 1966.

Hinton, William, 'Transformation in the countryside. Part Two: unresolved issues and the responsibility system', *US–China Review*, vol. 8, no. 4, 1984, pp. 12–19.

Honig, Emily and Hershatter, Gail, *Personal Voices. Chinese Women in the 1980s*, Stanford University Press, Stanford, California, 1988.

Honig, Emily, 'Socialist revolution and women's liberation in China – a review article', *Journal of Asian Studies*, vol. 49, no. 2, 1985, pp. 329–336.

Honig, Emily, *Sisters and Strangers. Women in the Shanghai Cotton Mills, 1919–1949*, Stanford University Press, Stanford, California, 1986.

Hooper, Beverley, 'Gender and education', in Epstein, Irving, ed., *Chinese Education. Problems, Policies, and Prospects*, Garland Publishing, New York and London, 1991, pp. 352–374.

Howard, Pat and Howard, Roger, 'The campaign to eliminate job security in China', *Journal of Contemporary Asia*, vol. 25, no. 3, 1995, pp. 338–355.

Hsu, Francis, *Under the Ancestors' Shadow. Chinese Culture and Personality*, Routledge & Kegan Paul, London, 1949.

Huang, Philip, *The Peasant Economy and Social Change in North China*, Stanford University Press, Stanford, California, 1985.

Huang, Philip, *The Peasant Family and Rural Development in the Yangzi Delta, 1350–1988*, Stanford University Press, Stanford, California, 1990.

Huang Xiyi, 'Changes in the economic status of rural women in the transformation of modern Chinese society', *Social Sciences in China*, no. 1, 1992, pp. 83–105.

Hull, Terence, 'Rising sex ratios in China: evidence from the 1990 population census', *Briefing Paper no. 31*, Australian Development Studies Network, Australian National University, Canberra, 1993.

Bibliography

Hussain, Athar and Liu Hong, 'Compendium of Literature on the Chinese Social Security System', *China Programme, Research Working Papers*, no. 3, STICERD, London School of Economics, 1989.

Inside China Mainland, vol. 15, March 1993, pp. 28–40 (a collection of articles on the 'Dismal agricultural situation').

Institute of Population Studies, Chinese Academy of Social Sciences, ed., *Sampling Survey Data of Women's Status in Contemporary China*, International Academic Publishers, Beijing, 1994.

Jacka, Tamara, 'Back to the wok: women and employment in Chinese industry in the 1980s', *Australian Journal of Chinese Affairs*, no. 24, 1990, pp. 1–24.

Jacka, Tamara, 'The public/private dichotomy and the gender division of rural labour', in Watson, Andrew, ed., *Economic Reform and Social Change in China*, Routledge, London and New York, 1992, pp. 117–143.

Jacobs, Bruce, 'Elections in China', *Australian Journal of Chinese Affairs*, no. 25, 1991, pp. 171–200.

Jaggar, Alison, *Feminist Politics and Human Nature*, Rowman & Allanheld, New Jersey, and Harvester Press, Sussex, 1983.

Jancar, Barbara, *Women under Communism*, John Hopkins University Press, Baltimore and London, 1978.

Jaschok, Maria, *Concubines and Bondservants: the Social History of a Chinese Custom*, Zed Press, London, 1988.

Ji Ping, Zhang Kaiti and Liu Dawei, 'Marriage motivated population movement in the outskirts of Beijing', *Social Sciences in China*, vol. 7, no. 1, 1986, pp. 161–180.

Johnson, Kay Ann, *Women, the Family and Peasant Revolution in China*, University of Chicago Press, Chicago and London, 1983.

Judd, Ellen, '*Niangjia:* Chinese women and their natal families', *Journal of Asian Studies*, vol. 48, no. 3, 1989, pp. 525–544.

Judd, Ellen, 'Alternative development strategies for women in rural China', *Development and Change*, vol. 21, no. 1, 1990, pp. 23–42.

Judd, Ellen, *Gender and Power in Rural North China*, Stanford University Press, Stanford, California, 1994.

Kane, Penny, *The Second Billion. Population and Family Planning in China*, Penguin Books, Australia, 1987.

Kato, Hiroyuki, 'Regional development in the reform period', in Garnaut, Ross and Liu Guoguang, *Economic Reform and Internationalisation: China and the Pacific Region*, Allen & Unwin, Sydney, 1990, pp. 116–136.

Khan, Azizur, Griffin, Keith, Riskin, Carl and Zhao Renwei, 'Household income and its distribution in China', *China Quarterly*, no. 132, 1992, pp. 1029–1061.

Kung, Lydia, *Factory Women in Taiwan*, UMI Research Press, Ann Arbor, Michigan, 1983.

Lavely, William, 'Marriage and mobility under rural collectivism', in Watson, Rubie and Ebrey, Patricia, eds, *Marriage and Inequality in Chinese Society*, University of California Press, Berkeley, 1991, pp. 286–312.

Levy, Marion, *The Family Revolution in Modern China* (2nd edn), Octagon Books, New York, 1963.

Li Kejing, 'Strategic approaches to eliminating illiteracy in China', *Social Sciences in China*, no. 2, 1992, pp. 23–33.

Li Xiaoyun, Lin Zhibin, Liu Yonggong and Li Ou (unpub.), 'The contribution of women to agricultural and household activities in rural areas. A case study in Ningjin County', Centre for Integrated Agricultural Development, Beijing Agricultural University, 1992.

Lloyd, Genevieve, *The Man of Reason. 'Male' and 'Female' in Western Philosophy*, Methuen, London, 1984.

MacCormack, Carol, 'Nature, culture and gender: a critique', in MacCormack, Carol and Strathern, Marilyn, eds, *Nature, Culture and Gender*, Cambridge University Press, Cambridge, 1980, pp. 1–24.

Matthews, Jill, *Good and Mad Women. The Historical Construction of Femininity in Twentieth-Century Australia* (2nd edn), Allen & Unwin, Sydney, 1992.

Mies, Maria, *The Lace Makers of Narsapur. Indian Housewives Produce for the World Market*, Zed Press, London, 1982.

Moore, Henrietta, *Feminism and Anthropology* (3rd edn), Polity Press, Cambridge, 1991.

Myrdal, Jan, *Report from a Chinese Village*, Penguin Books, Harmondsworth and Melbourne, 1967.

Nee, Victor and Su Sijin, 'Institutional change and economic growth in China: the view from the villages', *Journal of Asian Studies*, vol. 49, no. 1, 1990, pp. 3–25.

Ocko, Jonathan, 'Women, property, and law in the People's Republic of China', in Watson, Rubie and Ebrey, Patricia, eds, *Marriage and Inequality in Chinese Society*, University of California Press, Berkeley, 1991, pp. 313–346.

Odgaard, Ole, 'Collective control of income distribution: a case study of private enterprises in Sichuan province', in Delman, Jorgen, Ostergaard, Clemens Stubbe and Christiansen, Flemming, eds, *Remaking Peasant China. Problems of Rural Development and Institutions at the start of the 1990s*, Aarhus University Press, Denmark, 1990.

Odgaard, Ole, *Private Enterprises in Rural China*, Avebury, England, 1992.

Oi, Jean, 'The fate of the collective after the commune', in Davis, Deborah and Vogel, Ezra, eds, *Chinese Society on the Eve of Tiananmen. The Impact of Reform*, Harvard Contemporary China Series: 7, 1990, pp. 15–33.

Ortner, Sherry, 'Is female to male as nature is to culture?', in Rosaldo, Michelle and Lamphere, Louise, eds, *Woman, Culture, and Society*, Stanford University Press, Stanford, California, 1974, pp. 67–87.

Papanek, Hanna, 'To each less than she needs, from each more than she can do', in Tinker, Irene, ed., *Persistent Inequalities. Women and World Development*, Oxford University Press, New York and Oxford, 1990, pp. 162–184.

Parish, William and Whyte, Martin, *Village and Family in Contemporary China*, University of Chicago Press, Chicago and London, 1978.

Pepper, Suzanne, *China's Education Reform in the 1980s. Policies, Issues, and Historical Perspectives*, Institute of East Asian Studies, University of California, Berkeley, 1990.

Platte, Erika, 'The private sector in China's agriculture: an appraisal of recent changes', *Australian Journal of Chinese Affairs*, no. 10, 1983, pp. 81–96.

Potter, Sulamith and Potter, Jack, *China's Peasants. The Anthropology of a Revolution* (2nd edn), Cambridge University Press, Cambridge, 1991.

Pruitt, Ida, *A Daughter of Han. The Autobiography of a Chinese Working Woman*, Stanford University Press, Stanford, California, 1945.

Rai, Shirin and Zhang Junzuo, '"Competing and learning": women and the state in contemporary rural mainland China', *Issues and Studies*, vol. 30, no. 3, 1994, pp. 51–66.

Riskin, Carl, *China's Political Economy. The Quest for Development Since 1949*, Oxford University Press, Oxford, 1987.

Robinson, Jean, 'Of women and washing machines: employment, housework, and the reproduction of motherhood in socialist China', *China Quarterly*, no. 101, 1985, pp. 32–57.

Rofel, Lisa, 'Hegemony and productivity: workers in post-Mao China', in Dirlik, Arif and Meisner, Maurice, eds, *Marxism and the Chinese Experience*, M. E. Sharpe, Armonk, New York and London, 1989, pp. 235–252.

Rosaldo, Michelle, 'Woman, culture, and society: a theoretical overview', in Rosaldo, Michelle and Lamphere, Louise, eds, *Woman, Culture, and Society*, Stanford University Press, Stanford, California, 1974, pp. 17–42.

Rosaldo, Michelle, 'The use and abuse of anthropology: reflections on feminism and cross-cultural understanding', *Signs: Journal of Women in Culture and Society*, vol. 5, no. 3, 1980, pp. 389–417.

Ross, Heidi, 'The "crisis" in Chinese secondary schooling', in Epstein, Irving, ed., *Chinese Education. Problems, Policies and Prospects*, Garland Publishing, New York and London, 1991, pp. 66–108.

Rowbotham, Sheila, *Women, Resistance and Revolution*, Allen Lane, London, 1972.

Rozelle, Scott, 'Decision-making in China's rural economy: the linkages between village leaders and farm households', *China Quarterly*, no. 137, 1994, pp. 99–124.

Sacks, Karen, 'Engels revisited: women, the organization of production, and private property', in Rosaldo, Michelle and Lamphere, Louise, eds, *Woman, Culture, and Society*, Stanford University Press, Stanford, California, 1974, pp. 207–222.

Scott, Joan, 'Deconstructing equality-versus-difference: or, the uses of post-structuralist theory for feminism', *Feminist Studies*, vol. 14, no. 1, 1988, pp. 33–50.

Sen, Amartya, 'Gender and Cooperative Conflicts', in Tinker, Irene, ed., *Persistent Inequalities. Women and World Development*, Oxford University Press, New York and Oxford, 1990, pp. 123–149.

Shanin, Teodor, ed., *Peasants and Peasant Societies*, Penguin, Harmondsworth, 1971.

Shue, Vivienne, 'Emerging state-society relations in rural China', in Delman, Jorgen, Ostergaard, Clemens Stubbe and Christiansen, Flemming, eds, *Remaking Peasant China. Problems of Rural Development and Institutions at the Start of the 1990s*, Aarhus University Press, Denmark, 1990, pp. 60–80.

Sidel, Ruth and Sidel, Victor, *The Health of China. Current Conflicts in Medical and Human Services for One Billion People*, Zed Press, London, 1982.

Siu, Helen, 'The politics of migration in a market town', in Davis, Deborah and Vogel, Ezra, eds, *Chinese Society on the Eve of Tiananmen. The Impact of Reform*, Harvard University Press, Cambridge, Massachusetts and London, 1990, pp. 61–82.

Solinger, Dorothy, 'The Fifth National People's Congress and the process of policy making: reform, readjustment and the opposition', *Asian Survey*, vol. 22, no. 12, 1982, pp. 1238–1278.

Solinger, Dorothy, 'The Chinese work unit and transient labor in the transition from socialism', *Modern China*, vol. 21, no. 2, 1995, pp. 155–183.

Song Linfei, 'The present state and future prospects of specialized households in rural China', *Social Sciences in China*, vol. 5, no. 4, 1984, pp. 107–130.

South China Morning Post, 18 March 1993.

Stacey, Judith, *Patriarchy and Socialist Revolution in China*, University of California Press, Berkeley, 1983.

Strathern, Marilyn, 'No nature, no culture: the Hagen case', in MacCormack, Carol and Strathern, Marilyn, eds, *Nature, Culture and Gender*, Cambridge University Press, Cambridge, 1980, pp. 174–222.

SWB (Summary of World Broadcasts, BBC)

    5 October 1988 FE/W0046/A/1.

    15 February 1989 FE/0385 B2/7.

    22 August 1990 FE/0849 B2/3

    1 November 1990 FE/0910 B2/5.

    5 December 1990 FE/W0157 A/2.

    19 October 1992 FE/1515 C1/3-5.

    19 April 1995 FEW/0380 WG/12.

Taylor, Jeffrey, 'Rural employment trends and the legacy of surplus labour, 1978–86', *China Quarterly*, no. 116, 1988, pp. 736–766.

Terrill, Ross, *The White-Boned Demon. A biography of Madame Mao-Zedong*, William Morrow, New York, 1984.

Thorborg, Marina, 'Chinese employment policy in 1949–1978 with special emphasis on women in rural production', in *Chinese Economy Post-Mao. A Compendium of Papers Submitted to the Joint Economic Committee Congress of the United States, vol. 1 Policy and Performance*, US Government Printing Office, Washington, 1978.

Time, 11 November 1991.

Topley, Marjorie, 'Marriage resistance in rural Kwangtung', in Wolf, Margery and Witke, Roxane, eds, *Women in Chinese Society*, Stanford University Press, Stanford, California, 1975, pp. 67–88.

Wakeman, Frederic, *The Fall of Imperial China*, Free Press, New York, 1975.

Walker, Kathy Le Mons, 'Economic growth, peasant marginalization, and the sexual division of labor in early twentieth-century China', *Modern China*, vol. 19, no. 3, 1993, pp. 354–365.

Wang Shuhui, 'Educational level of female teenagers and young adults declines', *Chinese Education. A Journal of Translations*, vol. 22, no. 2, 1989, pp. 20–21.

Wang Tuoyu, 'Regional imbalances', in Byrd, William and Lin Qingsong, ed., *China's Rural Industry. Structure, Development, and Reform*, Published for the World Bank, Oxford University Press, Oxford, 1990, pp. 255–273.

Watson, Andrew, 'The management of the industrial economy: the return of the economists', in Gray, Jack and White, Gordon, *China's New Development Strategy*, Academic Press, London and New York, 1982, pp. 87–118.

Watson, Andrew, 'Agriculture looks for "shoes that fit": The production responsibility system and its implications', *World Development*, vol. 11, no. 8, 1983, pp. 705–730.

Watson, Andrew, 'New structures in the organization of Chinese agriculture: A variable model', *Pacific Affairs*, vol. 57, no. 4, 1984–85, pp. 621–645.

Watson, Andrew, 'The family farm, land use and accumulation in agriculture', *Australian Journal of Chinese Affairs*, no. 17, 1987, pp. 1–27.

Watson, Andrew, ed., *Economic Reform and Social Change in China*, Routledge, London and New York, 1992.

Watson, Andrew, 'The management of the rural economy: the institutional parameters', in Watson, Andrew, ed., *Economic Reform and Social Change in China*, Routledge, London and New York, 1992, pp. 171–199.

Watson, Andrew, 'Market reform and agricultural growth: the dynamics of change in the Chinese countryside in 1992', in Cheng, Joseph and Brosseau, Maurice, eds, *China Review 1993*, Chinese University of Hong Kong, 1993, pp. 1–20.

Watson, Rubie, 'Wives, concubines, and maids: servitude and kinship in the Hong Kong region, 1900–1940', in Watson, Rubie and Ebrey, Patricia, eds, *Marriage and Inequality in Chinese Society*, University of California Press, Berkeley, 1991, pp. 231–255.

White, Tyrene, 'Political reform and rural government', in Davis, Deborah and Vogel, Ezra, eds, *Chinese Society on the Eve of Tiananmen. The Impact of Reform*, Council on East Asian Studies, Harvard University, Cambridge, Massachusetts and London, 1990, pp. 37–60.

Wolf, Margery, *Women and the Family in Rural Taiwan*, Stanford University Press, Stanford, California, 1972.

Wolf, Margery, 'Chinese women: old skills in a new context', in Rosaldo, Michelle and Lamphere, Louise, eds, *Woman, Culture and Society*, Stanford University Press, Stanford, California, 1974.

Wolf, Margery, *Revolution Postponed. Women in Contemporary China*, Methuen, London, 1985.

Women in the Villages, Men in the Towns, 1984, UNESCO, Geneva.

Woon, Yuen-fong, 'From Mao to Deng: Life satisfaction among rural women in an emigrant community in South China', *Australian Journal of Chinese Affairs*, no. 25, 1991, pp. 139–170.

World Bank, *The Health Sector in China*, Report no. 4664-CHA, 1984.

Wu, Harry, 'The industrialisation of China's rural labour force since the economic reform', Working Paper no. 92/6, Chinese Economy Research Unit, University of Adelaide, 1992.

Wu, Harry, 'The rural industrial enterprise workforce', in Findlay, Christopher, Watson, Andrew and Wu, Harry, eds, *Rural Enterprises in China*, Macmillan, Houndmills and London, and St Martin's Press, New York, 1994.

Wu Jikang, 'Why young women are shying away from jobs in textile mills', *Chinese Sociology and Anthropology. A Journal of Translations*, vol. 20, no. 2, 1987–88, pp. 20–26.

Yanagisako, Sylvia Junko, 'Mixed metaphors: native and anthropological models of gender and kinship domains', in Collier, Jane Fishburne and Yanagisako, Sylvia Junko, eds, *Gender and Kinship. Essays Toward a Unified Analysis*, Stanford University Press, Stanford, California, 1987.

Yang, Martin, *A Chinese Village. Taitou, Shantung Province*, Columbia University Press, New York, 1945.

Young, Iris, 'Beyond the unhappy marriage: a critique of the dual systems theory', in Sargent, Lydia, ed., *Women and Revolution*, South End Press, Boston, 1980, pp. 43–69.

Young, Marilyn, 'Chicken Little in China: some reflections on women', in Dirlik, Arif and Meisner, Maurice, eds, *Marxism and the Chinese Experience*, M. E. Sharpe, Armonk, New York and London, 1989, pp. 253–268.

Young, Susan, 'Wealth but not security: attitudes towards private business in China in the 1980s', *Australian Journal of Chinese Affairs*, no. 25, 1991, pp. 115–138.

Zhang Ning, 'A conflict of interests: current problems in educational reform', in Watson, Andrew, ed., *Economic Reform and Social Change in China*, Routledge, London and New York, 1992, pp. 144–170.

Zhou Qiren and Du Ying, 'Specialized households: a preliminary study', *Social Sciences in China*, vol. 5, no. 3, September 1984, pp. 50–72.

Zweig, David, 'Peasants, ideology, and new incentive systems: Jiangsu Province, 1978–1981', in Parish, William, ed., *Chinese Rural Development. The Great Transformation*, M. E. Sharpe, Armonk, New York and London, 1985, pp. 141–163.

CHINESE LANGUAGE SOURCES

ACWF, '*Quanguo Fulian Shujichu xiang wujie changwei de gongzuo huibao*' ['Work report given by the secretariat of the All-China Women's Federation to the standing committee of the Fifth National Women's Congress'], *FNGZ*, April 1984, pp. 4–8.

ACWF, '*Xin shiqi nongcun funü gongzuo de xin renwu*' ['New tasks for rural woman-work in the new era'], *FNGZ*, August 1986, pp. 2–5.

ACWF, '*Guanyu zai quanguo gezu nongcun funü zhong shenru kaizhan xue wenhua, xue jishu, bi chengji, bi gongxian jingsai huodong de lianhe tongzhi*' ['Joint circular on the thorough development of activities to study culture and technology and compete in achievements and contribution amongst rural women of all nationalities across the country'], *FNGZ*, April 1989, pp. 11–12.

Bao Ronglan, '*Xin shenghuo de tiansuankula – nongcun nühetonggong shenghuo jilu*' ['The sweetness and bitterness of a new life – a record of the lives of rural female contract workers'], *ZGFN*, January 1989, pp. 6–8.

Cui Yuxiang, '*Guanyu funü canzheng wenti yanjiu zongshu*' ['A summary of research on women's participation in politics'], in Zhongguo Renmin Daxue Shubao Ziliao Zhongxin, Fuyin Baokan Ziliao, *Funü Zuzhi yu Huodong* [Press clippings on *Women's Organisations and Activities*, Centre for Books and Newspaper Materials, Chinese People's University], no. 6, 1993, pp. 42–45.

Dan Guangnai, *Zhongguo Changji – Guoqu he Xianzai [Prostitution in China – Past and Present]*, Falü Chubanshe, Beijing, 1995.

Fei Juanhong, '*Wo guo nongcun gaige yu liang xing laodong fengong*' ['China's rural reforms and the division of labour between the sexes'], Shehui Kexue Yanjiu [Social Science Research], no. 2, 1994, pp. 76–82.

FNGZ
    September 1984, p. 24
    July 1986, p. 12.

Guangming Ribao [Bright Daily], 14 October 1988.

Guo Furen, ed., *Chengdu Liudong Renkou [Chengdu's Floating Population]*, Chengdu Chubanshe, Chengdu, 1990.

Bibliography

Guo Zhigang, '*Bijiao jiating moshi bianhua dingliang yanjiu zhibiao de tantao*' ['An inquiry into research standards for comparing changes in family type'], *Renkou yu Jingji [Population and the Economy]*, no. 2, 1988, pp. 52–58.

Guojia Tongjiju [State Statistical Bureau], *Zhongguo Tongji Nianjian, 1986 [Statistical Yearbook of China, 1986]*, Zhongguo Tongji Chubanshe, Beijing, 1986.

Guojia Tongjiju [State Statistical Bureau], *Zhongguo Tongji Nianjian, 1989 [Statistical Yearbook of China, 1989]*, Zhongguo Tongji Chubanshe, Beijing, 1989.

Guojia Tongjiju [State Statistical Bureau], *Zhongguo Tongji Nianjian, 1990 [Statistical Yearbook of China, 1990]*, Zhongguo Tongji Chubanshe, Beijing, 1990.

Guojia Tongjiju [State Statistical Bureau], *Zhongguo Tongji Nianjian, 1992 [Statistical Yearbook of China, 1992]*, Zhongguo Tongji Chubanshe, Beijing, 1992.

Guojia Tongjiju [State Statistical Bureau], *Zhongguo Tongji Nianjian, 1994 [Statistical Yearbook of China, 1994]*, Zhongguo Tongji Chubanshe, Beijing, 1994.

Guojia Tongjiju Renkou Tongjisi [Population Statistics Department, State Bureau of Statistics], *Zhongguo Renkou Tongji Nianjian, 1991 [Chinese Population Statistical Yearbook, 1991]*, Zhongguo Tongji Chubanshe, Beijing, 1992.

Guojia Tongjiju Shehui Tongjisi [Social Statistics Department, State Bureau of Statistics], *Zhongguo Shehui Tongji Ziliao [Chinese Social Statistics]*, Zhongguo Tongji Chubanshe, Beijing, 1987.

Guowuyuan Yanjiushi [State Council Research Office], ed., *Geti Jingji Diaocha yu Yanjiu [Research and Investigation into the Private Economy]*, (Internal Document), Jingjikexue Chubanshe, Beijing, 1986.

Guowuyuan Yanjiushi Nongcun Jingjizu, Zhongguo Shehui Kexueyuan Nongcun Fazhan Yanjiusuo [Rural Economy Group of the State Council Research Office and Rural Development Research Institute of the Chinese Academy of Social Sciences], eds, *Bie Wu Xuanze – Xiangzhen Qiye yu Guomin Jingji de Xietiao Fazhan [There is a Choice – The Co-ordinated Development of Township Enterprises and the National Economy]*, Gaige Chabanshe, Beijing, 1990.

He Jianzhang and Zhu Qianfang (unpub.), '*Geti jingji de fazhan qushi ji duice – Shenyangshi diaocha baogao*' ['Development trends and policies on the private economy – an investigation report from Shenyang'], 1987, also translated in *Chinese Economic Studies*, vol. 21, no. 2, winter 1987–88.

Huang Qizao, '*Zai di si qi pinkun diqu xianji fulian zhuren peixun ban shang de zongjie jianghua*' ['Concluding speech at the fourth training class for heads of county level women's federations of poor areas'], *FNGZ*, November 1989, pp. 2–5.

Hunyin yu Jiating [Marriage and the Family], May 1986, p. 13.

Huo Da, '*Baomu*' ['Nanny'] in Yan Chunde, ed., *Xin Shiqi Nüzuojia Bai Ren Zuopin Xuan [A Collection of Works By One Hundred Recent Women Writers]*, Haixia Wenyi Chubanshe, Fuzhou, 1985, pp. 715–732.

Jiang Xuegui, ed., *Chengdu Xiangzhenqiye (1979–1988) [Chengdu's Township Enterprises (1979–1988)]*, Chengdu Chubanshe, Chengdu, 1989.

Jiao Fengjun, '*Nongcun jiaoyu de fazhan, kunjing yu chulu*' ['Developments, difficulties and solutions in rural education'], *Lilun Jianshe [The Construction of Theory]*, no. 2, 1994, pp. 60–63.

Jilinsheng Fulian Xuanjiaobu [Propaganda and Education Department of the Jilin Provincial Women's Federation], '*Tigao funü kexue wenhua suzhi shi bashi niandai funü yundong xin tedian zhi yi*' ['Improving women's scientific and cultural quality is a new characteristic of the women's movement of the '80s'], *FNGZ*, September 1984, pp. 14–15.

Jingji Ribao [Economics Daily], 4 August 1985.

Jingjixue Wenzhai [Selections on Economics], January 1986, p. 59.

Kang Keqing, '*Fenfa ziqiang kaichuang funü yundong xin jumian*' ['Let us rouse all our strength to initiate a new phase in the women's movement'], *Xinhua Yuebao [New China Monthly]*, no. 9, 1983, pp. 57–65.

Li Mengbai and Hu Xin, eds, *Liudong Renkou Dui Da Chengshi Fazhan de Yingxiang ji Duice [The Influence of the Floating Population on Large Cities and Policy Responses]*, Jingji Ribao Chubanshe, Beijing, 1991.

Li Qingzeng (unpub.), '*Lun nongcun shengyu laodongli de zhuanyi zhanlue*' ['A discussion of strategies for the diversion of rural surplus labour'], Rural Development Institute, Chinese Academy of Social Sciences, 1986.

Liu Jinxiu, '*Minjian funü xueshu tuanti yilan*' ['A guide to non-governmental academic women's groups'], in Beijingshi Funülianhehui and Beijing Funü Wenti Lilun Yanjiuhui, eds, *Zhongguo Funü Lilun Yanjiu Shi Nian* [Ten Years of Theoretical Research on Women's Issues], Zhongguo Funü Chubanshe, Beijing, 1992, pp. 580–584.

Liu Ying, '*Xianshi yu lixiang de chaju – tan nongcun jiating jiegou bianhua*' ['The gap between reality and ideals – a discussion of changes in family structure'], *Hunying yu Jiating [Marriage and the Family]*, no. 1, 1989, pp. 38–41.

Lu Ming and Si Xuelong, '*Qingnian nongmin de da shi*' ['The big event for rural youth'], *Nongye Jingji Congkan [Rural Economics Digest]*, January 1986, pp. 64–65.

Lu Zhonghe, '*Shanghai geti jingji fazhan de chengjiu, wenti ji guanli yijian*' ['Comments on the successes, problems and management of the development of Shanghai's private economy'], *Shanghai Jingji [Shanghai Economy]*, no. 2, 1988, pp. 55–58.

Ma Lizhen, '*Ba "shuang xue shuang bi" huodong tuixiang xin jieduan*' ['Advance the "double study, double compete" activities to a new stage'], *ZGFN*, March 1992, pp. 2–5.

Ma Yinan, '*Guanyu wanshan funü quanyi baozhangfa de ruogan sikao*' ['Some thoughts on how to perfect the Women's Rights Protection Law'], *Zhongguo Faxue [Chinese Legal Studies]*, no. 5, 1995, pp. 101–106.

Meng Xianfan, '*Gaige zhong nongcun nüxing de jingji jihui – dui liang ge cunzhuang de diaocha*' ['The economic opportunities for rural women during reform – a survey of two villages'], *Funü Yanjiu Luncong [Collection of Women's Studies]*, no. 3, 1994, pp. 27–31.

Meng Xianfan, ' "*Nan gong nü geng*" *yu Zhongguo nongcun nüxing de fazhan*' [' "Men working in industry and women ploughing" and rural women's development'], *Shehui Kexue Zhanxian [Social Sciences Frontline]*, no. 1, 1995, pp. 248–251.

Nan Ning, '*Xingbie qishi: jiaoyu de tanxi*' ['Sexual discrimination: the sigh of education'], *ZGFN*, February 1989, pp. 4–5.

NMRB

8 March 1985.

26 June 1985.

11 March 1986.

17 March 1986.

12 June 1986.

17 July 1986.
28 July 1986.
31 October 1986.
27 November 1986.
7 March 1987.
9 March 1987.
29 May 1987.
13 November 1987.
17 May 1988.
11 January 1989.

Nongcun Diaocha Bangongshi [Office of Rural Investigation], '*Nongcun gaige yu fazhan zhong de ruogan xin qingkuang*' ['Certain new situations arising in economic reform and development'], *Nongye Jingji Wenti [Issues in Agricultural Economics]*, no. 3, 1989, pp. 42–57.

Nongcun Diaocha Lingdao Xiaozu Bangongshi [Office of the Lead Group on Rural Investigation], *Nongcun zai biange zhong qianjin – lai zi jiceng de diaocha baogao [The Progress of Rural Areas in Reform – Report on a Grass-Roots Investigation]*, Nongye Chubanshe, PRC, 1987.

Qiangjiang Wanbao [Qiangjiang Evening Paper], 24 December 1992.

Quanguo Fulian Quanyibu Shengchanfulichu [Production Welfare Office, Legal Rights Department of the All-China Women's Federation], '*Xiangzhenqiye nügong laodong baohu ying yun er xing*' ['Labour protection for female workers in township enterprises must be carried out'], *FNGZ*, March 1988, pp. 6–7.

Renmin Jiaoyu [People's Education], October 1985, p. 12.

RMRB
9 April 1983.
18 April 1983.
13 September 1983.
27 January 1985.
31 October 1986.
2 March 1988.
21 April 1988.
9 July 1988.
17 September 1988.
11 October 1994.

Shandongsheng Fulian [Shandong Provincial Women's Federation], '*Weirao gaige jiaqiang jiceng funü zuzhi jianshe*' ['Strengthen the establishment of grass-roots women's organisations in line with reform'], *FNGZ*, October 1986, pp. 12–13.

Shanxisheng Fulian Diaoyanshi Quanyibu [Legal Rights Section of the Research Office of the Shanxi Provincial Women's Federation], '*Xiangzhenqiye nügong laobao xianzhuang de diaocha*', ['An investigation into labour protection for female workers in township enterprises'], *FNGZ*, September 1988, pp. 25–27.

Shanxisheng Huairenxian Fulian [Women's Federation of Huairen County, Shanxi Province], '*Tingyuan ziyou zhi fu lu*' ['The courtyard itself is a way to get rich'], *FNGZ*, September 1984, pp. 24–26.

Shi Chenglin, '*Lun xiandai nongcun funü zai laoli zhuanyi zhong de diwei he zuoyong*' ['A discussion of the status and function of rural women in the present movement of labour'], *Fujian Luntan: Jingji, Shehui Ban [Fujian Tribune: Economy and Society Edition]*, no. 9, 1987, pp. 54–56.

Song Meiya, '*Yi zhuang zhangfu qiangjian qizi an*' ['A case of a man raping his wife'], *ZGFN*, January 1991, pp. 14–15.

Tan Shen, '*Dangdai Zhongguo funü zhuangkuang de fenxi yu yuze*' ['Analysis and forecasts on the situation of women in contemporary China'], *Shehuixue Yanjiu [Sociological Research]*, no. 3, 1994, pp. 69–77.

Tan Yingzi, '*Jiceng fulian mianlin de xin wenti*' [New problems faced by grass-roots women's federations'], *FNGZ*, January 1989, pp. 23–25.

Tao Xiaoyong, '*Zhujiang sanjiaozhou diqu de dai geng jingying ji qi jingji, shehui yingxiang*' ['The subcontracting of land in the Pearl River Delta region and its economic and social implications'], *Nongye Jingji Wenti [Issues in Agricultural Economics]*, October 1986, pp. 16–18.

Wang Jinjin, '*Dangjin, Zhongguo, qiaoran xingqi de funü jiefang lang chao*' ['The tide of women's liberation that is softly rising in China today'], *ZGFN*, March 1991, pp. 8–11.

Wang Shuhui, '*Funü shengming zhouqi yu jiating jiegou*' [Women's life cycle and the structure of the family'], *Hunyin yu Jiating [Marriage and the Family]*, October 1987, pp. 14–16.

Wang Shuhui, '*Sichuan nongcun funü de zhiye jiegou*' ['The structure of women's work in rural Sichuan'], *Hunyin yu Jiating [Marriage and the Family]*, November 1987, pp. 20–29.

Wei Ziqian, '*Kaifa haizi danao de shenmi qianli*' ['Developing the mysterious potential of a child's brain'], *Nongjianü Baishitong [Rural Women Knowing All]*, no. 5, 1995, p. 39.

Wu Kaiti, '*Yao chongfen fahui funü de zuoyong*' ['We must bring women's abilities into full play'], *ZGFN*, May 1979, pp. 38–42.

Xu Yan, '*Liyong tingyuan gao te yang xinxi shichang shi guanjian*' ['Market information is the key to profiting from specialised production in the courtyard'], *Nongjianü Baishitong [Rural Women Knowing All]*, January 1995, pp. 60–61.

Yang Chengxun, '*Jingji tizhi gaige yu funü jiefang*' ['Economic reform and women's liberation'], *Funü Shenghuo [Women's Life]*, no. 1, 1986, pp. 4–5.

ZGFN

> April 1978, p. 16.
> March 1979, p. 5.
> July 1979, p. 9.
> July 1981, p. 29.
> September 1981, p. 46.
> May 1982, p. 30.
> June 1984, p. 20.
> July 1984, p. 17.
> October 1984, p. 48.
> July 1986, p. 11.
> September 1988, p. 30.
> July 1991, p. 24.

ZGFNB

> 20 June 1986.

4 July 1986.
18 August 1986.
11 January 1988.
ZGNMB
16 January 1983.
22 May 1983.
29 April 1984.
29 May 1984.

Zhang Jinyun and Hu Zhaoqing, '*Nongcun nü dangyuan shao, lao wenti ying yinqi zhongshi*' ['The problem of old age and scarcity of women Party members must be given attention'], *FNGZ*, July 1988, pp. 14–15.

Zhang Juan and Ma Wenrong, '*Daqiuzhuang "funü hui jia" de sisuo*', ['Thoughts on "women returning home" in Daqiu Village'], *ZGFN*, January 1988, pp. 8–10.

Zhang Qiti, '*Shixi wo guo de jiating leixing ji qi chengyuan goucheng*' ['An examination of China's family types and their membership'], *Renkou yu Jingji [Population and Economy]*, no. 6, 1988, pp. 46–50.

Zhang Ruihua, '*Nongcun tingyuan jingji chutan*' [A preliminary investigation of the rural courtyard economy'], in Zhongguo Renmin Daxue Shubao Ziliao Zhongxin, Fuyin Baokan Ziliao, *Funü Zuzhi yu Huodong* [Press clippings on *Women's Organisations and Activities*, Centre for Books and Newspaper Materials, Chinese People's University], no. 8, 1987, pp. 65–67.

Zhang Sehua and Liu Zhongyi, '*Zai Fujian Qingliuxian gao'e caili chengwei nongmin fudan*' ['In Qingliu County, Fujian, high bride-prices have become a burden for peasants'], *ZGFN*, December 1986, pp. 14–22.

Zhao Xishun, ed., *Gaige yu Nongcun Jiating [Reform and the Rural Family]*, Sichuansheng Shehui Kexueyuan Chubanshe, Sichuan, 1988.

Zhao Xishun, ed., *Nongmin Hunyin – Sichuan Nongcun Hunyin Yanjiu [Peasant Marriage – Research into Rural Marriage in Sichuan]*, Sichuan Renmin Chubanshe, Sichuan, 1990.

Zhonggong Zhongyang Zuzhi Bu and Zhonghua Quanguo Funü Lianhehui [Central Organisation Department of the CCP and The All-China Women's Federation], '*Zai gaige kaifang zhong jiaqiang peiyang xuanba nü ganbu de yijian*' ['Views on strengthening the training and election of women cadres during reform'], *FNGZ*, May 1988, pp. 9–10.

Zhongguo Jiaoyu Nianjian, 1949–1981 [Chinese Education Yearbook, 1949–1981], Zhongguo Da Baikequanshu Chubanshe, Beijing, 1984.

Zhongguo Laodong Renshi Bao [Chinese Labour Newspaper], 16 March 1988.

Zhongguo Nongcun Jingji [Chinese Rural Economy], June 1988, p. 63.

Zhongguo Xiangzhenqiye Nianjian, 1992 [Chinese Township Enterprise Yearbook, 1992], Nongye Chubanshe, Beijing, 1993.

Zhonghua Quanguo Funü Lianhehui Funü Yanjiusuo and Shaanxisheng Funü Lianhehui Yanjiushi [Research Institute of the All-China Women's Federation and Research Office of Shaanxi Provincial Women's Federation], *Zhongguo Funü Tongji Ziliao, 1949–1989 [Statistics on Chinese Women, 1949–1989]*, Zhongguo Tongji Chubanshe, Beijing, 1991.

Zhou Limin, '*Kaichuang xin jumian yao you "ban bian tian"*' ['In initiating a new phase we need "half the sky"'], *ZGFN*, November 1982, pp. 42–43.

Index

Printed in the United States
31221LVS00005B/11